DOUBLE CHAMPIONS

DOUBLE CHAMPIONS

THE MANCHESTER UNITED PLAYERS' ACCOUNT
OF THE 2007/08 SEASON

MANCHESTER UNITED

First published in hardback in Great Britain in 2008 by
Orion Books
an imprint of the Orion Publishing Group Ltd
Orion House, 5 Upper St Martin's Lane,
London WC2H 9EA
An Hachette Livre UK Company

3 5 7 9 10 8 6 4 2

A CIP catalogue record for this book is available
from the British Library.

ISBN: 978 0 7528 9843 8

Designed by Geoff Green Book Design, Cambridge
Printed and bound in the UK by CPI Mackays, Chatham ME5 8TD

The Orion Publishing Group's policy is to use papers that are natural, renewable and recyclable
and made from wood grown in sustainable forests. The logging and manufacturing processes are
expected to conform to the environmental regulations of the country of origin.

Every effort has been made to fulfil requirements with regard to reproducing copyright material.
The author and publisher will be glad to rectify any omissions at the earliest opportunity.

www.orionbooks.co.uk

CONTENTS

ACKNOWLEDGEMENTS

MUTV
ManUtd.com
United Review
Inside United
Manchester United Radio

Photographs: John and Matt Peters / Getty Images.

Thanks to everyone at the club for their cooperation and support during the writing of this book, especially Sir Alex Ferguson and his players for making it a truly memorable season.

Special thanks to the ever-obliging Karen Shotbolt, for her patience and help.

Thanks to: Ian Marshall, Sameer Pabari, James White and Phil Dickinson for their contributions.

This book is dedicated to all those who lost their lives in Munich on 6 February 1958, their families and friends. The red flag keeps flying high.

Steve Bartram and Gemma Thompson

DOUBLE CHAMPIONS

INTRODUCTION

Fate, eh? Bloody hell. In a season laced with pivotal anniversaries and landmarks, there was always a feeling that 2007/08 was going to be a special campaign at Old Trafford.

Some 50 years after the Munich air disaster and 40 since United's first European Cup triumph, the current Reds squad knew all too well that silverware would be the perfect way to honour their forebears.

The season started with exactly that: the Community Shield was secured at the expense of Chelsea in a penalty shoot-out. Just over ten months later in Moscow, United faced the same opponents, but this time the title of Europe's greatest was snared.

For Sir Alex Ferguson, it meant another taste of the continental glory he had sampled so briefly in 1999. The United manager's second Champions League triumph heightened his status as one of the all-time greats, while Ryan Giggs followed his gaffer's silver-laden lead to become the most-decorated player in the history of English football.

Only the most romanticised of football followers could have predicted Giggs' poignant climax to the campaign. Just ten days before the Reds ruled in Moscow, the veteran winger – in his 17th year as a senior player – secured United's 17th league title on the day he became the club's joint all-time record appearance-maker.

It was a fitting and just conclusion to a season typically laced with heart-stopping drama, plot twists and glory plucked from the brink of heartbreak.

For those who lost their lives in Munich or reigned supreme at Wembley, this was indeed the most fitting of tributes. It was the kind that only Manchester United could conspire to craft.

Steve Bartram and Gemma Thompson, June 2008

Chapter One

JULY – NEW SEASON, NEW FACES

It's an age-old adage at Old Trafford not to dwell on success. 'Today's the day. Tomorrow's the big day,' Sir Alex Ferguson often says. The challenges that lie ahead are greater than those conquered, and it's that ethos that has been the Manchester United way since the days of Sir Matt Busby.

The successful conclusion to the 2006/07 Premiership campaign was the ninth league title of Sir Alex's reign, but it provided a first triumph for a number of the squad's young charges, including the likes of Cristiano Ronaldo and Wayne Rooney. So when the team returned for pre-season training in July as the reigning champions, there was only one question on the United manager's lips – 'Can you do it again?'

'When it comes to the likes of Ryan Giggs, Paul Scholes and Gary Neville I never ask questions because they answer themselves. But to the ones who have won their first trophy, they need to ask themselves – will that be enough?' explained Sir Alex.

'If you achieve anything it creates excitement, develops you as a person and gives you the understanding not to lose and to go on and win again. After you have won a trophy, you enjoy it, but the next day it leaves you and the hard works begins again. You're looking for the next one, the next challenge, and that is what drives the best players on.'

And following through on those challenges year after year is what ultimately turns potential into greatness, according to goalkeeper Edwin van der Sar, whose career has spanned nearly two decades and yielded countless top honours.

'You do not become a legend overnight – you have to win things over a long period,' declared the Dutchman, already a four-time title winner with Ajax and owner of Champions League, UEFA Cup and European Super Cup winners' medals before his move to Old Trafford.

'The players showed their ability last season and we coped with anything that was put in our way. The squad is well positioned to achieve something special. It takes a long time to work towards something like this, but now the team must go on. It is not just about winning something once, but two or three times and that is the challenge.'

Maintaining a vice-like grip on their hard-earned crown was certainly the squad's main aim ahead of the new season, and it was a quest that would be further bolstered by a handful of new additions.

As usual during the transfer window 'silly' season, the Reds found themselves linked with a plethora of the game's top names. Tottenham's Dimitar Berbatov, Barcelona forward Samuel Eto'o, Klaas-Jan Huntelaar from Ajax, Atletico Madrid's Fernando Torres and Sampdoria front man Fabio Quagliarella were all touted as potential signings, with clubs, agents et al claiming United wanted their men.

When the Reds did start to splash the cash, however, those rumours all proved wide of the mark. Late on 30 May 2007, just 17 days after lifting the Premier League trophy, United caught everybody on the hop by announcing the arrivals, both for undisclosed fees, of Portuguese winger Nani from Sporting Lisbon and Brazilian attacker Anderson from FC Porto on five-year deals.

That assistant manager Carlos Queiroz and chief executive David Gill had been spotted in Portugal earlier that day had fuelled speculation something was afoot, but few were able to predict the outcome. According to Gill, however, United's scouting personnel had been monitoring the duo for some time.

'We've watched Nani and Anderson for the last year. Carlos has great knowledge of Portuguese football and our scouts have also been watching them for a quite a while,' he revealed.

Queiroz was even more elated by the captures and was unequivocal in his assessment of the pair's potential. 'It is a significant investment in United's prospects for the next ten years,' he stated. 'It's worth imagining a forward line with Rooney, Ronaldo, Anderson and Nani, these are players with enormous creativity. These signings mean the end of a long observation process. They are players who correspond to the club's intentions. They are young and have plenty of potential and talent.'

Anderson excitedly declared the switch 'a dream the size of the world', while Nani vowed to repay the faith already shown in him by the Reds.

'I cannot wait to play in the same team as Cristiano Ronaldo, Wayne Rooney and many more,' added Anderson, who would spend the next few weeks on international duty with Brazil at the Copa America. 'I could not imagine I would ever get to work with a manager like Sir Alex Ferguson, but it has happened. I am very happy.'

'United are one of the major clubs in Europe and any player would like to play at Old Trafford,' continued Nani. 'I have to keep working and giving my best to prove I am worthy of the confidence shown in me. I know I'm young and I have still many things to learn.'

The deal to bring Owen Hargreaves to Old Trafford on a four-year deal was the antithesis of the duo's discreet switch to United. Indeed, Hargreaves himself described the transfer 'as the worst kept secret in football' when negotiations were finally concluded on 31 May, almost a year after initial talks had begun with Bayern Munich.

'I was always quite positive and optimistic it would go through. When United want something they tend to get it,' he joked. 'But sometimes you just have to be patient. Bayern were quite particular in not wanting to sell me after the World Cup [in 2006], but I made it clear that I wanted to join United. That's why it came true really, because of my wish.'

Usually, when new arrivals come through the Carrington entrance doors, somebody has to make way. With Sir Alex adding substantial strength to his roster, the tabloid rumour mongers were frenzied in their speculation over who would be packing their bags. Alan Smith, Kieran Richardson, Gabriel Heinze, Mikael Silvestre and Louis Saha were, according to the British media, the most likely to be waving farewell. And, at the beginning of July, the manager himself admitted that some players may be forced to look elsewhere for regular first-team football.

'I don't expect anyone to leave, but it's possible it may happen simply because of the number of players we now have,' he said. 'Players understand today that in order to challenge for major trophies, you need a strong squad. No one will play all the games this season and, hopefully, the players will accept that and get on with the business of trying to achieve success for us. Some of them will view the situation we have at the moment and think they may not get enough games to satisfy them. But there are no decisions on anyone at the moment.'

One of those rumoured to be on his way out, Alan Smith, refused to get disheartened. 'You know at Manchester United that every year they will sign world-class players. It's an education that makes you mentally strong,' stated the Yorkshire-born striker. 'You also know that you are not guaranteed to play any games, week in, week out. Last season I came back from injury and played in the Champions League win over Roma and it was probably one of my best performances in a United shirt. But I knew it didn't mean I was guaranteed a start the following Saturday, but that makes you stronger mentally.

'It's a short career and you have to try to take every opportunity when it comes. That's how I was brought up and how I've been since I was a kid. I will never lose that and I will continue to give my best for United.'

Despite Smith's admirable determination to fight for his place, speculation was already starting to grow that the Reds were keen on adding to their bulging squad, most probably in attack. With Ole Gunnar Solskjaer and Louis Saha still struggling with knee injuries that had forced both into operations earlier in the summer, United appeared rather light in the striking department ahead of the new campaign with only Wayne Rooney and Smith as recognised front men.

David Gill added weight to that belief, revealing: 'We have looked at the striker area and we don't rule out another signing. We're not desperate for it, but if one came along that Alex felt would improve the squad, we're prepared to do that.'

Barcelona's Eidur Gudjohnsen was a possibility according to the tabloids, so too Bolton poacher Nicolas Anelka. As it turned out, West Ham striker Carlos Tevez was the surprise target. Despite struggling to settle in English football, the Argentine had become the Hammers' talisman during the second half of the previous season and it was he, ironically, who fired their winner at Old Trafford that ensured the East London club's top-flight status back in May. And Tevez was quick to make his feelings clear on the possibility of a permanent move to Manchester.

'For me, United would be a sensational destination and to be a member of Sir Alex's squad will be absolutely spectacular,' he beamed while on international duty at the Copa America. 'My dream is to be an idol in English football and I can achieve this now. I am a player who thrives on challenges. I went to England to triumph in the Premier League and with West Ham I have achieved that first stage. Now I'm ready to move on to the next stage.'

With both parties happy for the transfer to go ahead, things seemed straightforward. Not so. The wrangle over the forward's ownership was holding up proceedings, so much so that two weeks after the deal had looked to be settled, it was still up in the air as the Reds flew out for their four-game pre-season tour of the Far East on 15 July.

'We are working on it and clearly it's complicated – overly complicated in my humble opinion,' explained David Gill. 'We're working, effectively, with four other parties in order to sort it out: the player, West Ham, the companies who own his economic rights and the Premier League. Carlos is coming over to Manchester and will have a medical some time this week. The process is happening as we speak.'

Also ongoing was the seemingly likely departure of Gabriel Heinze. The Argentine left-back, away with Tevez at the Copa America, had stated earlier in the summer that he believed his future remained at Old Trafford, but comments from his brother, who also acted as his agent, were to the contrary.

Sir Alex maintained that the club were closely monitoring both situations involving the South American duo, but vowed to continue with the team's preparation for the upcoming season upon their arrival in Tokyo. Gary Neville, Louis Saha, Ole Gunnar Solskjaer, Ji-sung Park, Anderson, Heinze, Dong Fangzhuo, Ben Foster and Kieran Richardson were not among the 24-man travelling squad due to injury or international commitments. New signings Owen Hargreaves and Nani both made the trip, but minor knocks kept the pair out of the Reds' opening tour match, against Urawa Red Diamonds.

It may be a long way from Manchester, but the drizzly conditions brought some homely familiarity for the Reds, who donned their new home kit for the match. Some 59,000 United-daft locals packed into the Saitama Stadium, but it was Urawa Reds who opened the scoring on 25 minutes, completely against the run of play. Just moments after a Cristiano Ronaldo drive had stung the palms of Urawa goalkeeper Ryota Tsuzuki, Hideki Uchidate unleashed a swerving 25-yard shot that totally bamboozled Edwin van der Sar.

The Reds drew level two minutes after the restart through Darren Fletcher, before Ronaldo made it 2-1 in the 52nd minute with a superb individual effort that sent the Saitama faithful wild. However, Urawa's Shinji Ono ensured the game finished honours even with a cool finish 12 minutes from time, but the Reds had made a business-like start to their pre-season preparations.

'You always look to see whether the enthusiasm and desire is still there and whether the players are still enjoying their football,' remarked Sir Alex afterwards. 'I think we saw that they are.'

Wayne Rooney, sporting his new No.10 shirt for the first time against Urawa, echoed his manager's sentiments and highlighted the strength in depth within United's ranks following the new arrivals.

'It's definitely the strongest squad I've been involved in,' he declared. 'There are more players and better quality players as well. There's a good mix of youth and experience, which is great for the team.

'All the players are excited by the new signings,' he continued. 'I know all about Owen Hargreaves from my time with England. You know what you're going to get with Owen – he's a top player and a good lad. I haven't seen too much of Nani and Anderson, although I played against Anderson in a friendly once and he looked a good player. Nani hasn't been able to train with us yet, but I'm sure both of them will do really well for us.'

And Rooney was particularly excited about the imminent arrival of his new strike partner. 'It'll be great to play alongside Carlos Tevez and, hopefully, things will get sorted soon. He did brilliantly for West Ham last season and I think he'll be a great signing for us.'

As the Reds continued to finalise the deal to bring Tevez to the club, a fellow attacker was heading in the opposite direction. Winger Kieran Richardson opted to join Roy Keane's newly promoted Sunderland side, signing a four-year deal in the process.

'I'm delighted we've been able to bring Kieran to Sunderland,' said former United skipper Keane. 'Having worked with him in the past, I'm well aware of what a good player and a good lad he is. He's ready for a fresh challenge and, hopefully, Sunderland will provide that for him.'

Despite continual development, Richardson, who made 81 appearances and bagged 11 goals for the Reds, was never able to hold down a regular first-team spot. He was again used sparingly in the 2006/07 title-winning campaign and the arrivals of Hargreaves, Nani and Anderson seemed to spell the end of his United career.

Back in Asia and after a three-day stay in Japan, the Reds hot-footed it to Korea. The Far East is home to many millions of United fans and the team was afforded a hero's welcome at every destination, none more so than when they touched down at Seoul's Incheon Airport amid a cacophony of some 2,000 hysterical supporters.

'It's fantastic to see the reaction we get out here,' observed Sir

Alex. 'There are always thousands of fans camped in and around the hotel throughout the day and night. It's just one of these phenomena that we can create in certain parts of the world.'

It was the club's inaugural visit to Korea, an ever-growing hot-bed of United fans following Ji-sung Park's transfer to Old Trafford in 2005. Although unable to take part in the tour in a playing capacity while he recovered from knee surgery, Park was on hand to greet his team-mates on their arrival at their hotel.

'I feel very proud to be with the team in my country,' he beamed. 'For Korean people, United are the best club in the world, everyone supports them.'

Park earmarked a January return to action and insisted he was determined to play his part in another successful campaign.

'Last season I wasn't able to do as much for the team as I would have liked, because I had a couple of injuries. This time when I'm back from injury I hope to stay fit and play more games than I did last season,' he explained. 'I hope the team can be successful again – we won the title, but lost out in the Champions League and FA Cup, so I'd like to win those. I want to win as many trophies as possible.'

Despite being laid up on the sidelines, Park donned his scouting hat to act as United's local spy ahead of the team's match with FC Seoul.

'Ji has already warned me that they are a very strong side – he will be my assistant coach for the game!' joked Sir Alex at the pre-match press conference. 'We're all looking forward to the match, but we're expecting another tough test. The progress of Korean football has been fantastic and what the South Korean team achieved [in reaching the semi-finals] at the 2002 World Cup was extraordinary. Hopefully this match will be another good game between two good teams.'

That it was as the Reds demolished an FC Seoul side who never recovered from a quick-fire onslaught that saw United 3-0 up inside 21 minutes. Ronaldo, who turned in a virtuoso performance to the delight of the screaming locals, the impressive Chris Eagles and Rooney were all on target, before Patrice Evra, who revelled in his role on the left wing, added a fourth just after the hour.

But it was Ronaldo, the undisputed darling of the supporters, who once again stole the show.

'I feel fit and I'm very happy for that. But I must keep my form going,' he said at the final whistle. 'The Premier League starts soon and I must be ready for that. I hope to play well. My ambition is still the same – I want to play well, score goals and provide assists. I tried to do the same last year and I worked hard to do that. I hope things come good for me.'

Despite being only midway through their tour of the Far East, the signs already augured well for another impressive season from the winger. And, according to his manager, last season's multiple Player of the Year was more than capable of coping with the increasing media and public attention heaped upon him.

'He is an intelligent boy who looks after himself,' insisted Sir Alex. 'He has a lot of pluses. How players handle that celebrity kind of attention, you never know, but with Ronaldo he seems to do okay with that.

'The problem comes when players get flattered by it and start enjoying it. That's when you start worrying, but at the moment there's absolutely no sign that the boy will be wasted by it. When people ask to interview him, it doesn't worry me too much. He can cope.'

Factored into the team's hectic schedule on tour are a number of community visits, sponsorship appearances and signing sessions, much to the delight of the United-barmy locals.

'The support we have out here is unbelievable and I'm sure the additions of Ji [sung Park] and Dong [Fangzhuo] have increased that even more,' observed Rio Ferdinand. 'Manchester United, both as a football team and a brand, is huge in Asia and the adulation that we receive from the fans over here is unbelievable. So it's important we make time for the supporters when we're here.'

Ensuring the team's itinerary featured the right balance of train-ing, resting and fulfilling community and commercial obligations lay in assistant manager Carlos Queiroz's hands.

'It is important to ensure everything is right. How much sleep the players have and when they sleep. Every time you fly, it affects the water in your body. We try to move around those elements, so it limits the effects from a physiological point of view,' he explained. 'We look to manage all the training sessions to avoid clashes between the elements and keep going with the basic points. We believe, step-by-step, we will eventually reach the level it is possible to reach in these conditions. The most important thing is that the preparation makes them feel okay and not damage the performance of the players.'

Unfortunately, the Reds' arrival in Macau, ahead of their clash with Shenzhen FC at Macau's National Stadium, was marred by the news that Paul Scholes could be out for a month after suffering a knee injury in the win over FC Seoul. The midfielder was booked on the next flight home to undergo an exploratory operation to determine the extent of the damage.

It was certainly a blow for the Reds, who also looked likely to be without Owen Hargreaves for the remainder of the tour because of an ongoing knee complaint. However, the Reds were bolstered by the addition of Chinese international striker Dong Fangzhuo following China's exit from the Asian Cup.

The build-up to United's third tour game was dominated by newspaper reports linking Gabriel Heinze with a switch to Liverpool. Sir Alex was quick to rubbish such stories and was adamant the Argentine would not be able to join United's fierce rivals.

'I can assure you, Liverpool will not be getting Gabriel Heinze,' he said sternly. 'We can put that to bed right now and we have done so. We have had a couple offers for him and we have turned them down. Heinze's agents are rolling the ball all the time. But no matter what they think, we are in the driving seat.

'I don't exactly know what Gaby thinks because it is all coming from his agent, but this has been going on for a year and a half now. We're examining some of the statements coming from the agent regarding the first contact with Liverpool. We're not happy with the agent's conduct in the matter.'

On the pitch, United continued where they left off against FC

Seoul with another impressive and goal-filled display against Shenzhen FC. Nani marked his debut with a goal – and trademark somersault celebration – as the Reds ran out 6-0 winners. The outstanding Ryan Giggs opened the scoring before Wayne Rooney, Nani, John O'Shea, Cristiano Ronaldo and Chris Eagles – on the scoresheet for the second game in a row – completed the rout.

He may have only spent a limited amount of time in his company on the pitch, but Rio Ferdinand remarked afterwards that Nani has the potential to match Ronaldo's success at Old Trafford.

'He has looked very sharp in training and he reminds me of a young Ronaldo,' the defender enthused. 'I hope that won't be a burden for him – I'm sure it won't. He's played some great football in Portugal for the last few years and, hopefully, he can bring that form to our club.'

The Reds made the short hop across China to Guangzhou for the final match of their two-week trip against Guangzhou Pharmaceutical FC.

Having trained in such humid conditions for nearly two weeks, Rio Ferdinand felt the United squad had built up enough fitness to provide a sturdy platform for a successful season.

'The hot conditions are sometimes quite difficult in terms of training, but you reap the benefits of that at the end of the tour,' he said. 'You get your base fitness during pre-season, so it's a vital time. Ultimately that fitness helps you get through the season, especially during the physically demanding periods of the campaign at Christmas and during the run-in.'

The Reds' fourth and final tour game was anything but demanding as they cruised to a 3-0 victory. A youthful United side, including local boy Dong Fangzhuo, took to the pitch at the Guangdong Olympic Stadium in front of 50,000 fans. Wayne Rooney put the visitors ahead from the penalty spot on 20 minutes, before Nani's glorious chip from the left side of the area drifted over Guangzhou keeper Shuai and bounced in off the far post. But it was budding winger Lee Martin who produced the best moment of the match – capping a fine display with an unstoppable 30-yard strike after the break.

As the Reds headed home to Manchester, Sir Alex reflected on what he described as a 'hugely successful trip'.

'We're very happy with how the tour has gone,' he said. 'The hospitality and reception we've received from the fans has been unbelievable. Everything you could ask for on a trip like this, such as hotels, catering, facilities, has been absolutely superb and I'd like to thank everyone who has gone to so much effort to make that happen. On the playing side, we're very pleased. We're happy that everyone has had enough football to really prepare them for the new season.'

The question as to whether Carlos Tevez would be signed up as a United player for the new campaign continued to rumble on. Nevertheless, Sir Alex remained confident a solution would still be found before the 31 August transfer deadline and was even more defiant in his assessment of how Tevez would link-up with Wayne Rooney.

'I think Tevez and Wayne can play in the same side together. I know people say they both like to drop deep, but if you look at last season's FA Cup final, Wayne played up on his own and he was absolutely fantastic. That is where I see his future. He can drop in and give defenders a problem. Equally so, Tevez showed against us on the final day and against plenty of other teams, that when he plays right up there he is also a threat, because he can beat a man. That is the advantage of taking someone like Tevez.'

Ultimately, it seemed, Tevez's expected arrival was always going to mean curtains for one of United's attackers and, on the final day of July, the club announced the departure of striker Giuseppe Rossi to Spanish side Villarreal for an undisclosed fee. The Italian Under-21 international had spent the previous season out on loan, enjoying spells with Newcastle and his former club Parma in Serie A, where he scored nine goals in 19 appearances. Despite four goals in 13 appearances for United's first team during his three-year stay at Old Trafford, the New Jersey-born forward was never able to get a regular run in the side.

Ahead of the season kick-off, Sir Alex pondered the state of his squad and admitted to being surprised at what little transfer business United's title rivals had undertaken during the summer.

'I thought there would have been more spending. There's a lot of money in the Premier League at the moment, so I expected more activity. That's one of the reasons we wanted to do things so quickly. That allowed me to enjoy my holiday – I didn't have to be on the phone to David Gill every two minutes!

'Signing Hargreaves, Nani and Anderson and, hopefully, Tevez, gives us a really strong squad. That was maybe our downfall last season when we just didn't have enough of a squad to handle all the competitions we were in.

'To get Nani and Anderson at this point is great timing for us. They've got time to adapt into life at our club,' he added. 'They won't play every game this season, but they'll play a fair few. They give us a future. Owen brings different qualities to the ones we have at the moment. He'll bring real speed to the midfield and good energy, and he's got great European experience – playing in the Bundesliga for so many years brings a different type of experience that we're used to at this club – that will help us as well. So we're not short of options.'

Far from it. If Sir Alex was smacking his lips about how to deploy his reinforced arsenal of players, Edwin van der Sar was intrigued to see how the United boss would shape his side as a result.

'It will be interesting to see what the manager decides to do. He has the option to play a different system or keep things the same, so we'll just have to wait and see,' mused the Dutchman. 'There's still a lot of work to do and decisions to be made before the season starts.'

Despite being equipped with new ammunition in attack, the Reds seemed certain to be without the services of captain Gary Neville for the opening day. Nevertheless, he still felt hugely positive about the campaign ahead, especially having skippered the team to championship glory last time out, when many predicted United would fall short.

'Nobody thought we would win the league last season,' he recalled. 'But they underestimated us. They underestimated the knowledge and class of our manager. For two to three years we had been suffering. But the manager knew what he was doing over a period of two years in building a new team and now we are in a fantastic position. Last season we played the best football, the most attacking and entertaining football – and we deserved to win the trophy. I don't think any United fan could ever be as excited about the players, the team and about the way the club is, as today.'

Chapter Two

AUGUST – LATE-SUMMER GOAL DROUGHT

If giddiness was the mass mood around United going into the new season, August quickly provided the antidote with several sobering episodes. Three shock results, allied to key injuries and suspensions, meant that the pre-season headiness was rapidly deflating.

The beginning of the month continued the anticipatory theme of July, with Anderson joining his new colleagues at Carrington and a spate of pre-season friendlies taking place.

First up, Internazionale visited Old Trafford. Wayne Rooney put the Reds ahead with a blistering finish, but three quickfire goals from David Suazo (2) and a neat finish from Zlatan Ibrahimovic put the visitors 3-1 ahead before half-time. A spectacular own-goal from Brazilian striker Adriano handed United a route back into the match, but the reigning Serie A champions held firm for a victory that provided a dose of reality for Sir Alex Ferguson's side.

The manager criticised his team's display after the match, and Rio Ferdinand echoed those sentiments. 'The Inter game was definitely what the doctor ordered,' he said. 'We'd been on tour in Asia playing against teams who weren't really anywhere near the standard of teams we are going to face in the league. We got some positives out of it in terms of improving our fitness and we also got back to playing at a quick tempo. We probably learned a lot more against Inter than we did in the whole tour of the Far East.

'We didn't defend well at all. I don't know if the manager was talking about individuals when he criticised our display, it was more that as a team we didn't defend well. Playing against someone like

Inter raised questions that clearly needed to be answered. Those have been addressed.'

Attention quickly switched from the disappointment of defeat to Inter – in front of 73,738 fans, a club record attendance for a friendly – back to the transfer market. The Carlos Tevez saga took another twist when the striker began training with United, in order to keep his fitness ticking over.

The Argentine virtually passed Alan Smith on his way into Carrington, as the former Leeds United striker ended his three-year stay at United by signing for Sam Allardyce's Newcastle United. 'Smudge' as he was known to his United team-mates, made 93 appearances and scored 12 goals during his Reds career, and cited a need for regular first-team action as his motive for leaving.

The decision to allow Smith's departure was certainly a wrench for Sir Alex Ferguson. 'Alan has been a fantastic character in the dressing room and also a very important player for us,' he said. 'There are few characters as big as him in this country at the moment and it was a very difficult one for us to decide. I was very sad to see him go. He'll be remembered with great affection by everyone here and I'm sure that's the case with the fans.'

The irony that both Smith and Giuseppe Rossi before him had departed because of a lack of first-team openings at Old Trafford would soon become clear.

Back on the field, friendly victories over Peterborough (managed by Sir Alex's son, Darren) and Doncaster allowed a number of the Reds' fringe talents to boost their fitness, while the older heads prepared for a first competitive game of the season. The opposition and venue were exactly the same as those in the final game of the previous campaign – Chelsea at Wembley. Although the Community Shield lacks the same glamour and romance as the FA Cup, silverware is silverware – and it's always nice to get one over on your title rivals.

Saturday, 5 August 2007, Wembley Stadium

Attendance: 80,731

FA Community Shield
United 1 **Chelsea** 1 (United win 3-0 on penalties)

Three penalty shoot-out saves from Edwin van der Sar handed United victory over Chelsea on a sweltering afternoon at Wembley. The Dutch veteran beat away efforts from Claudio Pizarro, Frank Lampard and Shaun Wright-Phillips, while Rio Ferdinand, Michael Carrick and Wayne Rooney all fired home from the spot to ensure Community Shield triumph for United.

In normal time, Ryan Giggs opened the scoring ten minutes before half-time. Patrice Evra played a neat one-two with Cristiano Ronaldo before sliding the ball back to Giggs, who curled an effort into Petr Cech's top corner to register his first goal at Wembley on his 17th appearance at the famous old stadium.

United were pegged back before the break, however, as new Blues signing Florent Malouda out-muscled Ferdinand to reach a bouncing ball and poke a neat finish over the onrushing van der Sar.

The Reds enjoyed the better chances in the second period, with Ronaldo, Rooney and Giggs all coming close to snatching a winner in normal time. With the match mercilessly bereft of extra-time, however, United needed just six penalties – three saved, three scored – to bag their first silverware of the season.

UNITED: Van der Sar; Brown; Ferdinand, Vidic, Silvestre (Nani 68), Evra, O'Shea, Carrick, Ronaldo; Giggs (Fletcher 81), Rooney
Subs not used: Kuszczak, Piqué, Bardsley, Eagles, Martin

Goal: Giggs (35)

Penalty shoot-out
Scored: Ferdinand, Carrick, Rooney

CHELSEA: Cech; A. Cole (Diarra 68), Ben Haim, Carvalho, Johnson (Sidwell 78); Lampard, Essien, Mikel; Wright-Phillips, J. Cole (Sinclair 82), Malouda (Pizarro 52)
Subs not used: Cudicini, Worley, Hilario

Goal: Malouda (45)

Penalty shoot-out
Missed: Pizarro, Lampard, Wright-Phillips

Predictably, Sir Alex Ferguson was delighted with both the victory and what had been a strenuous workout, but conceded that the result would have little or no bearing on the season to come.

'It's always satisfying to win, no matter what competition you're playing in,' he said. 'But this result doesn't lay down any sort of marker. I think everyone in the country knows which teams are going to be contesting the title. Arsenal and Liverpool will play a bigger part this season and that may be good for the game.

'It was a difficult game and I think the heat played a part in that. I don't think either side was at their best, but in my experience you get that in Community Shield matches. You use them as a stepping stone to the big one next weekend when the season starts. It gave us a really good workout – that's the most important thing we got out of it. A lot of the players are tired, but it will bring them on a good deal in terms of the tempo and sharpness they need to win matches. The most important thing is we concentrate on ourselves and hopefully, come the start of the season, I'll have an even stronger squad available.'

With Ji-sung Park making great strides in his recovery from knee-ligament damage and a host of players gathering much-needed match fitness, the signs augured well. A further fillip came when Paul Scholes, who flew home early from the Asia Tour for exploratory knee surgery, completed 90 minutes of a friendly victory over Dunfermline. The depth of United's squad was emphatically underlined as Sir Alex travelled to Dunfermline, but simultaneously sent a side to Ireland to face Glentoran.

The Reds emerged victorious from both matches – 4-0 in Scotland, 3-0 in Ireland – and confidence was sky high ahead of the Premier League curtain-raiser against Reading.

'There's no chance of us giving up our title easily,' said Rio Ferdinand. 'I had a great end to last season and a great summer. You can't beat that kind of feeling or put it into words, and we'll be doing all we can to retain the title. But it's hard to win the league any year.

'The fact other teams have spent a lot of money poses questions,' he added. 'But will they gel? Will they become better teams? Will it be harder for their manager to cope with loads of players in their squad? Will he be able to juggle things around? It's all ifs and buts, really. We'll know by Christmas which teams have dealt with their new acquisitions well and how everyone is doing.

'We're very experienced in that capacity, so hopefully that will give us the step in front that we want. I don't really care what the likes of Chelsea or anyone else do. I'm happy with what we're doing – that's all I'm concentrating on.'

United's hopes of retaining their Premier League crown – and adding other silverware to an already bulging trophy room – were given a further boost when Carlos Tevez's arrival at the club was finally confirmed. After a long and winding transfer wrangle to secure his services, the Argentine became a Red on 10 August 2007 – two days before the start of the season.

Sir Alex resisted the temptation to field the striker against Reading, preferring instead to save him for the Manchester derby a week later. After all, United would have enough in the tank to overcome Steve Coppell's side at Old Trafford, wouldn't they?

Sunday, 12 August 2007, Old Trafford

Attendance: 75,655

FA Barclays Premier League
United 0 **Reading** 0

Reading failed to read the script as they put in a dogged performance to frustrate the champions at Old Trafford, and an afternoon of woe for United was capped by a fractured foot for Wayne Rooney.

The striker suffered the blow – the third such injury of his short career – as Michael Duberry tried to block his shot just before half-time. Rooney soldiered on for the rest of the half, but had to be replaced by debutant Nani at the interval.

The Royals, who survived the dismissal of substitute Dave Kitson, were indebted to a superb performance from goalkeeper Marcus Hahnemann, who repelled everything the Reds threw at him.

Countless chances came and went begging as Sir Alex Ferguson's side began their defence of the Premier League title with a teeth-grinding slog against the pragmatic visitors.

The limpet-like Nicky Shorey man-marked Cristiano Ronaldo for much of the match and restricted the Portuguese midfielder's influence on proceedings. Not that United were without creativity, as Rooney, Michael Carrick and Wes Brown were all thwarted by defence or goalkeeper, while Ryan Giggs slammed a volley against Hahnemann's near post.

Rooney then suffered a hairline fracture in his left foot under the challenge of Duberry – who clearly had no intent in mind – leaving United without any recognised strikers. Still the chances came, however, with Ronaldo denied by Hahnemann, Scholes' shot deflected wide and Evra scuffing a half-volley woefully off target.

John O'Shea was sent on as a makeshift striker and, shortly after Giggs had come close again with a curling free-kick, forced a fine reaction save from Hahnemann when he looked certain to score.

Nani fizzed an effort wide of the post before Royals substitute Dave Kitson was red-carded for his first act – a lunging challenge on Evra – and United subsequently laid frantic siege to the visitors' goal.

Carrick, Brown and Ronaldo all came close again in the dying stages, but Reading's point, garnered in the baking Manchester heat against relentless opposition, was undoubtedly hard-earned.

UNITED: Van der Sar; Brown (Fletcher 78), Vidic, Ferdinand, Silvestre (O'Shea 57); Carrick, Scholes, Evra; Ronaldo, Rooney (Nani 46), Giggs.
Subs not used: Kuszczak, Piqué

READING: Hahnemann; Murty, Gunnarsson, Duberry, Shorey; Hunt (Bikey 87), Harper, Ingimarsson, De la Cruz; Seol (Oster 57), Doyle (Kitson 72).
Subs not used: Federici, Cisse

The immediate post-match concerns predictably revolved not around the unexpected concession of two points, but the state of Wayne Rooney's left foot.

The United striker subsequently admitted: 'I knew straight away I'd broken it. I was really disappointed, particularly as I'd had a full pre-season and trained well and felt good. You're always disappointed when the team aren't winning games, and it's even harder when you can't do anything about it when you're injured because you want to be out there playing.'

'We're putting it down to two months,' was Sir Alex's diagnosis. 'But you never know with these kind of fractures. Hopefully it will be sooner, but that's the timescale we're putting on it at the moment. He should be back in training by that time, but I can't put an exact date on when he will be back playing. It is a bad blow, but we've got a good squad and we have alternatives to compensate for Wayne's loss.'

Michael Duberry was swift to pass his regards on to the injured United forward, but maintained that there had been no malice in his challenge. 'It was a complete accident,' insisted the Royals defender. 'I hope and wish him all the best and the speediest of recoveries, not just for Manchester United's sake but for England's too. He has already been through the trauma of the injury and I know myself what it is like. To be hurt in the first game of the season is even more disappointing and now he is facing the long haul of rehabilitation.'

Despite the transfer window remaining open, Sir Alex confirmed that he would not be making any knee-jerk signings to compensate for the loss of Rooney, and lingering questions over the fitness of fellow forwards Louis Saha and Ole Gunnar Solskjaer.

Although the manager was calm about his squad's long-term depth, there was no escaping the fact that United's striking department would be threadbare for the remainder of the month. Plans to save new boy Carlos Tevez for the Manchester derby had to be shelved.

'Carlos will start on Wednesday against Portsmouth,' confirmed Sir Alex at a press conference to announce the Argentine's arrival. 'I would have preferred to wait for the City game – that would have given him a few more days' training. But for the forthcoming few weeks, he will fill the position Wayne would have occupied.'

For his part, Tevez was champing at the bit to begin his United career after such an arduous transfer wrangle.

'I feel a wonderful amount of relief now to actually be here at Manchester United,' he said. 'I'm now getting myself prepared for the games that are coming up. It is a dream to wear the United shirt and it will also be a dream to win the title, which we will all be working for this season.

'I feel like I have grown a lot, particularly with a year at West Ham. I think every different club in football you are with, be it in Italy, Spain or Brazil, you learn different things and you try to take things from each club. It is a huge learning curve, but I feel I have grown as a player. Now I'm just getting ready to play for United. It's very important to be happy myself, but also to be able to make the people who support the team happy.'

Wednesday, 15 August 2007, Fratton Park

Attendance: 20,510

FA Barclays Premier League
Portsmouth 1 **United** 1

Two games into the new season, four points dropped. Just as Reading had survived an opening-day onslaught at Old Trafford to emerge without defeat, Harry Redknapp's Portsmouth registered a scarcely deserved point at Fratton Park.

Although Carlos Tevez shone on his debut, teeing up an opener for Paul Scholes, Benjani's second-half equaliser pegged United back. A procession of chances went begging, before Cristiano Ronaldo was red-carded just before full-time to put the seal on a truly miserable night on the south coast.

The Portuguese winger inflicted an ill-judged headbutt on Pompey's Richard Hughes, only five minutes after Sulley Muntari had been sent off for the hosts after garnering two bookings.

The undoubted positive for United, however, was the inspirational bow of Tevez, who gave a taste of his all-action attitude in an invigorating, sweat-soaked 90 minutes. The Argentine striker cut an isolated figure as the lone forward in the opening exchanges, but displayed immaculate close control and hold-up play as he laid on Scholes' 15th-minute opener.

The veteran midfielder crashed a stunning 25-yard effort past the helpless dive of David James to give United a deserved lead; it made him the Reds' all-time top scorer in the Premier League, with 96 goals.

United continued to dominate play in the first half, with James called upon to thwart Tevez after initially parrying Ronaldo's swerving effort. After the break, Nani's low left-footed effort was kept out at James' near post, before Tevez volleyed just over the bar after fashioning an opening from Scholes' clipped pass.

A United second seemed inevitable, until Pompey drew level with their first meaningful attack after 53 minutes. Matthew Taylor pinged a decent cross into the area, and the onrushing Benjani powered a header past the helpless Edwin van der Sar. The Reds were rattled, and David Nugent could have put the hosts ahead, but blazed over after van der Sar had parried Benjani's close-range shot.

After that brief wobble, the game returned to the previous theme of United dominance. Giggs saw a volley saved by James, before fizzing in a low cross that somehow eluded the lunging Scholes and Nemanja Vidic before trickling wide.

Hopes of a late winner were raised and then quickly dashed, as both Muntari and Ronaldo were red-carded by referee Steve Bennett, who blew the final whistle shortly after dismissing the Portuguese winger.

Not only had the Reds missed another glorious chance to post their first victory of the season, they would spend the next three games without the services of their most potent attacker.

PORTSMOUTH: James; Pamarot (Hughes 64), Cranie (Traore 46), Distin, Hreidarrson; Utaka, Davis, Mendes (Taylor 46), Muntari; Nugent, Benjani.
Subs not used: Ashdown, Kanu

Goal: Benjani (53)

UNITED: Van der Sar; Brown (Eagles 88), Ferdinand, Vidic, Evra; Ronaldo, Scholes, Carrick, Nani; Giggs (O'Shea 82), Tevez.
Subs not used: Kuszczak, Fletcher, Piqué

Goal: Scholes (15)

Sir Alex Ferguson admitted that Cristiano Ronaldo had fallen into a trap, and only had himself to blame after his red card at Fratton Park. The winger's act could only loosely be described as a headbutt, so minimal was the contact, and the United manager was far from enamoured by Steve Bennett's knee-jerk decision to issue a red card.

'I've looked at the replay a few times now and there's nothing conclusive – you can't really see anything,' he said. 'I believe he was provoked and he fell for it.'

'Cristiano was simply responsible for falling into a trap of intimidation. He was surprised about the decision, but really he's only himself to blame. It left us with ten men and now we're going to miss him for three games. It's a big blow. You get provoked and you have got to have the calmness to remind yourself you're a better player than these players and that is why they are doing it. He has fallen into the trap and paid the penalty for it.'

Given a few days to reflect on the events of the opening two games, Sir Alex had seen positives in his side's performances, but had noticed a worrying trend in the displays of referees.

'In a way, it's very difficult to be angry with Cristiano, because some of the things that happen to him on the pitch are not right,' he said. 'Late challenges worry me. We saw it again on Wednesday night. The referee let late challenges go unpunished time and time again. So there is a concern that way. People like Ronaldo are going to be the victims and people that watch the game are going to be the victims. It will end up with someone getting a serious injury.

'I think there is every chance that he might get a serious injury. You're not going to change Ronaldo. He likes to run at defenders and there is nobody in the game better at it than him. That's his game and what we want to see in him. That's where his courage comes into it. But the rest is down to the referee, and if you have got weak referees like against Portsmouth, you're going to be suffering.

'My fear is that I don't know if referees are a bit more tolerant of physical contact. I've noticed that in the last few months. Late challenges are going unpunished. Whether they [the referees] are getting instructions to manage these situations, I don't know.

'I thought these things were black and white. Late challenges should not be allowed. What disappointed me even more was when I heard [Sky Sports pundit] Andy Gray saying that the boy Dave Kitson shouldn't have been sent off for Reading against us. I think Andy Gray forgets that he was in the Seventies bashing into centre-halves. This is 2007. If Patrice Evra's foot had been on the ground it would have been a serious, serious injury. It could have killed his career. I know the boy Kitson is not that type of player but, nonetheless, it doesn't mean that he shouldn't be punished for doing stupid things on the pitch. Fortunately he was.'

But, more importantly, how did the boss feel about going into the Manchester derby below their local rivals in the Premier League table and still to register a first win of the season?

'I'm looking at the performances of the team in the first two games and saying to my players, "Well done",' he insisted. 'We're dropping points and that's disappointing and frustrating, because the performance levels have been very good. The important thing now is to be patient. The situation is recoverable.'

Sunday, 19 August 2007, City of Manchester Stadium

Attendance: 44,955

FA Barclays Premier League
Manchester City 1 **United** 0

Police around Eastlands must have been swarmed with concerned citizens at the final whistle – for some 40,000 people had just witnessed a mugging.

For the third game in a row, United were utterly dominant and oozed quality in a masterclass of passing and movement, but somehow failed to score again. And it got worse. The Reds' profligacy was rendered costly by Geovanni's first-half winner for Sven-Goran Eriksson's side.

The Brazilian – the scorer of a heartbreaking goal against United for Benfica in 2005 – struck a deflected long-range shot with City's only meaningful effort of the match. United, for their part, passed up another string of decent openings, and none were more inviting than an injury-time Carlos Tevez header, which was directed wide from inside the six-yard box.

City's victory owed much to United's charity in front of goal, but was reliant on outstanding performances from Richard Dunne and Micah Richards. Even when the Reds' forward line found a way past the City backline, they were thwarted by Kasper Schmeichel – son of United legend Peter.

Owen Hargreaves made his Reds' debut in a three-man midfield alongside Paul Scholes and Michael Carrick, and he was the outstanding performer as United ran their hosts ragged.

The midfield trio completely outplayed their City counterparts, and it was a neat flick from Scholes that played in Nani after five minutes. The Portuguese youngster tried to slot a low effort into the far corner, but was unable to beat Schmeichel, who saved well to his left-hand side.

Nani, Patrice Evra and Carlos Tevez all came close to putting United ahead, but instead it was City who took the lead just after the half-hour mark. Geovanni's speculative effort looked to be covered by van der Sar, but the wicked swerve generated by a deflection off Nemanja Vidic took the ball away from the Dutchman and into the bottom corner.

It was City's only attacking contribution of the match. United, however, continued to toil in vain. Vidic headed a Ryan Giggs corner against Schmeichel's crossbar, before Richards slid in to deny Tevez a certain tap-in.

Sir Alex Ferguson introduced teenage striker Fraizer Campbell for his senior debut, while Chris Eagles and John O'Shea were also thrown into the fray as the United manager looked for someone, anyone, to get a telling touch and beat City's resolute defence.

Time and again attacks faltered at the final hurdle as either Richards or Dunne made a telling interception, but it seemed that United had finally bagged the point they so richly deserved in the first minute of injury-time.

Giggs' inswinging right-wing cross evaded a mass of bodies and time slipped into slow motion as the ball bounced in front of Tevez. He instinctively directed the ball goalwards with a diving header inside the six-yard box, but somehow it fizzed past the post and into the perplexed United fans behind the goal.

It was the perfect embodiment of another frustrating afternoon, when yet again United's luck had stayed on the team coach.

MANCHESTER CITY: Schmeichel; Corluka, Dunne, Richards, Garrido; Johnson, Hamann, Geovanni (Ball 74), Petrov; Bojinov (Mpenza 8), Elano (Bianchi 63).

Subs not used: Hart, Onuoha

Goal: Geovanni (31)

UNITED: Van der Sar; Brown (O'Shea 73), Ferdinand, Vidic, Evra; Carrick (Campbell 73), Scholes, Hargreaves; Nani (Eagles 60), Giggs, Tevez. Subs not used: Kuszczak, Silvestre

Sir Alex Ferguson's post-match mood after his side's unlikely defeat at Eastlands was one of bemusement. Two points from three games was scant reward for three sterling performances and the manager was aware that his side needed a victory to kick-start their season, but he was still struggling to condemn his side's performances.

'We really should have sewn the game up even before they'd crossed the halfway line,' he said. 'We've only got ourselves to blame – let's make no mistake about that. I thought we were absolutely outstanding and completely dominated the game. But you have to say, with all these chances, we had to take one or two at least.

'You look around that field and there's not one bad performer. Everyone played their part. At this moment in time we'll use our experience to make sure we don't get carried away and have a knee-jerk reaction to it. What we do need, of course, is a win and we've got a home game against Tottenham next week. We've given ourselves an uphill fight; I don't think there's any question of that. Over the past few years we've always been able to overcome these things and we'll have to do that again.'

Owen Hargreaves was suffering a conflict of emotions after making his long-awaited United bow in such a bizarre defeat, with pride and despair in equal measure.

'To make my debut in a Manchester derby was the biggest moment of my career so far,' admitted the midfielder. 'But I was disappointed not to win. I am sure there will be more wins in the future though.

'We need to score goals. The most important thing is to have those chances. We have made them, but not utilised them. We could have scored one or two and they are things we have got to work on. We are missing Ronny [Cristiano Ronaldo] and Wazza [Wayne Rooney] and they are key players. We are going to miss those players at any time, but we still had enough on the pitch to win the game.

'It's a shame that we only have two points from three matches, because in those games we have pretty much dominated possession and could easily have won all three.'

With the Reds' title defence already being called into question by the media, the club needed a dose of good news. While the dust was still settling at Eastlands, that timely fillip filtered through from the Far East.

United's youngsters had jetted to Malaysia earlier in August to take part in the inaugural Champions Youth Cup, a prestigious competition pitting youth teams from some of world football's biggest clubs against each other. The Reds emerged from the group stages with victories over Porto and Boca Juniors, while a final-match defeat to Internazionale proved inconsequential. Barcelona and Brazilian side Flamengo were then ousted as United booked a berth in the final against Juventus.

A solitary goal from teenage striker Febian Brandy was enough to swing the final – and the trophy – in United's favour, and it marked a massive success: the Reds were the world's top youth side. Coach Andy Welsh led the team after a brief return from his role at Royal Antwerp, and he was elated with his side's triumph.

'I'm delighted with the result and extremely pleased with the performance of the players,' he enthused. 'It has been a fantastic tournament and we had a wonderful two-and-a-half weeks. The boys got to play teams from different parts of the world and it was a learning experience for them all.'

While Welsh and his young champions were returning from Kuala Lumpur with silverware in tow, Sir Alex Ferguson's senior squad were at Carrington in training for the looming visit of Tottenham, or out on international duty with their respective countries.

With a number of key players already on the sidelines, United's roster was further depleted by the sale of Gabriel Heinze. The Argentine was denied a move to Liverpool by a tribunal hearing, on the basis of a letter from United to the player's agents. The letter stipulated that the defender could leave Old Trafford for a set amount, but not to any of the club's English rivals.

Heinze's response to the verdict was swift. The next day he joined Real Madrid, bringing down the curtain on a three-year Old Trafford career that started so brightly – with him winning the 2004/05 Sir Matt Busby Player of the Year award – but ultimately fizzled out after injury problems and the emergence of Patrice Evra.

With that transfer saga finally done and dusted, Sir Alex had one less issue to occupy his thoughts as he prepared for the arrival of Martin Jol's side to Old Trafford. Despite the Reds' goal-shy start to the season, the boss was in confident mood.

'We will win the game on Sunday,' he said. 'Our performance level will win the game for us. There is no question Tottenham will come here with great determination. But with the ability in this team, I know the results we have been having will not carry on for long.'

Sunday, 26 August 2007, Old Trafford

Attendance: 75,696

FA Barclays Premier League
United 1 **Tottenham Hotspur** 0

After playing beautifully with scant reward in the three previous matches, United resorted to good, old-fashioned winning ugly to finally kick-start their season against Tottenham.

It took a moment of magic from Nani, with a 30-yard pile-driver 22 minutes from time, to settle the match in United's favour, but Tottenham could consider themselves highly unfortunate not to have taken anything from the game.

United started the match with only Derby County below them in the table, and anything other than victory would have turned what had merely been an eyebrow-raising blip into a full-scale crisis. There were plenty of hearts in mouths, then, when Robbie Keane clipped the crossbar for Spurs after just 20 seconds.

In an understandably nervous atmosphere, United took some time to settle. Rio Ferdinand saw a volley turned away by England team-mate Paul Robinson as the hosts slowly clicked into gear, before Michael Carrick and Paul Scholes both came close to breaking the deadlock.

The Reds' lack of attacking options remained at the fore, however, and a formational reshuffle saw Chris Eagles introduced on the wing at the expense of Carrick, with Ryan Giggs pushed up alongside Carlos Tevez.

The reaction was almost immediate, and almost disastrous. Dimitar Berbatov tangled with Edwin van der Sar and the ball trickled towards goal, only for Ferdinand to slide the ball heroically to safety. Moments later, irate Tottenham players surrounded the referee amid incorrect claims that Wes Brown had handled another Berbatov effort inside the area.

Tottenham's start to the season had only been marginally better than United's, so their desire to kickstart a winning run of their own was understandable. Those hopes were laid to rest in emphatic style, though, as Nani hit his first United goal – although Carlos Tevez may, in his brasher moments, cheekily claim that it should be credited to him.

Nani skipped past the challenge of Tom Huddlestone and lashed an unstoppable drive towards goal. The shot took the slightest nick off Tevez's head en route past Robinson, but it was the young Portuguese star who rightly took the plaudits and treated the Old Trafford faithful to a spectacular celebratory somersault.

The stadium erupted in joy, but any such emotions turned to nerves as the seconds ticked away. Berbatov – who had been the subject of a United club statement two days earlier, in which they denied any interest in signing the Bulgarian – came close to levelling matters with a superb long-range effort, only to see it dip narrowly over the bar.

That was the final noteworthy effort of the match, and United's season had finally begun.

UNITED: Van der Sar; Brown, Ferdinand, Vidic, Evra; Nani, Scholes, Hargreaves, Carrick (Eagles 57), Giggs; Tevez (Fletcher 78).
Subs not used: Dong, O'Shea, Kuszczak

Goal: Nani (68)

TOTTENHAM HOTSPUR: Robinson; Chimbonda, Rocha (Zokora 83), Gardner, Lee (Taarabt 75); Malbranque, Huddlestone, Jenas, Bale; Berbatov, Keane (Defoe 75).
Subs not used: Stalteri, Cerny

Nervy but not bothered was Sir Alex Ferguson's take on the Reds' first victory of the 2007/08 season.

'I thought we lacked a bit of confidence in the early part of the match,' he admitted. 'The players were anxious because expectation is high here, but once the first ten minutes were over, it was a reasonable performance from us, not brilliant, not as good as in previous games.

'What was required during the second half and right through the game was to dig in, play with great commitment and show the right discipline to win a football match. 1-0 was a great scoreline today simply because it was going to be a difficult game anyway. I can look on this result as the first time this season that we've had a little break. Hopefully it will give us the confidence to enjoy our football and we can now go on a long run.'

The roles of Nani and Carlos Tevez in United's victory, and their all-round adaptation to life at Old Trafford during a difficult period, drew high praise from Rio Ferdinand after the match.

'It isn't easy for the new signings to slot in, especially when there are a lot of injuries and the side's a bit fragmented,' said Ferdinand. 'It's been a difficult period for them, but they've done well. Carlos' movement, his know-how and his nous around the pitch have been very, very good.

'Nani's a young player with huge potential. It's fantastic for him, having come to a big club like United, to hit the target like that. In that respect he's similar to Ronaldo; he can hit the ball so hard that as long as he hits the target he's got a chance of scoring... Hopefully we're going to see a lot more goals like that in the future.'

However, while Rio had one eye on a bright and prosperous future at Old Trafford, another old head had taken the difficult decision to call time on what had been a simply wonderful United career. Ole Gunnar Solskjaer, with 12 major honours and over a decade of service to his name, decided that his ongoing knee injuries could not allow him to continue playing, and he confirmed the news two days after United's victory over Spurs.

A statement from the striker read: 'I would like to thank the manager, the coaching and medical staff and most of all the fans, who have supported me through my career. They have been fantastic and were a real inspiration to me when I was out injured. The support the fans and the staff showed me during that time was the main motivation for me making my comeback. I feel proud to have represented Manchester United for 11 years and have some very special memories.'

Sir Alex Ferguson quickly moved to retain the Norwegian's services and Solskjaer agreed to remain at Carrington as part of the club's coaching set-up. With his know-how and undoubted pedigree as a penalty-box predator, Sir Alex had no doubts that his new appointment was a coup.

'Ending your playing career is a sad day for anyone. In the case of Ole, he has 11 fantastic years [at Old Trafford] he can look back on,' said the manager. 'He has achieved everything a player could ever wish to achieve. He has been a great servant to the club and has always remained a model professional in his responsibility as a player, in his demeanour, and his manners have always been exemplary. Ole will hopefully go on to be a good coach.'

With Ole set to bid a personal farewell – in playing terms at least – to Old Trafford, and with Roy Keane due to make his first return as an opposition manager, Sunderland's visit to Manchester would be an emotional way to kick off September.

Chapter Three

SEPTEMBER – OFF AND RUNNING

Forty-eight hours after being pitched with AS Roma, Sporting Lisbon and Dynamo Kyiv in the Champions League group stages, the Reds were handed a home tie against Coventry City in the third round of the Carling Cup.

The Sky Blues were the early pace-setters in the Championship, leading the table with seven points from three games after beating Barnsley and Cardiff, and drawing with Hull.

Manager Iain Dowie was named August's Championship Manager of the Month as a result, and his side's good form had continued in the Carling Cup. Coventry were yet to concede a goal in the competition, having booked their trip to Old Trafford with comfortable 3-0 and 2-0 victories over Notts County and Carlisle respectively.

The game was scheduled to take place on Wednesday, 26 September but, before that, there was the small matter of three league games, against Sunderland, Everton and Chelsea, plus a Champions League trip to Sporting Lisbon to focus on.

As Sir Alex readied his troops for the tea-time clash with Roy Keane's Sunderland, he confirmed that Louis Saha was available for the first time this season following knee surgery, while Anderson was pencilled in for his United debut having shaken off a hamstring strain.

A first victory of the season against Tottenham six days earlier had got the Reds up and running in the league, and Sir Alex was hoping his side would continue against Sunderland where they had left off against Spurs.

Saturday, 1 September 2007, Old Trafford

Attendance: 75,648

FA Barclays Premier League
United 1 **Sunderland** 0

On a day of ovations for two United legends, it was a second-half cameo from the returning Louis Saha that stole the show and handed the Reds another vital three points.

The French striker, who had not been seen in action since last season's brief run-out in the Champions League semi-final defeat to AC Milan, returned with a bang, heading home Nani's 72nd-minute corner to bring the visitors' stubborn resistance – inspired by a fine performance from goalkeeper Craig Gordon – to an end.

Earlier, former Reds skipper Roy Keane – making his first appearance at Old Trafford as an opposition manager – was afforded a rapturous reception as he strode down the touchline towards the dug-out. He, along with both sets of players, then assembled to form a guard of honour for the recently retired Ole Gunnar Solskjaer. Old Trafford rose as one (including the generous travelling support) to salute the striker, whose deadly toe-poke at the Nou Camp in '99 will forever be part of the club's folklore.

After two legends of the modern era had been suitably recognised, it was time for the focus to switch to the present. All four of United's summer signings started the game, with Brazilian playmaker Anderson the latest debutant in attack. It was another new boy, Nani, however, who had the game's first sight of goal, but the winger's left-footed shot was scrambled away, albeit unconvincingly, by Gordon.

Clear-cut chances were at a premium during a fairly lacklustre first half, with Sunderland focused on stifling United's attack rather than mounting any real attacking threat of their own.

As half-time approached, both Carlos Tevez and Paul Scholes went close to breaking the deadlock. Gordon denied the Argentine, while a deflection off Danny Collins took Scholes' drilled shot fractionally wide of the Scot's right-hand post.

Having seen his side left frustrated in the opening 45 minutes, Sir Alex opted for both a change of approach and personnel with the introduction of Louis Saha for Anderson and a switch from a 4-3-3 formation to 4-4-2. It worked a treat. The presence of a target man up front injected a real thrust and purpose into the Reds' attacking play.

On 56 minutes Saha produced United's best moment of the match, brilliantly controlling the ball, before swivelling and lashing a volley goalwards. Gordon, the thorn in United's side all afternoon, plunged to his right to turn the effort away.

The Black Cats keeper managed to parry and gather a Hargreaves shot soon after but, 18 minutes from time, the Reds finally found a way through.

Nani fizzed in a superb left-wing corner that Saha converted, rising between Daryl Murphy and Nyron Nosworthy to head the ball home.

As the game entered its final stages, Hargreaves fired a shot just over the angle of post and crossbar, before substitute Darren Fletcher scooped an effort into the stands.

It mattered little, though. Saha had already made his mark and had crucially turned what only seemed like being one point into three.

UNITED: Van der Sar; Brown, Ferdinand, Vidic, Evra; Hargreaves, Scholes, Eagles (Fletcher 66); Anderson (Saha 46), Tevez, Nani (O'Shea 84).
Subs not used: Carrick, Kuszczak

Goal: Saha (72)

SUNDERLAND: Gordon; McShane, Nosworthy, Higginbotham, Collins; Etuhu (Miller 82), Leadbitter, Yorke, Wallace (Stokes 82); Chopra, Jones (Murphy 70).
Subs not used: Ward, Kay

Match-winner Louis Saha's relief and joy of being back in action and back among the goals was palpable as he faced the cameras after the game.

'It was a great feeling to score, but the most important thing was to win because we couldn't allow the gap [between United and the other top-four teams] to get any bigger,' he said.

'Being out injured is never easy for a footballer, but I've worked very hard to get back. I think any United player who has been out injured has to work twice as hard, because we have so many games across the course of the season. So I'm just glad to be back.'

Sir Alex was equally delighted to have the Frenchman at his disposal once more.

'Louis is such an important player for us. He gave us a good target to play to today and it improved our play enormously,' stated the boss. 'He showed his penetration, strength and speed. They're great assets to have and, of course, we've missed them for the last eight months now.

'It's a delight to have him back, particularly as he's got us the win today. He's come through fine, which we're pleased about as well.'

Another player also beaming with pride after the game was United debutant Anderson, who thoroughly enjoyed his 45-minute run-out.

'It was amazing to step out at Old Trafford,' he declared. 'It was a very proud moment, not just for me, but for my family as well. As a young boy it was always my dream to play for a big European club. I was lucky enough to do it with FC Porto and now I'm at United. I feel proud to be here and I want to do my best.'

Though disappointed to see his side come up short against the Reds, Sunderland boss Roy Keane took time out to pay tribute to the Old Trafford faithful for their warm welcome.

'I have to say the reception I got from the United fans was fantastic. They've always been great to me and I appreciate that very much. It's small consolation at this moment in time, though, because we lost the game. Nevertheless, I'm very grateful because they've always given me nothing but great support.'

Things got even better for United 24 hours later when goals from Zat Knight and Gabriel Agbonlahor condemned Chelsea to their first defeat of the season at Villa Park. However, Arsenal maintained their good form with a 3-1 win over Portsmouth at the Emirates, which put them level on points with leaders Liverpool who, a day earlier, had charged to the top of the table with a thumping victory over struggling Derby County at Anfield.

While a host of Reds headed off on international duty, there was still plenty going on at Old Trafford. Budding young defender Danny Simpson, who had recently been sidelined by a hernia problem, signed a new contract to keep him at the club until 2010, while, having been omitted from the Brazilian squad for their friendlies against USA and Mexico, Anderson continued to hone his fitness with a 64-minute outing in the reserves' defeat to Manchester City.

While some pundits had been somewhat underwhelmed by the midfielder's debut against Sunderland, Sir Alex remained confident in the Brazilian's ability, insisting that he simply needed a little more time to settle into English football's top flight.

'He's 19 years of age and is a player with great skill. I'm sure he'll be okay,' said the Reds manager. 'I thought he found it difficult against Sunderland because of the speed of the game and the way they set their stall out made it difficult for us.

'Also if you look at four of the lads that played – Anderson, [Chris] Eagles, [Carlos] Tevez and Nani – they've never played with each other before. We were pleased to get 45 minutes behind Anderson and, hopefully, the two weeks before the Everton game will give him a chance to improve.'

Anderson's arrival, allied to that of Owen Hargreaves, Nani and Carlos Tevez, meant competition for places was fierce within the camp. Sir Alex maintained that everyone would be given their chance to shine and that patience would be fully rewarded.

'We have to have players here who understand the dynamics of the operation of the club. When we're going for everything, some of them will have to be patient. They're going to get chances and play games, and in those matches they can be important players,' he declared.

'It's a challenge for me and the staff to make sure we're being fair and picking the right team. It's also a challenge for the players to show loyalty to us, and if they don't think that we're being fair, then they have every right to come and see me. The door is always open.

'Look at players like Phil Neville and Nicky Butt. For three or four years they weren't regular starters, but they loved the club, they were patient and prepared to accept that they wouldn't play every game, but they always got 20-odd matches a season. You can't do it forever and you have to be fair to them, and let them move on when they want to. But Nicky and Phil can still sit back and think, "I've got eight or nine medals from my time there," which is a fantastic achievement.'

Aside from the abundance of riches in the first-team dressing room, Sir Alex was equally buoyed by the club's strength in reserve following the return of a number of young players from loan spells.

'I think we've got a terrific bunch with Dong [Fangzhuo], [Fraizer] Campbell, [Lee] Martin, [Darron] Gibson and [Chris] Eagles – who has come on unbelievably well – [Gerard] Piqué, [Jonny] Evans, [Danny] Simpson... they're all excellent,' insisted the boss. 'The hardest thing will be to manage the situation, but we have plans that'll ensure they get enough football.'

There was mixed news from the treatment room as the Reds prepared for their lunchtime trip to Goodison Park following the latest round of international games.

On a positive front, the United boss would once again be able to call upon Wayne Rooney following his recovery from a broken foot (although Sir Alex admitted that he may save the striker for the midweek trip to Lisbon) and Cristiano Ronaldo was available after serving a three-match suspension following his dismissal at Portsmouth.

Not so good was the news that Owen Hargreaves, who missed both of England's Euro 2008 qualifiers with a thigh strain, remained a slight doubt, while Darren Fletcher and John O'Shea were all but certain to miss out after both were injured playing for their countries. Fletcher limped off in Scotland's famous win over France and seemed likely to be out for around six weeks, while O'Shea appeared to pick up a knee injury during the Republic of Ireland's loss to the Czech Republic and faced a week or so on the sidelines.

Skipper Gary Neville was also struggling after straining a thigh in training as he stepped up his recovery from ankle-ligament damage.

'I probably did a bit too much. I was a bit over-excited at getting back and I just felt my thigh a little bit. It's very frustrating,' he admitted. 'Hopefully in the next week or two I'll be back and I hope to be playing games in the next couple of weeks definitely. Because I've been out for such a long time I think the Everton game is going to be too soon. I think it [his return to action] will probably be after that.'

Saturday, 15 September 2007, Goodison Park

Attendance: 39,364

FA Barclays Premier League
Everton 0 **United** 1

Nemanja Vidic has become a cult hero at Old Trafford and after a performance like this it's easy to see why.

After a rock-solid defensive display throughout the 90 minutes, the big Serbian showed he can be just as deadly at the other end, powering home United's winner with just seven minutes to go.

In the build-up to the game – the Reds' first for two weeks following the international break – there was talk of Wayne Rooney making a surprise comeback at his former stomping ground. But with Cristiano Ronaldo returning from suspension, Carlos Tevez getting sharper by the game and Louis Saha available on the bench, Sir Alex Ferguson opted not to risk the striker.

United controlled large periods of possession and attacked with purpose from the start. Patrice Evra, playing in a more advanced role on the left flank, had United's first sight of goal latching on to a brilliant through-ball from Tevez, only to lash his effort into the side-netting. Soon after, Joleon Lescott managed to divert Ronaldo's fizzing shot away from danger as United continued to pile the pressure on the home side.

The half ended on a sour note, however, when Mikael Silvestre was stretchered off after slipping and twisting his knee. Nani replaced the Frenchman and took up duties on the left wing, with Evra dropping back into his familiar left-back role.

Everton began to find their feet after the break with Yakubu proving a handful for United's backline. The Nigerian set up Phil Jagielka to strike just wide two minutes after the re-start, and then won a corner from which Paul Scholes was forced to clear off the line from Andy Johnson's header.

United kept on probing, but to no avail. A neat interchange between Ronaldo and Tevez, saw the Argentine clipping the ball over the Everton defence and into Scholes' path, but the midfielder uncharacteristically fired over.

Saha entered the fray just after the hour as the Reds looked to step up their attacking exertions. Ronaldo thought he'd earned a penalty in the 70th minute, but referee Alan Wiley gave Everton a free-kick and booked the winger for diving instead.

It looked like being one of those days for United, until Evra won a corner on the left, which Nani duly swung in. Vidic darted to the near post and bulleted a header past the helpless Wessels. Remarkably, it was United's first attempt on target.

The Serbian international looked to have sealed the points, but there was still the odd scare or two to be had. James McFadden came on for former Red Phil Neville and immediately tested Edwin van der Sar with a 20-yard effort. The Dutchman palmed it away, but it fell to substitute Victor Anichebe inside the six-yard area. United's fans, hearts in mouths, winced, but Rio Ferdinand came to the rescue to block the Nigerian's shot, before Yobo fired wide.

United may not have been at their most fluent best but, after a stuttering start, a third 1-0 win in a row ensured the Reds' title charge continued to gather momentum.

EVERTON: Wessels; Hibbert, Yobo, Lescott, Baines; Osman (Pienaar 72) P Neville (McFadden 84), Jagielka, Arteta; Johnson, Yakubu (Anichebe 72) Subs not used: Turner, Carsley

UNITED: Van der Sar; Brown, Ferdinand, Vidic, Silvestre (Nani 40, (Piqué 84)); Ronaldo, Carrick, Scholes, Evra; Giggs (Saha 62), Tevez
Subs not used: Kuszczak, Gibson

Goal: Vidic (83)

'It was a great result,' declared Sir Alex after the match, paying tribute to his team's resolve. 'A lot of teams will drop points here. It was a real battle and it looked like it was going to be a draw, until we got a lifeline with Nemanja's goal.

'It wasn't a great performance, but the whole team worked very hard and we defended very well. They had a chance at 1-0, but Edwin made a terrific save and Rio made a fantastic block from the follow-up. That's determined defending, and it's the kind you need to win the title. If we can keep that going then, once we've got all our top players back and got the consistency of our performance, we'll be alright.'

The same couldn't be said for Mikael Silvestre, who, it was confirmed, had suffered cruciate-ligament damage and was likely to miss the remainder of the season.

Defensive team-mate and goalscoring hero Nemanja Vidic highlighted United's togetherness and their ability to defend in numbers as being the key to the victory.

'We played like a team,' he said. 'It's not just two players; everyone played well and that helped us get the result. Yakubu is strong and Johnson is quick and likes the ball in the channels. But we knew about them and stopped them from getting chances.

'With our ability going forward, we knew we'd be able to score, and we did. We came for the win and got it. Sometimes you have to make sure you don't lose a goal.

'It's always difficult after the international break,' he added. 'We knew that it would be hard against Everton and that we'd need to play a compact game. And we did that.'

Vidic and his comrades soon switched their attentions to United's opening Champions League Group F game in Lisbon, with stand-in skipper Ryan Giggs stressing the importance of getting off to a winning start.

'If we play to our best ability, we should get out of the group quite comfortably,' declared Giggs. 'It's a tough group because they're all good teams and the away games will be particularly hard.

'But we are better equipped for Europe than we were last year. We have brought in players who have experience in Europe and, hopefully, the younger lads can learn from their experience last year.

'I remember when I was a young lad. I learnt something new from every game I played in Europe, especially away from home. Each game you play you get better and have more confidence. Hopefully that will be the case for the team this year.'

Who would lead the line in Lisbon remained unclear, as Sir Alex admitted a lack of match fitness among his attackers had given him plenty to ponder.

'Carlos Tevez has been doing exceptionally and is getting better and better, but on Saturday, in the last 20 minutes, he tired again,' explained the manager. 'Louis Saha is someone we're gauging match to match. The plan is to ease him into games as we go. Remember, he's been out for eight months. As for Wayne Rooney, he's only played a game and a half this season, which was more than a month ago.

'I don't know if I'll start him, put him on the bench, start him with Carlos Tevez... Maybe I'll do the same as we did at Goodison Park and play Tevez up front with Giggs. Do I bring Saha and Rooney on at half-time? There are decisions to make. We have to make sure we make the right team selection because we want to win.'

Wednesday, 19 September 2007, Estadio Jose Alvalade

Attendance: 39,514

UEFA Champions League Group F
Sporting Lisbon 0 **United** 1

Cristiano Ronaldo returned to haunt his former club with a superb headed winner to get United's Champions League campaign off to the perfect start.

The ex-Sporting winger was afforded a standing ovation from the Estadio Jose Alvalade faithful following his deliberately muted celebration, after diving to meet Wes Brown's excellent cross just after the hour.

In truth though, the Reds owed as much to Edwin van der Sar as they did to Ronaldo for ensuring they left Lisbon with three points in the bag. The Dutch stopper enjoyed one of his finest nights in a red shirt, fending off countless long-range efforts from the hosts and making two superb saves either side of Ronaldo's breakthrough.

In addition to securing an opening win in Group F – the Reds' 100th Champions League victory in total – another major positive was the 72-minute outing for Wayne Rooney, who was making his first appearance since breaking his foot on the opening day of the season.

Lisbon bossed the opening exchanges and came close to taking the lead on 28 minutes. Liedson bent a shot towards the top corner, but van der Sar hurled himself towards it and somehow managed to claw the ball round the post.

There were further nervy moments for the Reds, most notably a deflected free-kick from Brazilian defender Ronny, but van der Sar once again had it covered.

Having ridden their luck somewhat, United began to grow in stature as the half wore on. Nani went close with a deflected shot after a rapid counter-attack, while Sporting had Anderson Polga to thank when his last-ditch intervention prevented Rooney from tapping home Ryan Giggs' low centre.

The Welshman himself spurned United's most clear-cut chance of the evening on 58 minutes, heading over the bar after a run fine run and cross from Ronaldo.

Four minutes later, however, the Reds went ahead when Ronaldo stooped to head home Brown's right-wing centre.

The winger's decision not to rub salt into Lisbon's wounds, by barely celebrating, was sportingly recognised by the home fans and applause began to ripple round the ground.

Another former Sporting starlet, Nani, almost doubled the tally in the 70th minute, but his powerful shot was parried clear by Vladimir Stojkovic.

With 12 minutes left, United had van der Sar to thank once again. Tonel ghosted onto the end of a left-wing cross, but the Dutch stopper plunged low to his right and averted the ball to safety.

After testing Stojkovic once more with a winding run and low shot, Ronaldo was given a standing ovation by both sets of fans as he left proceedings four minutes from time. It had indeed been the perfect homecoming.

SPORTING LISBON: Stojkovic; Abel, Tonel, Anderson Polga, Ronny (Pereirinha 74); Izmailov (Vukcevic 55), Veloso, Joao Moutinho, Romagnoli (Purovic 67); Djalo, Liedson.
Subs not used: Tiago, Paredes, Farnerud, Gladstone

UNITED: Van der Sar; Brown, Vidic, Ferdinand, Evra; Ronaldo (Tevez 85), Carrick, Scholes, Giggs (Anderson 76), Nani; Rooney (Saha 72).
Subs not used: Kuszczak, Piqué, J Evans, Eagles

Goal: Ronaldo (62)

The victory was only United's third in 15 Champions League away games and provided a timely tonic for those who doubted the Reds' ability to perform away from Old Trafford. What's more, it provided the perfect start to a new Champions League campaign.

'It was a good night for us. Winning your first match of the group away from home – just like we did last season – sets the tone. Getting off to a good start is always important,' insisted Sir Alex.

'This victory will give the players a good confidence boost, because we went a couple of years without winning away from home in Europe. Last season we changed that trend and it got us back to how we were eight or nine years ago when we were a constant threat away from home.

'Tactically things were, in the main, very good. Our penetration was better in the second half and there was more purpose to our game. They had some opportunities from the edge of the box, but they never really opened us up and that was our plan.'

The United boss was also pleased to see Ronaldo get off the mark in the goalscoring stakes after what had been, on a personal level, an opening month to forget.

'It's good he's got his first goal. His suspension derailed him a little bit, but I'm sure he's back on track now,' maintained Sir Alex.

The man himself was bursting with pride at heading the winner in his homeland, but admitted he felt a tad guilty that it resulted in defeat for his former club.

'Red is my colour and I want to win for United,' he said. 'I said before the game that Sporting is my second home and I feel a little bit sad, but the most important thing is United. They are my team and I'm very happy with the victory.'

Four wins out of four ensured the Reds went into their biggest game of the season so far, against Chelsea, in fine fettle. Less could be said of the Blues who, just three days before their visit to Old Trafford, announced they had sensationally parted company with manager Jose Mourinho by mutual consent. Speculation had been rife about the Portuguese's future after the Blues' indifferent start to the campaign, but the news still sent shockwaves through the game.

Chelsea confirmed former director of football Avram Grant, a close friend of club owner Roman Abramovich and the former coach of Israel, Maccabi Tel-Aviv and Maccabi Haifa, as Mourinho's successor alongside his previous assistant Steve Clarke.

At the pre-match press conference, Sir Alex Ferguson paid a brief, but glowing, tribute to Mourinho and admitted that he was going to miss the challenge of squaring up to his Portuguese counterpart.

'Jose leaving is a disappointment for the game,' he said genuinely. 'I think he was terrific for football and, of course, for Chelsea. I enjoyed the competition with him and I think he brought something fresh and new to our game. I've sent him a message and told him I'll miss my glass of wine with him on Sunday.

'He's been fantastic and brought unparalleled success. It's certainly a challenge for the man that replaces him. At the moment it's Avram Grant.

'I wish Jose well, but that's as far as I want to put it. What happens at Chelsea doesn't matter to us. We've got to focus on our game, because we will still be facing the same set of players. And that's a challenge enough for us. If you look at the record between the two teams over the last three or four years, there is nothing in it. Very few goals are scored. It's always a tight, tight game.'

Sunday, 23 September 2007, Old Trafford

Attendance: 75,633

FA Barclays Premier League
United 2 **Chelsea** 0

Chelsea arrived at Old Trafford Mourinho-less and winless in their last three games, and they were left point-less come full-time after Carlos Tevez and Louis Saha sent United second in the table.

Soon after John Obi Mikel's first-half sending-off, Tevez headed home his first goal in a red shirt, before Saha compounded Chelsea's and Avram Grant's misery a minute from time, when he converted from the spot.

The build-up to the game had been dominated by Jose Mourinho's shock departure, but Sir Alex Ferguson called for the Reds to focus on their own game, rather than worry about the managerial antics at Stamford Bridge. And they did that to good effect almost immediately.

Wayne Rooney latched on to a ball won by Ryan Giggs in midfield, cut inside Tal Ben-Haim, before curling a shot towards the far top corner, which Petr Cech somehow managed to tip away.

With his attacking options somewhat blunted by the absence of Didier Drogba and Frank Lampard through injury, new Blues' boss Grant stuck to his predecessor's 4-5-1 template as the visitors looked to contain and frustrate United.

They were lucky not to concede a penalty on 20 minutes, however, when Joe Cole tangled with Patrice Evra inside the area. The Stretford End bellowed as one for a spot-kick, but referee Mike Dean ushered away the protests.

United continued to enjoy the lion's share of the goalscoring opportunities with Giggs the next player to go close, volleying Rooney's cross just over the bar. The Reds' were further boosted just after the half-hour mark when John Obi Mikel was given his marching orders following a two-footed mid-air challenge on Evra. Thankfully for the Frenchman, he didn't follow through, but referee Dean still deemed Mikel's intent worthy of a straight red card.

Things got even better for United on the stroke of half-time as Tevez darted into space and dived to head home Giggs' inviting centre, prompting wild celebrations in front of an ecstatic Stretford End.

Deprived of their full midfield arsenal following Mikel's dismissal, the visitors opted to sit back and hit United on the counter-attack after the break. But the Blues' tactics bore little fruit in the face of an outstanding display from United's rock solid backline.

Grant was lucky not to see his side reduced to nine men midway through the second period after Joe Cole brought down Cristiano Ronaldo in full flight and got away with just a caution.

United made the result safe a minute from time when substitute Louis Saha, on for the industrious Tevez, was clipped in the area by Ben-Haim. The striker dusted himself down, before firing the spot-kick down the centre of the goal.

Just as his predecessor had done, Chelsea's new boss bemoaned the refereeing decisions that he felt had swung the match in United's favour. In truth, though, the better team – and the hungrier one – deservedly walked away with all three points.

UNITED: Van der Sar; Brown, Ferdinand, Vidic, Evra; Ronaldo, Carrick, Scholes, Giggs; Tevez (Saha 79), Rooney.
Subs not used: Kuszczak, O'Shea, Nani, Piqué

Goals: Tevez (45), Saha (89, pen)

CHELSEA: Cech; Ferreira, Ben-Haim, Terry, A. Cole; J. Cole (Pizarro 76), Mikel, Makelele, Essien, Malouda (Wright-Phillips 69); Shevchenko (Kalou 59).
Subs not used: Cudicini, Alex

Ryan Giggs saluted his side's impeccable timing after the victory over Chelsea moved United second in the table and within two points of leaders Arsenal, who had run out 5-0 winners against Derby County 24 hours earlier. The captain admitted the dismissal of John Obi Mikel could have worked against the Reds, especially if the visitors had reached the break on level terms.

'When you play against ten men, they all get behind the ball and it can be difficult,' said the winger. 'But we scored at the right time.'

Giggs was the provider for United's opener as Carlos Tevez opened his account for the club.

'You get the ball into the area and hope the centre-forwards get in there,' added Giggs. 'Carlos made a great run – you score loads of goals running across the near post and he managed to do that. I was really pleased to see it go in.'

Sir Alex Ferguson hailed the Argentine's all-round display, labelling him 'brave as a lion and tough as nails'.

'I think this will only help him,' insisted the manager. 'I was pleased that he got off the mark, because he had a good goalscoring record with West Ham. He's got a lot of excellent qualities, he's a clever player and is still only a young lad, 23 years of age. Carlos has got a cocky confidence in his own ability as well as great awareness. He will only get better.'

Tevez's fellow striker Louis Saha also had a lot to be pleased about having come on to fire his second goal of the season. The Frenchman insisted he was finally beginning to feel more like his old self after a series of injury setbacks and remained determined to silence the critics who believe he doesn't have the mental strength to succeed.

'Anyone who says I am not willing to play until I am 100 per cent fit is not telling the truth,' he declared. 'I have never refused to play for the team, yet last season I was hearing claims about me not being psychologically committed.

'The people who criticise me don't know that three years ago I was playing games despite having a knee that I couldn't bend more than 90 degrees. I now feel I am close to last year's top form. I am not far away and the more minutes I gain on the pitch, the better I will play. My aim this year is to stay fit and show people the real Louis Saha.'

Saha, like a number of first-team regulars, would be given a breather for the Reds' Carling Cup third-round tie with Coventry City at Old Trafford. Almost a dozen reserves and fringe players – including Gerard Piqué, Chris Eagles and Tomasz Kuszczak – looked set to be given their chance to shine, while senior squad members Nani, Anderson and John O'Shea were also expected to be involved.

'This is a really important night for these players,' declared Sir Alex prior to kick-off. 'They all want regular first-team football and that's not easy to manage. I'm trying to get them games in the Premier League and in Europe too, but Wednesday is a great opportunity for them.

'You have to use your squad throughout the course of the season, and I'll be doing that when the time is right. At the moment they might not see that, but it will happen and I know they won't let us down.

'A lot of these players have already shown great improvement. There's real promise there and that's what we want to see on Wednesday. We want them to play with the kind of commitment they see from the first-team players every week.'

Unfortunately for Sir Alex he was to be left very disappointed.

Wednesday, 26 September 2007, Old Trafford

Attendance: 74,055

Carling Cup, Third Round
United 0 **Coventry City** 2

Given United's history of producing homegrown talent down the years, much is always expected whenever a new crop of young charges are given their chance to shine at the Theatre of Dreams.

Unfortunately for the Reds, a serious case of stage fright set in during the Carling Cup third-round clash with Coventry City, which resulted in United's budding youngsters falling at the first hurdle and crashing out of the competition.

Sir Alex selected a starting XI with an average age of just 21 with club debuts for centre-half Jonny Evans and full-back Danny Simpson. Eight of the starting line-up – Nani, Anderson and John O'Shea excluded – were handed their first starts of the 2007/08 campaign. But, as with all infrequently assembled sides, it took this United team time to find their feet, especially under the close attention they received from Coventry's players, who were prepared to fight for every ball.

The opening 20 minutes promised much as the Reds grew in confidence. Gerard Piqué started solidly at the back; Lee Martin and Nani looked lively on the flanks; while Anderson showed some nice touches and a wide range of passes. And, after 17 minutes, the Brazilian sliced open the Coventry defence with a ball to Nani, which ended with Martin's deflected volley dropping just wide.

Unfortunately that was as close as United came for the rest of the evening as the visitors took a stranglehold on the game. They crucially took the lead on 27 minutes with Sky Blues skipper Michael Doyle crossing for Michael Mifsud to tap home. The Maltese forward almost grabbed his, and Coventry's, second moments later when he flicked Robbie Simpson's cross onto the post.

United began the second period as they had started the first, with Nani and substitute Fraizer Campbell trying their luck from distance, while Dong Fangzhuo and sub Michael Carrick had efforts deflected away from danger.

Having stood firm in defence, Iain Dowie's side struck the killer blow 20 minutes from time as Mifsud doubled his tally for the night. Breaking down the left, he evaded Piqué's challenge, played a one-two with Jay Tabb and lashed his shot past Tomasz Kuszczak. He

Cristiano Ronaldo, the undisputed darling of the Asian supporters, Wayne Rooney and new signing Nani were all on the scoresheet as United hit Shenzhen FC for six during the 2007 pre-season tour.

Sir Alex parades two of his summer signings. The deal for Anderson came out of the blue, but it took months of negotiations before the Reds finally sealed the capture of Carlos Tevez.

Owen Hargreaves was forced to sit out the opening three games of the season, while fellow new arrival Nani made an instant impact on his first start at Old Trafford, firing a vital winner against Spurs.

Edwin van der Sar saved all three of Chelsea's penalties in the shoot-out at Wembley as the Reds lifted the Community Shield.

The squad celebrate their first piece of silverware of the season.

With the league season just 35 minutes old, the curse of the metatarsal strikes Wayne Rooney yet again in the 0–0 draw against Reading.

Paul Scholes celebrates his first goal of the season, a rasping effort against Portsmouth at Fratton Park, but the game ended in a draw as United dropped two more points.

Even when United's front men found a way past the City backline, they were thwarted by Kasper Schmeichel, son of United legend Peter, and ended up 1–0 losers.

It took a moment of magic from Nani, with a 30-yard piledriver, to seal United's first league win of the campaign, against Spurs.

Old Trafford stands as one to salute Ole Gunnar Solskjaer before the Sunderland game, following the Norwegian's decision to call time on his career.

Fellow United legend Roy Keane was given a warm welcome on his first return to Old Trafford as a manager, but Louis Saha's goal secured victory for United.

Nemanja Vidic rises to power home Nani's corner and claims a vital victory for United at Goodison Park seven minutes from time.

Cristiano Ronaldo enjoyed a 'perfect night' on his return to his homeland, scoring the only goal against former club Sporting Lisbon whose fans gave him a standing ovation. Wayne Rooney's return from injury provided further cause for cheer for United.

Carlos Tevez becomes an instant United hero as he celebrates his first goal in a red shirt in the September win over Chelsea, playing their first game under new manager Avram Grant.

Sir Alex Ferguson admitted he was 'shocked and flabbergasted' by United's performance in the 2–0 Carling Cup defeat to Coventry City.

Wayne Rooney opens his account for the season with a smart, first-time finish past Roma's Gianluca Curci to secure the points in the Champions League Group F fixture on 2 October.

United moved top of the table with an emphatic, irresistible second-half display against Wigan.

could have completed his hat-trick soon after when the Polish stopper spilled Michael Doyle's low free-kick, but he fired wide.

It may have been a night to forget for United's youngsters, but at least it provided them with a lesson they would never forget.

UNITED: Kuszczak; Bardsley (Brown 46), Piqué, Evans (Carrick 56), Simpson; Martin (Campbell 46), O'Shea, Anderson, Nani; Eagles, Dong.
Subs not used: Heaton, A Eckersley

COVENTRY CITY: Marshall; Borrowdale, Ward, Turner, Osbourne (McNamee 88); Simpson, Doyle, Hughes, Tabb, Mifsud; Best (Adebola 90).
Subs not used: Konstantopoulos, De Zeeuw, Thornton

Goals: Mifsud (27, 70)

A visibly stunned Sir Alex Ferguson admitted he was 'shocked and flabbergasted' by United's performance against the Sky Blues. A young Reds team never really got going against Iain Dowie's men and that disappointed the boss, who had given a number of the club's emerging talents the chance to shine on the first-team stage in front of 75,000 fans.

'You take it on the chin,' insisted the boss. 'But that was an absolutely flabbergasting performance, I didn't expect that. I'm not interested in giving reasons; it was just a bad performance. We have great faith in the young players. It's a big shock to us all.

'Coventry made it a cup tie – that was certainly an issue in the first half. They were first to every ball and maybe some of our players were not used to that kind of cup football. And it was typical of cup football that, after a great save from their goalkeeper, they go up the other end and kill the game.'

The players themselves were equally horrified by such an uncharacteristic display, and Gerard Piqué admitted he felt 'horrible' at the final whistle.

'Looking up at the scoreboard and seeing 2-0 was a horrible feeling, especially when you're up against a Championship side at

Old Trafford,' said the bewildered Spaniard. 'I thought we started the game well and had some good possession. But their first goal brought them alive. After the break we didn't feel good and when they scored the second it was a horrible feeling.

'Some people will think we've missed our chance. We know we did a lot of things wrong and we're all very disappointed. We gave everything we could on the pitch, but things just didn't go our way. You can always learn from these situations and hopefully we will grow as players.'

The Carling Cup had been viewed as an opportunity to give United's young starlets the platform to show what they could do. But with that avenue now cut off, Sir Alex admitted there would be loan moves for a number of youngsters.

'We looked at the League Cup as a chance for these players to play. Now that's gone we'll have to review the situation with one or two of them going on loan, because they do need football,' revealed the boss.

'With [Gary] Neville and [Owen] Hargreaves on their way back [from injury], we've got a good strong squad. There'll have to be some that we have to keep. Piqué was excellent on Wednesday. He was our best player, along with Anderson. We'll probably keep Simpson as he can play both full-back positions. But I'm looking at the rest going out on loan as they need to play football.'

At a club like United there are always new challenges just around the corner as soon as one has passed, and a Saturday tea-time trip to Birmingham City ensured the Carling Cup defeat soon became a distant memory as attentions turned back to the Reds' title charge.

Owen Hargreaves, who had not featured since the win over Sunderland, had an outside chance of making the bench, while Sir Alex confirmed Gary Neville was edging ever closer to a return to action, initially for the reserves.

There was more good news on fellow defender and cruciate-ligament victim Mikael Silvestre. Initial reports had claimed the Frenchman would miss the rest of United's 2007/08 campaign, but Sir Alex said he now expected him be fit for the title run-in.

'I'm sure Mikael will be back in March,' revealed the boss. 'We had him operated on in France recently and it all went well. It was pleasing to see there was no further damage other than the cruciate ligament. That was a big bonus.'

Prior to kick-off, the Reds received news of Chelsea's failure to beat South London neighbours Fulham. The Blues were unable to find a way past the Cottagers in the 0-0 stalemate at Stamford Bridge and also lost Didier Drogba (sent off) and John Terry (cheekbone injury) in the second half. Fellow title contenders Arsenal and Liverpool both enjoyed away victories at West Ham and Wigan respectively. It meant that only three points would do for United at St Andrews.

Saturday, 29 September 2007, St Andrews

Attendance: 26,526

FA Barclays Premier League
Birmingham City 0 **United** 1

Friends turned foes can so often return to haunt you in football, and former United skipper Steve Bruce very nearly got one over on his old side at St Andrews. A piece of opportunism from Cristiano Ronaldo ensured the Reds left the Midlands with exactly what they came for – three points – but it was close, very close.

Sir Alex made wholesale changes to the side that lost to Coventry in the Carling Cup, with all 11 who started in the victory over Chelsea returning to action.

United looked shaky from the off, particularly in defence, and Edwin van der Sar was twice called into action in the opening two minutes. After Paul Scholes was caught in possession, Cameron Jerome let fly with a shot that required quick reactions from the Dutch goalkeeper. Frank Queudrue was first to meet the resulting corner and his powerful downward header forced another smart save from van der Sar.

Those early scares may have failed to jolt the Reds' attack into life, but there was no doubting their defensive qualities. It was epitomised by Rio Ferdinand who, in the 18th minute, brilliantly hooked Gary McSheffrey's header off the line after Patrice Evra had dallied too long in attempting to shepherd the ball out of play.

Cristiano Ronaldo mustered the Reds' first sight of goal with a low drive soon after, but his effort was directed straight at Blues goalkeeper Maik Taylor.

Birmingham continued their onslaught on United's goal with the visitors doing little to help their own cause. Shortly after receiving treatment on his toe on 23 minutes, van der Sar left his area to deal with a through-ball, but his scuffed clearance fell straight to Jerome. Thankfully, the striker was unable to muster enough elevation in his strike to clear the covering Nemanja Vidic.

With van der Sar visibly struggling, Ferdinand assumed responsibility for goal kicks until Polish stopper Tomasz Kuszczak replaced the Dutchman at the break.

The Reds began the second period in a much more positive fashion, with Carlos Tevez forcing Taylor into action after good link-up play with Ryan Giggs.

Moments later, Taylor was beaten as United went ahead. Ronaldo pounced on sloppy defending from Queudrue on the edge of his own box before brilliantly rounding Taylor and slotting home. It was the Portuguese winger's first league goal from open play since February and it gave the Reds a vital, if not wholly deserved, lead.

Kuszczak showed his worth on 56 minutes when a McSheffrey shot flicked off Ferdinand and looked set for the top corner before the Pole intervened with a flying save at the near post.

The action continued at both ends – McSheffrey fizzed a free-kick inches wide of the post, Wayne Rooney saw his shot cleared off the line and Tevez blasted over from 18 yards. Ten minutes from time Ronaldo skewed an effort wide from 12 yards when he should have scored.

It mattered little in the end, though. The Portuguese star had already done the necessary damage and ensured Sir Alex reigned victorious over his former pupil.

BIRMINGHAM CITY: Taylor; Kelly, Djourou (Schmitz 76), Ridgewell, Queudrue; Larsson, Nafti (O'Connor 84), Muamba (Palacios 71), McSheffrey; Kapo, Jerome.
Subs not used: Kingson, Danns

UNITED: Van der Sar (Kuszczak 46); Brown, Vidic, Ferdinand, Evra; Carrick, Scholes, Ronaldo, Giggs (Saha 64); Tevez (O'Shea 89), Rooney.
Subs not used: Anderson, Piqué

Goal: Ronaldo (51)

Sir Alex was unconcerned by the narrow margin of victory against Steve Bruce's side, believing his team had shown further signs that they were close to hitting peak form.

'I think we're getting towards top gear,' declared the boss. 'You could see signs of that today. Some of the movement up front was very good. Rooney, Ronaldo and Tevez are big threats for all our opponents and the forward line is looking much better now.

'I actually thought that Birmingham were by far the better team in the first half, although we did carve out some good chances for ourselves. I would say it was the hardest game of the season so far. Even at 1-0 we were just praying to get through the match. Late on, they kept pumping balls into the box, but we coped with that well. They're a big side, very athletic, and we had to be on our toes in the second half. It's a good result for us, a very good result.

'Ronaldo's goal might have come from a mistake by one of their players, but his composure in beating the man, beating the goalkeeper and then finishing was excellent. He was sensational today. The boy is so good it's frightening. His capabilities are unending.'

The man himself was pleased to cap his performance with the winning goal and insisted his best form was still to come.

'I always try to work hard in training and, hopefully, I will keep improving and more goals will come as well,' said Ronaldo. 'But my main concern is the team – I think only about that. The most important thing in football is getting the three points and I was pleased we did that against Birmingham. We didn't play as well as we can, but sometimes you can win matches without playing well. Our good football is coming. We have great players at the club and great staff and we will improve.'

It was an ominous warning indeed for United's upcoming opponents.

Chapter Four

OCTOBER – FOUR-MIDABLE REDS

United began October in a strange state of unfamiliar familiarity – winning, but not in the way they were accustomed. The Reds' 1-0 victory at Birmingham was their fifth single-goal triumph of the season, although defender Nemanja Vidic was far from concerned.

'We're delighted as long as we win,' said the Serbian defender. 'It's always important to keep a clean sheet, especially when we only score once. But we are proud and happy because it was an important three points.

'It wasn't a great game. We started badly and made a couple of mistakes in the first 20 minutes, which gave Birmingham a bit of hope. We gave them a few half chances, but we'll improve on that for the next match.'

Having watched Edwin van der Sar sustain a toe injury at St Andrews, Vidic would be lining up for the Reds' next outing, against AS Roma, ahead of Polish goalkeeper Tomasz Kuszczak.

The Pole would be making his European debut, but Sir Alex Ferguson had no qualms about the incoming custodian.

'I'm very confident that Tomasz can step up to the Champions League,' Sir Alex said in the pre-match press conference. 'The boy just needed the opportunity. Especially with the ability and experience of Edwin, it is difficult for any young goalkeeper to get games. But he showed on Saturday against Birmingham, as he has done in the past, that he can do very well. I was very pleased with his performance against Birmingham.'

With Roma back at Old Trafford just six months after their 7-1 quarter-final humiliation, there was no doubt the *giallorossi* would be seeking vengeance in Manchester. Certainly anybody expecting a repeat scoreline would be disappointed, according to Owen Hargreaves.

'There will be no repeat of the 7-1,' said the midfielder. 'Those results happen perhaps once every four years in the entire competition. It's not going to happen again. As long as we get the three points, I'll be happy.'

Tuesday, 2 October 2007, Old Trafford

Attendance: 73,652

UEFA Champions League Group F
United 1 **AS Roma** 0

It never scaled the heights of the Romans' 7-1 slaughter of six months previously, but Wayne Rooney's solitary strike gave United a vital victory and a three-point lead at the top of Group F.

Against a Roma side focused on avenging their all-too-recent capitulation at Old Trafford, United's victory was impressive – although not without a couple of scares along the way.

European debutant Tomasz Kuszczak had to be alert as early as the tenth minute to clutch a long-range effort from Roma talisman Francesco Totti. The early exchanges were far cagier than the seven-goal salute of the previous April, with both sides still cautiously looking to establish group-stage supremacy.

United's first period in the ascendancy started just shy of the half-hour mark. Nani claimed a penalty for handball, which was waved away, before crossing for Cristiano Ronaldo, only for the Portuguese star to fire narrowly off target. The game suddenly shifted into an end-to-end spectacle. Nani's overhit cross had to be clawed away by Roma goalkeeper Gianluca Curci, who then thwarted Louis Saha by palming away his shot, before Totti again tried his luck from distance – this time with a free-kick that had Kuszczak scrambling.

Nani was at the heart of all of United's best play, in arguably what turned out to be his best display to date in his burgeoning Reds' career. The young winger was involved once again as he crossed for Rooney, who could only volley over from close range.

Half-time came with the scoreline still blank – a far cry from the 4-0 lead United had taken back to the dressing room six months earlier. If that didn't underline the opposition's improvement, the Reds were handed a timely wake-up call just after the restart, when Totti burst into the area and clipped an effort just over the crossbar.

Nani came slightly closer moments later, but his cross-shot clipped the top of Curci's bar before bouncing to safety. As the clock ticked towards the 70th minute, Ronaldo finally found the net with an impudent backheel through Curci's legs, only to see his effort ruled out for offside.

There was no questioning the validity of Wayne Rooney's strike moments later, however. Again Nani was involved, this time poking a neat pass to release Rooney inside the area, and the England striker drove a first-time shot in off Curci's far post to put United into the lead.

Carlos Tevez fired narrowly wide from distance shortly afterwards, but it was Roma who forged all the late chances. Rio Ferdinand had to be alert to block a shot from Ludovic Giuly and Max Tonetto miscued a back-post volley, before Ahmed Esposito blasted wide with the goal at his mercy with just three minutes remaining. It was a let-off for United, and the closest thing to a satisfactory defeat Roma manager Luciano Spalletti will ever sample. His side had restored their pride, but United had taken the points. Surely Sir Alex Ferguson would have taken that deal before kick-off.

UNITED: Kuszczak; O'Shea, Vidic, Ferdinand, Evra; Carrick, Scholes, Ronaldo, Nani (Giggs 80); Rooney (Anderson 85), Saha (Tevez 66)
Subs not used: Heaton, Piqué, Simpson, Eagles

Goal: Rooney (70)

AS ROMA: Curci; Cicinho, Juan, Mexes, Tonetto; De Rossi, Aquilani (Pizarro 61), Giuly (Esposito 80), Perrotta, Mancini (Vucinic 74); Totti
Subs not used: Sergio, Antunes, Barusso, Brighi

'Maybe we can count ourselves a little lucky,' Sir Alex conceded after the game. 'Tomasz made a couple of good saves and a good block in the second half. Roma had a few decent chances.'

With United still some way shy of top form – particularly in front of goal – questions were being raised about when they would click into gear. The manager was in little doubt that the real United would soon stand up.

'We've got the players,' he said. 'Sometimes you go through these spells, but it won't last forever. Some day we're going to hit a few goals. Hopefully that will come soon. All the players are working hard and all are showing a lot of experience. I'm pleased with the win, because Roma are a good team. It was a good game and a good European night. It was a bit tactical at times, but an excellent result for us.'

French defender Patrice Evra was similarly undeterred by the narrow margin of victory and focused instead on United's strong position as early leaders of Group F. 'Of course, I'd prefer us to score more goals,' he said. 'But we've won 1-0 and you still get the same number of points no matter if the score is 1-0, 7-1 or 2-0. It's still three points and I'm happy with that. I'm also very happy for Wayne Rooney. He's worked hard to come back from injury and it's great to see him score. It was a great result tonight.'

Having emerged from his European debut with a clean sheet, three points and a number of key saves under his belt, Tomasz Kuszczak was predictably delighted with life. Now he wanted the chance to prove himself as the Reds' undisputed starting goalkeeper.

'I know I am a good goalkeeper, I just need the opportunity to show it,' he said. 'I don't think about how long I have got to do that. Edwin is injured at the moment, so I have the chance to play in big games and I need to do well. I want to play more. That is why it's important for me to perform in every single game. I enjoy every match at Old Trafford because the fans are great, and when you have a full stadium it is a dream to play there.

'I have been happy with my form and feel I did well in pre-season. I was determined to fight for my place but, unfortunately, I started the season on the bench again. Most importantly, the team is in good shape and we are keeping clean sheets and defending well.'

The tentative feel-good factor creeping back into the club was tempered slightly by the news that Michael Carrick would be out for roughly six weeks. The midfielder fell awkwardly against Roma and subsequent scans revealed that he had fractured his elbow. With Owen Hargreaves and Darren Fletcher sidelined by a recurring tendonitis problem and a slight leg fracture respectively, United's midfield was beginning to look threadbare.

Carrick remained in a philosophical mood, however, as he prepared for an enforced spell on the sidelines. 'It's hard to take, but it happens,' he said. 'Injuries are a part of football and it's something I have to deal with and try to get back as soon as possible.

'When I first did it, I knew I'd done something. I didn't know how bad it was, but I couldn't really move it too much and it was very painful. So when I did find out it was broken it wasn't too much of a shock.

'I have to rest for a few weeks now. I'll be out for four to six weeks. I'd say six weeks and anything less is a bonus. I'm very disappointed because I was really enjoying my football.'

For Carrick's cohorts, attentions had long since been switched to the visit of struggling Wigan Athletic. For Sir Alex Ferguson, another 1-0 win would do just fine – but he wasn't expecting his side's goal drought to continue for long.

'I've got no worries about our form,' the manager said at the pre-match press conference. 'It's great, we get criticised for winning 1-0, but if we won 5-1 people would say the defence has gone to pieces!

'There are valid reasons for the delay in reaching form: Rooney's injury, Ronaldo's suspension, the international breaks that every club has had to contend with. And it's difficult to keep the continuity going when your players are away for two weeks at a time. But it is going to happen. I just hope it's sooner rather than later. But it's all coming together with this team and we will score goals.'

Saturday, 6 October 2007, Old Trafford

Attendance: 75,300

FA Barclays Premier League
United 4 **Wigan Athletic** 0

Finally, the dam burst. After scoring more than one goal only once in 11 games, United rediscovered their goal touch in an emphatic second-half display to bury Wigan at Old Trafford.

Goals from Carlos Tevez, Cristiano Ronaldo (2) and Wayne Rooney accounted for Chris Hutchings' Latics, who had thoroughly frustrated United during a bruising first half in which the Reds lost Nemanja Vidic and John O'Shea to injuries – with concussion and a dead leg respectively.

A patched-up defence saw Gerard Piqué and Danny Simpson included alongside Rio Ferdinand and Patrice Evra, and the fledgling pair turned in outstanding performances. Not that they were regularly tested by a Latics side intent on stifling United from the outset.

For the first 45 minutes, the gameplan worked a treat. Visiting goalkeeper Chris Kirkland was only forced into meaningful action once, to keep out a misguided header from his own defender, Salomon Olembe; while referee Mike Riley denied Ronaldo a strong shout for a penalty after he was hauled down inside the area by Michael Brown.

After that, it was a case of musical defenders. Nemanja Vidic was replaced by Anderson after suffering concussion, a move which took O'Shea to centre-back. The big Irishman then sustained a dead leg and had to be replaced by Simpson. Meanwhile, Piqué and Evra both picked up knocks from bruising challenges.

Such upheaval hardly helped United's cause, and it came as no surprise that the Reds struggled to turn their possession and attacking menace into clear-cut chances. After the interval, however, they began to flow. Ryan Giggs volleyed Ronaldo's half-cleared cross against the bar, before Tevez took Anderson's brilliant pass in his stride, beat Titus Bramble and Kevin Kilbane before rounding Kirkland and lashing the ball into the net.

The lead was doubled almost immediately, as Kilbane flicked Giggs' cross towards his own goal and, although Kirkland parried it away superbly, Ronaldo was on hand to gently nod in the rebound.

Tomasz Kuszczak, a virtual spectator for the first hour, made a fine reaction save from substitute Antonio Valencia's fierce shot as Wigan finally showed some semblance of attacking intent.

The visitors' newfound ambition created sizeable gaps for the Reds to exploit, and they duly took advantage of one shortly afterwards. Piqué released Rooney down the left wing, the England striker slid a fine ball across the area and Ronaldo steamed in, slotted the ball home and ended the game as a contest.

By now Wigan were forlorn, and Rooney promptly registered the goal his fine performance had deserved. Simpson strode down the right wing onto Paul Scholes' pass, and swung in a perfect cross for Rooney to power a header past Kirkland. Simpson took many of the plaudits, and only a decent save from Kirkland prevented the young full-back from capping a memorable outing with his maiden United goal.

But four was enough for the Reds, particularly after a period in which goals had been at such a premium. They would come, Sir Alex had assured the media before the visit of Wigan, and his words had been validated in spectacular fashion.

UNITED: Kuszczak; Piqué, Ferdinand, Vidic (Anderson 21), Evra; Ronaldo, Scholes, O'Shea (Simpson 28), Giggs; Rooney, Tevez (Nani 80)
Subs not used: Heaton, Eagles

Goals: Tevez (54), Ronaldo (59, 76), Rooney (82)

WIGAN ATHLETIC: Kirkland; Melchiot (Hall 51), Boyce, Bramble, Kilbane; Skoko, Brown, Koumas, Scharner, Olembe (Valencia 66); Bent.
Subs not used: Pollitt, Landzaat, Aghahowa

Temporarily at least, Old Trafford had a new hero – young full-back

Danny Simpson, who caught the eye with a superb display on his Premier League debut. And the Salford-born defender, a lifelong Red, was more than a touch pleased with a clean sheet and an assist.

'It was magnificent, I'm buzzing,' he beamed after the game. 'It's a Premier League game, playing with Ronaldo on the right wing and it's a good feeling. I don't know what else to say. Hopefully there'll be a few more feelings like this to come.

'I had family and friends here, so obviously I've had a few texts from everybody. I'm looking forward to going and seeing them now, to see what they have to say. The gaffer has said I'm staying here as cover. Obviously we've got a few injuries and, hopefully, I've shown him today that, when the lads are injured, I can come in and do a job for him.'

While yet another clean sheet was welcomed with open arms, the Reds' return to free-scoring form was a source of great delight for veteran winger Ryan Giggs.

'We know there are goals within this team, goals from everywhere,' he said. 'It's always nice to see Carlos, Wayne and Cristiano, lads who want to score goals, on the scoresheet.

'At the back we looked really solid, and we have done throughout the season really. Today again, we limited them to hardly any chances. The one chance they did have, Tomasz made a great save, so everyone's contributed to keeping a clean sheet.'

Giggs also reserved special praise for the eye-catching performances turned in by a number of United's younger players.

'Piqué came in at centre-half and did a good job, and so did Simmo,' he said. 'They got two assists really, so overall it was a really good performance from them both. In the second half Anderson was really involved in a lot of the play. He worked hard, showed some great touches, some great passes, and he's still only young and finding his feet, but he put in a really good performance.'

As a glut of United stars jetted off on international duty, there was still plenty of activity around Carrington, as Sir Alex reacted to the lack of Carling Cup football by farming some younger players out on loan. Darron Gibson, Fraizer Campbell, Phil Bardsley and

Adam Eckersley joined Wolves, Hull City, Sheffield United and Port Vale respectively on temporary deals in a bid to further their football education.

While United's youngsters were heading away from Carrington on short-term deals, Ryan Giggs penned a one-year contract extension until the end of June 2009. 'I am delighted to have signed for a further season. I am enjoying football more than ever and I hope to carry on playing football for United for as long as I can,' said the delighted Welshman. 'I would like to thank Sir Alex, the fans and everyone at the club for the great support I have received over the years.'

The feeling was more than mutual, and Sir Alex was quick to publicise his own elation at securing Giggs' services for an extra 12 months. 'I am absolutely delighted,' he said. 'Ryan epitomises the word loyalty. He signed here as a 14-year-old schoolboy and is still with the club 20 years on. Apart from his playing ability he has a fantastic demeanour and is a great role model to the younger players. I am sure he will be at the club for a long time to come.'

Amid talk that he would almost certainly now surpass Sir Bobby Charlton's all-time appearances record, Giggs continued to retain a short-term focus. First up on the agenda was a trip to Aston Villa.

With the Villans flying high in the league and playing some scintillating football, Sir Alex Ferguson was delighted to welcome Edwin van der Sar back from a toe injury, although it seemed likely that the game would come too soon for Nemanja Vidic. The Reds' superb record at Villa Park augured well, but the United manager would not allow any complacency, particularly after an international break, and against a side so well managed by Martin O'Neill.

'We have a good record against Villa, but we don't take that for granted and we know we're going to have to work hard,' he said. 'Martin has done a great job and galvanised the club again, and one of the great respects that you can give to Martin is that he has given young players a go.

'There are quite a few young players breaking into the first team at Aston Villa, which is very encouraging for the management and the fans. It's always tough to go there. The interesting thing is that when we go to Villa, there are never a lot of goals.'

With both sides in such rich attacking form, however, caution was never going to be on the agenda.

Saturday, 20 October 2007, Villa Park

Attendance: 42,640

FA Barclays Premier League
Aston Villa 1 **United** 4

Villa fans must truly loathe playing United. The Villans haven't tasted victory over the Reds since 1999, and even that was against a weakened League Cup side.

Martin O'Neill's side were in such good form ahead of this latest visit of United that countless pundits and soothsayers were readying themselves for a home victory. For roughly half an hour, they were onto something. Then, in devastating fashion, United clicked into overdrive and were 3-1 up at the interval. Two second-half red cards later, Villa fans were thankful to be going home on the end of only a 4-1 drubbing, so dominant were the Reds.

Wayne Rooney, scorer of two goals, would have had more but for the crossbar and a saved penalty, while strike partner Carlos Tevez was in similarly scintillating form. Between them, the duo ripped Villa to shreds.

That never seemed likely as the Midlanders burst out of the traps, and took the lead after 13 minutes. In flicking Ashley Young's fizzing cross past Edwin van der Sar, Gabriel Agbonlahor became the first player to score a Premier League goal against United in over two months, during which time the Reds had notched up six successive clean sheets.

Undeterred, United weathered the storm and began to create opportunities of their own. Nani volleyed over from Rooney's nod down, before Scott Carson raced from his line to prevent Tevez in a one-on-one.

Nine minutes before the interval, the Reds drew level and embarked on a wanton scoring spree. Nani's low cross from the right wing prompted hesitancy in the Villa defence, with Zat Knight and Carson failing to deal with it, and Rooney nipped in to tap home from close range.

On the stroke of half-time, United moved ahead. Tevez cut inside from the left flank and, using space created by a decoy run from Ryan Giggs, slotted a pinpoint pass to Rooney, who took a touch before placing a neat finish past Carson. The game had turned on its head in just eight minutes, but there was more to come. In stoppage time, Gerard Piqué's header was cleared off the line, Rio Ferdinand half-connected with the loose ball, but Craig Gardner inexplicably sliced his attempted clearance against the underside of his own bar, and the ball flew into the net.

A telling five-minute spell around the hour mark totally ended Villa's resistance, as Nigel Reo-Coker was dismissed for two bookings, while Carson was also shown the red card for hauling down Tevez inside the area. Replacement Stuart Taylor had a memorable first touch, however, as he parried away Rooney's spot-kick to deny the striker a treble. Moments later, when Rooney smashed a close-range shot against the bar, it seemed that the hat-trick was not meant to be.

As the game wound down to a comfortable close for United, Giggs added a fourth goal, albeit via two huge deflections. Cutting in from the right flank, the veteran winger's shot first struck Wilfred Bouma and then Martin Laursen before drifting past the helpless Taylor.

A classic Giggs goal it was not, but a classic United performance it most certainly was.

ASTON VILLA: Carson; Bouma, Mellberg, Laursen, Knight (Taylor 67); Gardner (Osbourne 54); Barry, Reo-Coker, Young; Agbonlahor, Moore (Maloney 54)
Subs not used: Davies, Petrov

Goal: Agbonlahor (13)

UNITED: Van der Sar; Piqué, Brown, Ferdinand, Evra; Nani, Anderson, Scholes (O'Shea 77), Giggs (Ronaldo 77); Tevez (Fletcher 73), Rooney
Subs not used: Kuszczak, Simpson

Goals: Rooney (36, 44), Ferdinand (45), Giggs (75)

'We are delighted, the performance in particular was absolutely superb and I think it's probably our best of the season,' declared a smiling Sir Alex Ferguson after his side had run riot at Villa Park.

'I don't think the red cards made a difference to the scoreline, but they did give us an easier task. Reo-Coker was unlucky, but he made two bookable offences as they were both late tackles. You can't afford to do that in the modern game. As for Carson being sent off, there is a lot of sympathy in that situation, but the letter of the law says he has to go.'

Having turned in a swashbuckling attacking display at Villa Park, the United manager conceded that the Reds may need to be cagier in their next outing, a Champions League trip to Dynamo Kyiv.

'We're in a good position with Sporting beating Dynamo Kyiv,' said the Reds' boss. 'We've got Kyiv in the next two matches, home and away, but their two defeats mean they have to beat us, which is good. We can set our stall out to play on the counter-attack.

'Kyiv have always been a difficult side to beat, especially at home. We drew 0-0 against them there a few years ago. They'll be a real handful. They have always been a club that have been able to produce good young players. Their set-up was designed purely to produce players. So we expect a tough game, but we're in a good position.'

United were dealt a blow on the eve of the game when Paul Scholes suffered a knee injury in training. It was decided that the veteran midfielder would remain with the squad, then undergo a scan upon returning to England.

Having started the 2006/07 Champions League campaign with three victories, then slipped to two unlikely defeats before qualifying on matchday six, United were eager to get qualification wrapped up as soon as they could.

'Last season we started off well in Europe, but then we got ourselves into difficulty by losing twice and needing to win in the last game,' said Edwin van der Sar. 'The first thing you want is to qualify and the second is to do it as quickly as possible. But we can't underestimate the opposition. We know that it can be difficult on these nights. The home crowd will be fanatical and there's also the cold weather to contend with.

'We've watched the videos and had the analysis from the scouts and the coaching staff, but the games can sometimes be different. We want the best at United and that means qualifying as quickly as we can.'

Victory in the Olympiyskiy Stadium would take United a huge step closer to that aim.

Tuesday, 23 October 2007, Olympiyskiy Stadium

Attendance: 42,000 (estimated)

UEFA Champions League Group F

Dynamo Kyiv 2 **United** 4

It's a bold plan to try and outgun United, and one that rarely works. So it proved for Dynamo Kyiv coach Jozsef Szabo, whose 4-3-3 formation allowed the Reds to run riot in the Ukraine.

Trying to recall a more open Champions League tie is quite a task and the match total of six goals could easily have been doubled by the final whistle, and how United only notched four remains a mystery.

Having struggled for so long to get into the goalscoring groove, this was the third match in succession in which United registered four goals – and it took them just ten minutes to get off the mark.

Tiberiu Ghioane brought Cristiano Ronaldo crashing to the ground on the left wing, Ryan Giggs curled in a superb free -kick and Rio Ferdinand thumped a header into the roof of the net. Rather than sit on the lead, though, United continued to press and were rewarded by a second goal eight minutes later.

Ronaldo fed Wes Brown on the right-hand side of the penalty area, and the defender slid a teasing cross into the box. Goran Gavrancic slid in vain to intercept, but could only divert the ball to Rooney, who tapped the ball into the unguarded net.

Two up in less than 20 minutes, but United continued to chase more goals and both Rooney and Carlos Tevez came close to adding a third, but were denied by Kyiv goalkeeper Olexandr Shovkovskiy.

With their first meaningful attack, however, Kyiv halved the arrears when veteran striker Diogo Rincon rose unmarked to head home a right-wing corner, despite the best efforts of Ronaldo on the goal-line.

The concession of such a slack goal clearly irked United, and they poured forward in search of a killer third. Shovkovskiy was immediately forced into a smart save from Ronaldo, while the Ukrainian stopper could only thank his lucky stars when John O'Shea shot straight at him from six yards out.

He was helpless just before half-time, though, when United did re-establish their two-goal lead. Giggs took advantage of acres of space on the left wing to deliver a perfect cross for Ronaldo, who back-pedalled slightly before powering a header high into the top corner.

In comparison to a breathless first half, the second 45 minutes was a largely tame affair. Kyiv fashioned the better chances, going close through Rincon's header and a curling free-kick from Carlos Correa, but United were handed the chance to bury the game when Gavrancic was adjudged to have handled inside his own area. Ronaldo duly stepped up and sent Shovkovskiy the wrong way to seal the win.

Ismael Bangoura pulled a late goal back from 20 yards, but United ultimately strolled to the victory that put them on the brink of sealing early qualification for the knockout phase.

DYNAMO KYIV: Shovkovskiy; Ghioane (Belkevich 46), Gavrancic, Yussuf, Diakhate; Gusev, Correa (Rotan 83), Nesmachniy; Bangoura, Rincon, Shatskikh (Milevskiy 46)
Subs not used: Rybka, Vaschuk, El Kaddouri, Markovic

Goals: Rincon (33), Bangoura (78)

UNITED: Van der Sar (Kuszczak 80); Brown, Ferdinand, Vidic, O'Shea; Ronaldo, Anderson, Fletcher, Giggs (Simpson 80); Tevez (Nani 73), Rooney
Subs not used: Piqué, Evans, Eagles

Goals: Ferdinand (10), Rooney (18), Ronaldo (41, 68 pen)

'We planned to win this one and we did it,' stated goalscorer Rio Ferdinand. 'A good start was vital for us and we scored two quick goals. We allowed them a way back into the game from a set-piece, which is quite uncharacteristic of us, but we restored our lead quickly and never looked like giving anything more to Kyiv.

'We had to work hard tonight because there were a lot of long balls coming into the area. I think we did well at the back and they had to attack at a slower pace or stick to the wings.'

Central defensive partner Nemanja Vidic concurred that three points were imperative for United, and was already contemplating a home victory over the Ukrainian champions a fortnight later, in order to seal qualification with two group games to spare.

'It is important to beat Kyiv at home,' declared the Serb. 'Whenever we are at home, it is important to win. If we win that game I think we will be there. Then the group will be finished before the end. We have nine points now, so we can be more relaxed in the next couple of games. The forwards did very well, but most importantly we got the three points.

'It has clicked for us in terms of scoring goals. We have got four away from home in the Champions League, we have to be happy with that. And we could have scored more. Even after we scored, we didn't just sit back and defend. We wanted to play good football and score more goals. That is the way we play.'

It was bad news for Kyiv, who would visit Old Trafford 15 days later, and also bad news for Middlesbrough, who travelled to face the rampant Reds just three days after they landed back in Manchester.

With Sir Alex's men having overcome a bumpy start to the season and hit a goal-laden winning streak, Ryan Giggs was keen for United to keep in the groove against Gareth Southgate's Boro.

'If we play like we have been recently, I'd back us against anyone,' said the winger. 'Confidence is high at the moment and we look very dangerous going forward. We also look really solid at the back. Individually, the defenders have done brilliantly this season. Rio has scored in the last couple of games and Vidic always weighs in with goals. We defend as a team and attack as a team.

'Middlesbrough have quality in their side and we expect a difficult game. They'll be thinking that we've had a long trip to Kyiv in midweek and that now will be a good time to catch us. We need to apply ourselves and perform like we have been in recent weeks.'

One player who would definitely sit out the Teessiders' visit to Old Trafford was Paul Scholes, who discovered, after two scans on his knee, that he would be out of action for three months.

It came as a timely boost, then, that Owen Hargreaves was in contention to face Boro after his recurring tendonitis problem. 'Owen is ready to play and he should start,' Sir Alex said at the prematch press conference. 'We did the right thing. We tried our best to get him through without an injection, but he had it and is ready to play. It's been a frustrating time for him, but it's a long season and if he's back, and stays back, then that is terrific news.'

Saturday, 27 October 2007, Old Trafford

Attendance: 75,720

FA Barclays Premier League
United 4 **Middlesbrough** 1

When you're hot, you're hot. Even Middlesbrough, who traditionally hold something of a hoodoo over United, were powerless to stop a bloodthirsty attacking display from the Reds' insatiable, in-form forward line.

Following Wigan, Aston Villa and Dynamo Kyiv, Middlesbrough became the fourth team in a row to suffer a heavy defeat against in-form United, as the Reds equalled a club record fourth-consecutive four-goal haul, set 100 years earlier.

In recent years, Boro sides have enjoyed success against United largely through stifling Sir Alex Ferguson's side, but the Teessiders' chances of doing that were ended after just three minutes, when Nani hit an unstoppable opener.

The winger picked up the ball on the left flank, just inside the Boro half, advanced past three defenders, cut inside and unleashed a scorching 30-yard drive that arced over the flailing Schwarzer.

The veteran Australian may have been helpless to keep Nani's bullet of an effort out but, two minutes later, he made a crucial save from Carlos Tevez in a one-on-one situation. United would rue that miss moments later, as Jeremie Aliadiere headed in Tuncay Sanli's cross to level the scores.

Six minutes gone, two goals. This was nothing like the war of attrition many had expected before the game. Boro remained a menace on the counter-attack, and Stewart Downing headed waste-fully wide after 24 minutes, following more good work from Tuncay.

The England winger was heavily involved again as United retook the lead after 33 minutes. Downing won the ball back inside his own area, dwelled in possession long enough for Nani to nick it to Rooney, and the striker hammered a shot past Schwarzer.

United finished the first half in a flurry, and wasted a glorious three-on-one break involving Tevez, Rooney and Ronaldo against Boro's David Wheater. The Reds took a single-goal advantage into the break, but could have widened the gap within a minute of the restart as Tevez fed Rooney, only for the striker to fire narrowly over.

The signs of Rooney and Tevez's burgeoning partnership had been apparent against Aston Villa and Dynamo Kyiv, and they combined again in some style to add to United's lead.

Tevez flicked Anderson's clipped pass into Rooney and continued his run into the box, slipping below Boro's radar, as the visiting defence were all magnetised to Rooney. Without so much as a glance, Rooney neatly back-heeled the ball straight to Tevez, who slid home a simple finish.

Old Trafford roared its appreciation, and there was further cause for cheer when Tevez hit a fourth in the game's dying moments. Rooney embarked on a long, winding run before picking out the Argentine, who cut inside and, although his goal-bound shot struck Andrew Taylor's arm, it bounced down into the ground and past the hapless Schwarzer.

With that, United had equalled a century-old record and moved to the top of the Premier League table, with a tantalising trip to title rivals Arsenal next up.

UNITED: Van der Sar; Brown, Vidic, Ferdinand (Piqué 73), O'Shea; Ronaldo, Hargreaves (Fletcher 66), Anderson (Giggs 78), Nani; Tevez, Rooney. Subs not used: Kuszczak, Simpson

Goals: Nani (3), Rooney (33), Tevez (55, 85)

MIDDLESBROUGH: Schwarzer; Young, Woodgate, Wheater, Taylor; O'Neil, Cattermole (Boateng 90), Rochemback, Downing; Tuncay (Lee 80), Aliadiere (Hutchinson 55). Subs not used: Turnbull, Hines

Goal: Aliadiere (6)

'For weeks people were going on about our 1-0 wins, but now they're going on about us scoring four. It's amazing!" laughed Sir Alex Ferguson after the record-equalling four-goal haul. 'Some of the attacking play today was very good, although when we got in front we took our foot off the pedal. We started running with the ball, didn't play the way we normally play and paid the penalty.

'We weren't getting to the ball quick enough and I think the players really needed a wake-up call, and that's exactly what their goal did to us. Credit to Middlesbrough for that 20-minute period when they got in and about us. But there was no doubt we were on top in the second half. There was far more concentration, our attacking play improved and we could have scored a lot of goals.'

The United manager was particularly impressed with Carlos Tevez and Wayne Rooney, who scored three goals between them and linked up superbly for United's third.

'I think that goal sums up their partnership,' he said. 'It was all about quick-thinking, great vision and, you know, the courage to even try that. Wayne could have taken another touch, but he knew Tevez was making that run and a little back-heel put him in on goal. It was a fantastic move and hopefully we're going to see a more complete partnership.'

One half of the on-song duo, Wayne Rooney, was more than happy to salute the efforts of his strike partner, who was looking increasingly settled after his drawn-out arrival from West Ham.

'Playing with Carlos is brilliant,' said Wayne. 'He's a clever player, very intelligent, and I think we both work well together. We've both been scoring a few goals lately, so we're pleased with that.

'The best way to play football is to pass and move, and as soon as Carlos gave me the ball I could see him starting his run out of the corner of my eye. He got on the end of my back-heel and I'm delighted for him to have scored two today. He's worked very hard over the last two games and he deserves those goals.'

Having scored six times in five matches, Rooney also conceded that he was delighted with his own form, saying: 'I know it's my job to score goals and I try to do that in every game. I'm happy with how things are going and I hope that can continue. To play in this team is an honour. We're playing fast, attacking football and that's the football I want to be involved in.'

For Owen Hargreaves, delighted to be back in action, there was still some way to go before United would hit their peak. It was ominous news for the rest of the Premier League and Europe.

'We look good, our offensive play is great,' said the midfielder. 'But we have some things we can work on, even going forward. We had some wonderful moments against Middlesbrough, but at times we were a bit complacent. We could have, if we'd wanted, scored more goals, so we have some things we can work on, and that's a great thing. We're winning comfortably and we're not even hitting top gear yet.'

Chapter Five

NOVEMBER – TIGHT AT THE TOP

After a perfect record in October – five wins out of five, 17 goals for, four against – the Reds went into their opening clash of November at table-topping Arsenal on the crest of a wave.

They were further boosted by the news that Rio Ferdinand would be fit for the game, despite press reports claiming that he had aggravated an old groin injury in the win over Middlesbrough.

'I don't know where that story has come from,' said a bemused Ferdinand in the build-up to the trip to North London. 'I think it's newspapers making up stories again. I've been training fully this week so there's no problem.'

Also back in contention were Michael Carrick, following a four-week lay-off with a fractured elbow, Owen Hargreaves, who came through the Boro victory unscathed after returning from a knee injury, and Patrice Evra and Anderson, who had both shaken off minor knocks. Louis Saha was also available again after spending the last four games on the sidelines.

Howard Webb was confirmed as the man in the middle, but his appointment came under fire from former referee Graham Poll, who expressed his concern at Webb taking charge of his second Arsenal game in a row, following the Gunners' 1-1 draw with Liverpool, just days earlier.

'Never before have you seen a referee in the Premier League get appointed to the same team in consecutive weeks,' remarked Poll. 'It doesn't happen. There are all sorts of connotations with it. Is Howard Webb going to have to prove his impartiality and will that mean he is going to favour Manchester United? It's unfair pressure on a very good referee.'

The Premier League defended Webb's appointment, insisting his recent performances in the Arsenal-Liverpool match and Germany's Euro 2008 qualifier against the Czech Republic made him the best man for the job.

'Howard Webb is the best performing referee at the moment and it's only right he takes charge of the highest-profile games,' said a spokesman for the Premier League. Up to this point in the season the South Yorkshire-based Webb had refereed one United match, the 1-0 home win over Tottenham in August.

Sir Alex Ferguson did not seem concerned by Webb's recent familiarity with the Gunners, but admitted that the outcome of the clash could have a significant bearing on the outcome of the title race, especially as the only factor separating the two teams was goals scored.

'It's still an open race, but Arsenal have had a great start and they're the ones we are chasing at the moment,' he said. 'Everything is coming together, as I thought it would, and in good time to take on Arsenal in what could be a key match in our title defence.

'Both teams will be hell-bent on winning and that's the kind of mouth-watering aspect about the game. Anyone who has got a ticket will be rubbing their hands together, because without question the form of both teams, the football they are playing, the goals they are scoring, points to a big occasion. It's always going to be tense. Tenacity and intensity are part of these encounters and it won't escape Saturday's game.'

The two sides' excellent run of form prompted many pundits to predict a two-horse race between United and Arsenal for the title. Sir Alex, however, was far from convinced.

'People are saying it will rest between the two of us, but then you look at Chelsea's form of last week,' he declared in reference to Chelsea's 6-0 demolition of Manchester City at Stamford Bridge. 'They played some sparkling football and looked very impressive, and the strength of Liverpool's squad means you cannot discount them.

'At this moment in time both us and Arsenal are enjoying a good spell, but I know from my experiences there are rough days ahead. You maybe lose a game or two, but that's the nature of football. It's a tough league and I would certainly like to be top on Saturday night.'

Rio Ferdinand echoed those sentiments and insisted victory at the Emirates would send out an ominous warning to United's title rivals.

'I don't think it will determine where the league is going to go, but a win would be a great marker to put down. There are only a handful of games gone, but we need to make sure we give a good account of ourselves.

'We're scoring goals and it's a big difference from the start of the season,' he added. 'We were creating chances, but weren't converting them. Now we seem to be putting them in the back of the net and that bodes well. It's looking good, but it's got to continue. We have to sustain it over a long period of time. This is just the start. Hopefully we'll be saying this after the Christmas period and we can say we've got a consistent strike force and a consistent team.'

Two days before the clash, club captain Gary Neville completed almost an hour of the reserves' Manchester Senior Cup win over Stockport County, posting his first action since March. The defender enjoyed a stern test in a fiercely-fought local derby, which United won 6-1 through goals from Chris Eagles, Sean Evans and braces from Febian Brandy and Dong Fangzhuo. Aside from one or two hints of ring-rustiness – predictable after seven months on the sidelines – Neville looked solid throughout, and did well in the centre of defence alongside Jonny Evans.

The trip to North London came too soon for the skipper, who was still in need of some more reserves' action to hone his fitness. Nonetheless, Sir Alex insisted it was 'great to have him back'.

Saturday, 3 November 2007, Emirates Stadium

Attendance: 60,161

FA Barclays Premier League
Arsenal 2 **United** 2

There was a definite feeling of déjà vu for United after William Gallas' injury-time strike at the Emirates Stadium, but thankfully for the Reds at least they left North London with a share of the spoils this time round, having gone down to a last-gasp Arsenal winner in the corresponding fixture last season.

The Frenchman found the net at both ends, starting and ending the scoring after Cesc Fabregas had hauled Arsenal level and Cristiano Ronaldo had given United what had seemed a decisive late lead.

The match began at a frantic pace with both sides looking to stamp their authority on each other. Emmanuel Adebayor and Carlos Tevez saw half chances go begging, before Nemanja Vidic's shirt tug on Aleksandr Hleb drew shouts for a penalty. Referee Howard Webb waved away the appeals.

Ryan Giggs poked an effort just wide soon after and blasted a shot just over the bar after a knock-down from Tevez. At the other end, Edwin van der Sar saved well on his line from Gallas, who headed Cesc Fabregas' free-kick goalwards.

Gallas found himself on the score-sheet on the stroke of half-time, but at the wrong end as he inadvertently deflected Wayne Rooney's effort past Manuel Almunia to hand United the advantage.

The lead was short lived, however, when, three minutes after the restart, Fabregas fired the hosts level. Van der Sar bravely blocked Adebayor's close-range effort, but Bacary Sagna quickly squared the loose ball for the Spaniard to sidefoot home.

United weathered the Arsenal storm and began to look increasingly like the team that would snatch a winner in a tightly poised game. Rooney went close on 64 minutes after a one-two with Giggs, but was unable to guide his header on target.

Rooney flicked a ball through to Patrice Evra soon after, but the Frenchman's cut-back eluded Ronaldo, who was unable to get there in front of a cluster of Arsenal defenders.

The Portuguese winger was not to be denied eight minutes from time, however, as United snatched the lead once more. Louis Saha, on for Tevez, slid a superb ball into the onrushing Evra's path, and the defender crossed brilliantly for Ronaldo to slot the ball home.

That looked to be it, until Gallas struck the killer blow. Gael Clichy swung in a superb left-wing cross that eventually landed at the feet of Gallas, who volleyed sweetly goalwards. Van der Sar looked to have saved it, but an eagle-eyed linesman spotted that the Dutchman was behind his goal-line when he clawed the ball clear.

It was a deflating moment for Sir Alex's men, but the point gained may well prove to be a very valuable one come May.

ARSENAL: Almunia; Sagna, Toure, Gallas, Clichy; Eboue (Walcott 74), Flamini, Fabregas, Rosicky (Eduardo 81); Hleb (Gilberto 81), Adebayor. Subs not used: Lehmann, Diarra

Goals: Fabregas (48), Gallas (90)

UNITED: Van der Sar; Brown (O'Shea 71), Ferdinand, Vidic, Evra; Ronaldo, Anderson (Carrick 76), Hargreaves, Giggs; Tevez (Saha 76), Rooney. Subs not used: Kuszczak, Nani

Goals: Gallas o.g. (45), Ronaldo (82)

A fuming Sir Alex Ferguson faced the cameras at the end of a dramatic 90 minutes, clearly irked by his side's inability to hold on to the lead after twice being in the box seat.

'We threw it away. We were in a winning position twice,' raged the United boss. 'The goal that angered me most was the goal we gave away after half-time. To lose a goal from taking a throw-in at their corner flag was criminal.'

The goal in question, scored by Cesc Fabregas, came only three minutes after Wayne Rooney had given United the lead – albeit with the half-time interval in between.

'It was a marvellous time for us to score, just before the break,' continued Sir Alex. 'We should have been buoyed by that and we did start the second half well with good possession. Then we gave the goal away and for the next five to ten minutes after that they got at us.

'To be honest I couldn't see either team scoring a second goal. To then score our second when we did and give it away in injury time is hard to take, really hard to take. Arsenal got out of jail. The result doesn't tell you anything as both teams are going to be challenging, but the draw is good for Chelsea and Liverpool and there are a lot of twists and turns to come.'

Despite having to settle for a share of the spoils, Sir Alex insisted the Reds emerged from the trip to North London with a psychological advantage over their great rivals.

'Our players were in the dressing room feeling absolutely sick after the game, but their dressing room was elated. They were celebrating as if they'd won the World Cup, which I found very interesting. Our players took something out of that, psychologically,' declared the boss.

'I think we are a better side than Arsenal now. They're a young team and they're going to be a very good team – there's no question of that – but we went there when they were on top form and they hardly managed a shot on goal. There were definitely a lot of positives for us.'

Ryan Giggs agreed, adding: 'I think some of their players thought they'd won the game when the final whistle went. I'm not sure we would have celebrated like that if we'd have drawn at home, but I suppose they were just excited to score right at the death.'

Later in the day, Chelsea moved closer to the coat-tails of United and Arsenal after goals from Frank Lampard and Juliano Belletti handed them a 2-0 win at Wigan and a fourth consecutive league victory to nil. Liverpool, however, were unable to gain any ground on the leaders, drawing 0-0 at Blackburn.

Despite letting things slip at the Emirates, there was still plenty to be positive about, not least the fact that Louis Saha's latest return to

Ryan Giggs netted his first league
goal of the season at Villa Park as
the Reds cantered to a 4–1 victory.

Rio Ferdinand set the Reds on
their way to a 4–2 victory in Kyiv,
bagging his second goal in as
many games.

The Reds produced another vibrant attacking display against Middlesbrough and equalled a century-old club record with a fourth consecutive four-goal haul.

The Reds were left deflated at the Emirates in November as William Gallas claimed an injury-time equaliser for the Gunners. John O'Shea, Nemanja Vidic, Edwin van der Sar and Michael Carrick lament the missed opportunity.

Gerard Piqué leaps to head home his first goal in a red shirt in the 4–0 win over Dynamo Kyiv.

Cristiano Ronaldo's sucker punch of two goals in two minutes ensured victory over Mark Hughes' Blackburn.

The Reds turned in an uncharacteristically subdued performance against Bolton at the Reebok Stadium, resulting in their second league defeat of the season. Louis Saha sums up the disappointment.

Cristiano Ronaldo was the match-winner against Sporting Lisbon for the second time of the season, firing home a stunning injury-time free-kick.

Midfield magician Anderson uses sleight of foot to conjure a route past Fulham's packed midfield during the Reds' 2–0 win at Old Trafford.

Over 16 years after scoring his first league goal against Manchester City, Ryan Giggs slotted home his 100th in the 4–1 win over Derby County.

Having constantly pestered Sir Alex for the armband, Wayne Rooney skippered a young side to a respectable 1–1 draw at the Stadio Olimpico in Rome.

Carlos Tevez's first-half strike in front of the Kop sealed United's fifth league win in six years at Anfield.

Cristiano Ronaldo ensures a merry Christmas for United by firing home a dramatic late penalty against Everton.

The Reds barely broke sweat at the Stadium of Light as goals from Wayne Rooney, Cristiano Ronaldo and a Louis Saha double sealed a fifth away win of the season.

Sir Alex was forced to watch from the stands as United's attempts to end 2007 on a high were scuppered by West Ham, who earned a third consecutive win against the Reds.

Carlos Tevez starts the new year with a winning goal – and a celebratory shout-out to his family back in Argentina.

United were again paired with Aston Villa in the FA Cup, and Cristiano Ronaldo's late opener set the Reds on the road to yet another win at Villa Park.

At long last, Cristiano Ronaldo celebrates his first United hat-trick as the Reds run riot against Newcastle at Old Trafford.

Wayne Rooney roars with delight as his goal finally breaks down Reading's stubborn resistance at the Madejski Stadium.

Patrice Evra samples the local transport during United's mid-season trip to Saudi Arabia.

fitness had enabled Sir Alex to name his best 16 of the season to date against Arsene Wenger's men. The French striker was one of five internationals on the United bench, alongside Nani, John O'Shea, Tomasz Kuszczak and Michael Carrick.

'I had the strongest bench that we've had all season, which is encouraging for us,' remarked Sir Alex ahead of the Champions League clash with Dynamo Kyiv. 'The lads who have been playing all this time have been fantastic and we are very proud of them. But we can now alternate our teams a little bit better.'

Things were certainly looking up in terms of availability of players, but that in itself gave Sir Alex an alternative headache – who to leave off the bench?

The Reds boss used the example of having to omit Darren Fletcher from United's 16-man squad at the Emirates as a major reason why he'd like to see the Premier League up the number of permitted substitutes from five to seven.

'Having to tell Darren Fletcher he wasn't in the 16 was a real kick in the teeth for the boy, especially as he'd been absolutely fantastic in Kyiv ten days before that,' explained the manager. 'He deserved to be part of the squad and that decision did not sit well with me.

'When you look at the profile of the Premier League and the money available, there should be seven substitutes. Nowadays, every club in the Premier League have big squads of more than 16 players. In our case, we have around 25. We've tried to get this changed for some years now and I believe if the coaches were to make the decision then it would pass.'

Unfortunately for Sir Alex he would not be able to call on skipper Gary Neville in the immediate future after the defender picked up a calf strain in training prior to the Reds' Group F game at Old Trafford.

'It's a real dampener for the boy and for us and is something we could have done without,' admitted Sir Alex. 'I don't think it's a long one, but it is a setback because he really needs to get his season on the road.'

Wednesday, 7 November 2007, Old Trafford

Attendance: 75,017

UEFA Champions League Group F

United 4 **Dynamo Kyiv** 0

The Reds claimed their place in the last 16 of the Champions League thanks to an efficient display against a Dynamo Kyiv side with just one intention – damage limitation.

'They didn't seem to want to play, which spoilt the game,' commented Wayne Rooney afterwards. What remained unblemished, however, was United's immaculate Group F record – four wins out of four and just two goals conceded.

Sir Alex, who celebrated his 21st anniversary at Old Trafford a day earlier, made five changes to the team that faced Arsenal at the Emirates Stadium, but there was no place in the starting line-up for Louis Saha, who took up a seat on the bench, while Rio Ferdinand and Owen Hargreaves were left out of the squad entirely.

Youngster Danny Simpson started at right-back, while Spaniard Gerard Piqué came in for Ferdinand for his first-ever European start. And it proved to be a memorable evening for the centre-back. Defensively solid throughout, he also made his mark at the other end on 31 minutes, rising to head home his first goal in a United shirt after Ronaldo's free-kick had arrived at him via deflections off Michael Carrick and Carlos Tevez.

Six minutes later, the Reds had a two-goal advantage after some inspired chasing from Tevez. Winning possession from Carlos Correa in midfield, the Argentine swapped passes with Rooney and smashed his shot high into the net.

Having sat back for the majority of the opening period, Dynamo, temporarily managed by former Arsenal defender Oleg Luzhny, nearly found a way back into proceedings immediately after the restart when substitute Diogo Rincon fizzed an effort in from the edge of the area. Tomasz Kuszczak, a half-time replacement for Edwin van der Sar – who was suffering from a toe complaint – was alert to the situation and saved brilliantly.

Rincon was inches away from latching onto Marjan Markovic's cross just after the hour, but United always looked capable of upping the tempo whenever required. That they did on 76 minutes when Rooney calmly converted Nani's pin-point cross.

Two minutes before full-time Cristiano Ronaldo rubberstamped the romp, turning inside to beat Pape Diakhate, before unleashing an unstoppable drive into the far corner.

UNITED: Van der Sar (Kuszczak 46); Simpson, Piqué (Evans 73), Vidic, Evra; Ronaldo, Carrick, Fletcher, Nani; Rooney, Tevez (Saha 67).
Subs not used: Brown, Anderson, O'Shea, Eagles

Goals: Piqué (31), Tevez (37), Rooney (76), Ronaldo (88)

DYNAMO KYIV: Shovkovskiy; Markovic, Diakhate, Fedorov, El Kaddouri; Ghioane, Vaschuk, Correa; Gusev (Rebrov 46), Milevskiy (Bangoura 76), Rotan (Rincon 46).
Subs not used: Rybka, Gavrancic, Ninkovic, Dopilka

Sir Alex, understandably delighted to see United progress to the knock-out stages, took time to wax lyrical about the performances of some of his young troops, most notably goalscorer Gerard Piqué, Danny Simpson and late substitute Jonny Evans.

'They'll have got some good experience from this match and also the understanding that they have a great chance [to make it] at this club,' he said. 'Piqué, Simpson and Evans are all terrific young players. They know what's required when they go into the first team and they know their futures are with this club. Tonight only gives them encouragement that they are doing the right things.'

Hearing such praise having just been handed his first-ever Champions League start was music to Danny Simpson's ears.

'It means everything,' beamed the Salford-born defender. 'When the manager said "You and Gerard are playing at the back with Nemanja [Vidic] and Patrice [Evra]", it was a hell of a compliment. He didn't even have to say anything to me – just, "Go out there and do what you normally do." It is everything to get a start. It gives you that confidence that he trusts you.

'The gaffer has always said if there is a young lad he will give them a chance, and he proved that. After that he might feel that now we are through to the knock-out stages he could give me another game against better teams. For the likes of myself, Gerard and Jonny it is looking good for the future.'

Twenty-four hours after helping the Reds secure their place in the last 16, Nemanja Vidic committed his future to the club by signing a two-year extension to his current contract until 2012.

'Playing in this team is a great privilege,' declared the popular defender. 'This is such a great club and I am delighted to be able to extend my stay here. The fans and everyone at the club have been very special to me. I hope I can do my bit to win even more trophies in the years ahead.'

Sir Alex was equally pleased and paid tribute to the Serb's ever-improving partnership with Rio Ferdinand at the heart of the Reds' defence.

'Nemanja has made a terrific impact at the club and the partner-ship he has forged with Rio was a major part in us winning the title last year,' said the manager. 'He is an extremely popular member of the squad both with staff and fans alike. It's great news that he wants to be part of this exciting side for years to come.'

Vidic looked set to be reunited with his defensive sidekick for the visit of Blackburn Rovers, after Ferdinand had been handed a well-earned rest for the Kyiv game. Gary Neville was still suffering from a calf strain, while a knee condition would, it seemed, see Louis Saha used more sparingly.

'The situation Louis finds himself in with his knee condition means he won't play every game,' revealed Sir Alex at the press conference prior to United's next home match, against Blackburn. 'The dilemma is whether to start him or to bring him on.

'If you look at the composition of the side, he is different from everyone else, so he makes a bigger impact as a substitute. He makes a great impact. Therefore, my inclination is to use him as a sub. He's fine with that.'

Just hours later, however, Sir Alex was forced to rethink that strategy and revert to Plan B, after a freak training-ground accident left Wayne Rooney with an injured ankle and facing a month on the sidelines.

'He was playing a game of head tennis and he caught his foot on the stanchion that holds up the net,' revealed Sir Alex. 'It's a sickening blow, but hopefully he'll be back in four weeks.

'He's been in red-hot form recently, but that's football. He'll miss our games against Blackburn and Bolton and it's obviously a big loss for England too. I think Rooney was the man who could take England to the European Championships.'

Sir Alex remained hopeful of having the striker – recently named the Barclays Player of the Month for October – available for the trip to Anfield on 16 December.

Despite being shorn of the services of arguably United's main talisman, the boss was confident he had the resources to cope. In fact, in his programme notes for Blackburn's visit, he even went as far as to say that the current squad might just be his best yet.

'I believe this is the strongest squad I have ever had, so much so that I think I would be pushed to name my overall best team,' he declared. 'It will vary, dependent on fitness, form, opposition and the way the fixtures fall – especially on the last lap as the various competitions reach a climax.

'But this is what I have been working towards. I don't like the short-term fix. I prefer to see a pool of players emerge and develop into something special, which, believe me, is what's happening at Old Trafford this season. We have the young players led by Wayne Rooney and Cristiano Ronaldo and now joined by the likes of Carlos Tevez, Nani and Anderson. In fact, it is difficult to know where to stop when I am talking about our important players with Hargreaves, Carrick and Saha in the ranks along with our home-produced players like Fletcher, Wes Brown and John O'Shea.

'I am not becoming youth-obsessed either, with experience represented by Scholes and Giggs, both now into their 30s, but who in my view will play until they are 36, such has been their lifestyles. There is many a pitfall for celebrity players, but those two have avoided all the traps and set fine examples for those coming up behind them.'

As it turned out, the latter of the pair would maintain that model with a virtuoso second-half display against a Blackburn side more than capable of holding their own against English football's finest.

Sunday, 11 November 2007, Old Trafford

Attendance: 75,710

FA Barclays Premier League
United 2 **Blackburn Rovers** 0

Having seen Arsenal, Chelsea and Liverpool all fail to defeat Mark Hughes' men, the Reds knew victory over Blackburn at Old Trafford was not going to be a mere formality. And so it proved, as both sides traded blows early on. But as he's already proved on a handful of occasions so far this season, Cristiano Ronaldo can be the difference between one point and three.

The Portuguese winger's two goals in two minutes just after the half-hour mark put the Reds in the ascendancy, and David Dunn's sending off early in the second half practically extinguished Rovers' chances of taking anything from the game.

It was a somewhat different story early on. Carlos Tevez tested Brad Friedel with a powerful shot, forcing the American stopper to turn the ball around the post at full stretch.

At the other end, Patrice Evra was called upon to avert the danger after a frenzied scramble in the area just before the 15-minute mark. Christopher Samba then struck the woodwork after referee Chris Foy had waved play on despite Dunn's foul on Ronaldo on the edge of United's box.

The unpunished foul on Ronaldo left both the United players and the Old Trafford crowd incensed, so much so that it galvanised the Reds into mounting a sustained period of attack.

Ronaldo saw his left-foot volley from Ryan Giggs' corner cleared off the line, but the duo's link-up on 34 minutes led to United's opener. Giggs – imperious throughout – swung the ball in and Ronaldo climbed above Aaron Mokoena and planted a header past David Bentley on the post.

A minute later, the winger doubled his and United's tally. Louis Saha, in for the injured Wayne Rooney, won possession in midfield before feeding a pass to Tevez. The Argentine surged forward with intent and curled a delicious ball across goal with the outside of his right foot, allowing Ronaldo to slot home.

Not long after the restart, Dunn received his marching orders after an earlier tug on Tevez's shirt was followed by a late challenge on Saha. In truth, it seemed a little harsh, and Mark Hughes was particularly aggrieved at the decision.

Ronaldo went close to bagging his first United hat-trick just after the hour with a rasping 20-yard shot that flew inches past Friedel's post.

The Reds saw out the final period with ease to make it ten games unbeaten. The championship charge had certainly started to gather pace.

UNITED: Van der Sar; Brown, Ferdinand, Vidic, Evra; Ronaldo, Hargreaves (Carrick 76), Anderson, Giggs; Tevez, Saha (Nani 68).
Subs not used: Kuszczak, O'Shea, Fletcher

Goals: Ronaldo (34, 35)

BLACKBURN ROVERS: Friedel; Emerton, Nelsen, Samba, Warnock; Bentley, Dunn, Mokoena, Pedersen; McCarthy, Santa Cruz (Derbyshire 78).
Subs not used: Brown, Ooijer, Tugay, Berner

Cristiano Ronaldo might have been the man grabbing all the headlines once again after his first-half double took the Reds temporarily top of the table, but it was the vintage display of another winger that caught Sir Alex Ferguson's eye.

'I thought Ryan Giggs was absolutely fantastic, particularly in the second half,' said the manager. 'You look at him today and see the freshness he shows. I think he can go on for years. He's been a wonderful servant for us.'

Getting the most out of Giggs – fast approaching his 34th birthday – entailed selecting the winger's deployment carefully, and affording him as much rest as possible.

'We have to be careful with Ryan these days,' said Sir Alex. 'He didn't play last Wednesday and we've now got a two-week break before we play Bolton. Retiring from international football has helped him, there's no question of that.'

The man himself was in full agreement.

'I made the decision to retire [from international football] hoping it would make me fresher, and I think that has definitely been proved right this season,' he stated. 'I have had no injuries, played a lot of games and felt good. That was my aim at the start of the season.

'It was a tough decision. I loved playing for my country, but there were young players coming through and it was the right time to do it.'

He also insisted that he was happy to allow Sir Alex to nurse him through the season, even though it has meant more hours on the training pitch.

'I've adjusted to being in and out of the team – you have to. I have realised that as I get older I have to prepare that little bit differently. I don't play in every game, but I sometimes do a bit more training just to make sure I'm ready when the manager does pick me,' revealed United's most-decorated servant.

'It's not different training, just more. When you play every game, like I was a few seasons ago, it's just play-rest-play-rest and it's all about recovery. When you're not playing every week, you can do a lot more training and hopefully that can help. I'm not disappointed when I'm not on the team sheet, because I'm experienced enough to know I'll play enough games and, if I'm playing well, I'll play in the big games.

'I want to play all the time, but I've got to be sensible. The manager is looking at the bigger picture, and we have got a lot of players to choose from. When he doesn't want me to play, he might give me a couple of days off and tell me to spend them in the gym. I hope what he's done will help prolong my career.'

Giggs was given further time off as the majority of the squad headed off on international duty for the final batch of Euro 2008 qualifiers. Things did not exactly go as planned for United's international performers after a dramatic final night of qualifying. The upshot of the evening's events meant that the Reds could have as few as five representatives at the finals in Austria and Switzerland.

United's contingent of England players were not the only ones disappointed to miss out on qualification after their 3-2 defeat to Croatia at Wembley. Serbia – without Nemanja Vidic, who didn't even make the bench – drew 2-2 with Poland, extinguishing their hopes of making Euro 2008.

Northern Ireland also harboured slim hopes of qualifying, but their 1-0 defeat to Spain in Gran Canaria saw them miss out. Young United defender Jonny Evans missed the match through injury.

Despite a disappointing night for most of the squad, there was good news for some, with Edwin van der Sar, Cristiano Ronaldo, Nani, Patrice Evra and Tomasz Kuszczak all playing their part in qualification.

On his return to Old Trafford from international duty, Wes Brown, an unused sub for England, spoke of his disappointment at seeing his country fall at the final hurdle, but insisted he was fully focused on United's upcoming trip to Bolton.

'It was very disappointing not to qualify, but that's football and you always have something else to aim for. It's important to focus on the next challenge when another has gone,' he said. 'International goings-on can sometimes affect club form. Whenever we've come back from international get-togethers we never seem to play very well. It could be the travelling, I don't know. But it can sometimes have an impact.'

Wes' words were unfortunately prophetic when, 48 hours later at the Reebok Stadium, the Reds slipped to their second defeat of the season.

Saturday, 24 November 2007, Reebok Stadium

Attendance: 25,028

FA Barclays Premier League
Bolton Wanderers 1 **United** 0

Few would have predicted it. A contest between the current and seemingly would-be champions and a side struggling for results and deep in relegation territory looked to have only one outcome. But as any United fan will tell you, you learn to expect the unexpected, and this result certainly fell under the surprising category.

On the face it, though, this was an uncharacteristically subdued display from Sir Alex's men. Coupled with a clinical first-half finish by Nicolas Anelka, it resulted in United's second league defeat of the campaign and vital lost ground in the title race.

The Reds began proceedings without the injured duo of Nemanja Vidic (back) and Cristiano Ronaldo (thigh). In came Nani and young Spaniard Gerard Piqué, for only his second Premier League start for the Reds. Unfortunately, his inexperience told after just 11 minutes when he misjudged the flight of Ivan Campo's clipped free-kick, allowing Anelka to take full advantage and sweep a tidy finish past Edwin van der Sar.

Buoyed by taking a shock early lead, Bolton set about protecting what they had as if their lives depended on it. United, meanwhile, continued to look decidedly out of sorts, particularly in attack, despite enjoying the lion's share of possession. Wayward shots from Louis Saha and Owen Hargreaves were all they had to show for their first-half endeavours.

While the home side continued to stand firm at the back, their somewhat boisterous tactics visibly irked Sir Alex Ferguson, who had more than a few choice words for referee Mark Clattenburg as the officials made their way off the pitch at the interval. The United boss was subsequently banished to the stands for his remonstrations and would later be charged by the FA.

The second half was played out in a similar fashion and, with half an hour remaining, Sir Alex had seen enough. Via mobile phone from his new, elevated view, the boss replaced Piqué with Anderson, switching Wes Brown to the heart of the defence and Owen Hargreaves to right-back.

And it was Hargreaves himself who drew an excellent save from Jussi Jaaskelainen, who tipped the midfielder's 25-yard free-kick over the bar. Nani was next to go close with a fizzing effort past Jaaskelainen's near post.

With 20 minutes remaining, Carlos Tevez was presented with a golden opportunity to draw the visitors level but, with the goal gaping, the striker somehow contrived to flick Patrice Evra's cross wide. It was an astonishing miss.

Ricardo Gardner survived a strong penalty claim after Nani's shot ricocheted off his upper arm; Evra blazed over when a lay-off to the unmarked Saha was the better option; and Hargreaves saw another set-piece clip the roof of the net in stoppage time.

It was a fitting end to what had been a day to forget for United.

BOLTON WANDERERS: Jaaskelainen; Hunt, Meite, A O'Brien, Gardner; Guthrie (Wilhelmsson 74), Nolan (McCann 82), Campo, Diouf; Davies (Speed 70), Anelka.
Subs not used: Al-Habsi, Michalik

Goal: Anelka (11)

UNITED: Van der Sar; Brown (O'Shea 89), Ferdinand, Piqué (Anderson 59), Evra; Nani, Hargreaves, Carrick, Giggs; Tevez, Saha.
Subs not used: Kuszczak, Fletcher, Eagles

Sir Alex was understandably deflated at the final whistle, but he was more concerned by the lack of protection afforded to his players by the match officials.

'I can't believe some of the things that were going on,' proclaimed the manager. 'I thought there were two or three very dodgy, late tackles, and you hope the referee is strong in those situations. We play our football and it was important to keep playing football. But you need the protection and we did not get that.

'I made my feelings known to the referee and he did not like it. I think we improved in the second half, in terms of our passing. And the movement was better. It was difficult to break Bolton down because after they went 1-0 up they just defended.'

United's off day at the Reebok was made worse by late goals from William Gallas and Tomas Rosicky, that earned Arsenal a 2-0 win over Wigan at the Emirates and sent the Gunners three points clear at the top of the table. Chelsea kept themselves in contention with a 2-0 win at Derby, thanks to goals from Salomon Kalou and Shaun Wright-Phillips.

Away from the action on the pitch, the Reds announced that John O'Shea had signed a three-year extension to his current contract, keeping him at Old Trafford until June 2012, while Sir Alex confirmed that the club had already made tentative enquiries about making Carlos Tevez's stay at Old Trafford a permanent one. The striker would remain on loan until the end of the 2008/09 season, but the Reds' boss remained hopeful of making the deal permanent.

'There is no question about his long-term future here. David Gill has spoken to his agent and told him we are very happy with him,' he insisted. 'The fee is in place. I won't tell you what it is, but it is still cheap. I want to make this happen. He has impressed everyone with his appetite for the game. He'll get me 15 goals a season and, what's more, they will be important goals.'

Somewhat appropriately, Tevez was on the scoresheet 24 hours later, as the Reds claimed their fifth-consecutive Champions League victory of the season.

Tuesday, 27 November 2007, Old Trafford

Attendance: 75,162
UEFA Champions League Group F
United 2 **Sporting Lisbon** 1

It's safe to say Sporting Lisbon are sick of the sight of Cristiano Ronaldo. Once a hero at Sporting, the Reds' winger returned to haunt his former club back in September and he left them reeling once more with a last-minute winner that cemented United's place as Group F winners.

The winger fired a trademark dipping, swerving free-kick past the helpless Rui Patricio in the second minute of injury time to maintain the Reds' 100 per cent record in this season's Champions League and dump his old team out of the competition altogether.

A draw looked the most likely result after the Reds had drawn level through substitute Carlos Tevez after Sporting defender Abel had given the visitors a shock lead on 21 minutes.

Prior to that point, Louis Saha had gone closest to opening the scoring, latching on to Ronaldo's brilliant backheel, but unfortunately firing wide of the far post.

Two minutes later, the visitors went ahead in the unlikeliest of fashions. Miguel Veloso – who, earlier in the week, Carlos Queiroz had revealed featured on United's scouting radar – fed Abel on the wing. As the Reds' defence, including goalkeeper Tomasz Kuszczak, prepared to deal with a cross, the right-back opted to go for goal instead, despite being virtually on the touchline, and somehow squeezed a powerful effort inside the near post.

The goal, later described as a 'freak' strike by Sir Alex, stunned Old Trafford into silence. It nearly turned worse for the Reds four minutes later when Brazilian forward Liedson found the net, but a linesman's flag ensured the scoreline remained the same.

With the Reds struggling to get into their stride, Sir Alex changed things around at the break, with Ryan Giggs and Tevez replacing Darren Fletcher and Nani respectively.

The impact was almost immediate, as Ronaldo and Nemanja Vidic both went close with headers from two Giggs set-pieces, before Saha found himself with a sight of goal thanks to Tevez's through-ball, but Sporting snuffed out the opportunity.

Parity was restored just after the hour, although goalscorer Carlos Tevez knew little about it. Patrice Evra did well to rescue a loose ball and fizzed in a cross that deflected to Ronaldo via Saha. The winger's subsequent effort on goal looked to be heading wide, but somehow ended up in the back of the net after a double deflection off Marian Had and Tevez.

There may have been a touch of fortune about United's equaliser, but they certainly deserved to be level.

Veloso went close with a scorching drive two minutes later, but United dominated the remaining half-hour. Ronaldo sent a diving header into the side netting, before clipping a shot past the top corner of the goal from just inside the area.

He was not to be denied as the game entered stoppage time, though. Setting himself 25-yards out, he blasted a sublime set-piece past Patricio to send the Reds through as group winners and his old club packing.

UNITED: Kuszczak; O'Shea, Ferdinand, Vidic, Evra; Fletcher (Giggs 46), Carrick, Anderson, Nani (Tevez 46); Ronaldo, Saha (Hargreaves 79).
Subs not used: Van der Sar, Brown, Piqué, Simpson

Goals: Tevez (61), Ronaldo (90)

SPORTING LISBON: Patricio; Abel, Tonel, Polga, Had; Veloso, Moutinho, Izmailov (Pereirinha 81), Romagnoli (Vukcevic 68); Purovic (Farnerud 80), Liedson.
Subs not used: Tiago, Silva, Gladstone, Paez

Goal: Abel (21)

After helping to guarantee his side top spot in Group F with a second-consecutive victory over his former club, Cristiano Ronaldo claimed the Reds had the wherewithal to win the competition for a third time.

'It's fantastic, I think we're in a good way,' said the winger, who days later found himself nominated alongside AC Milan star Kaka and Barcelona's Argentine prodigy Lionel Messi for the FIFA World Player of the Year award.

'We've won all our games and we're playing well. We play the way we like to see Manchester play and in the second round I hope we do the same job. I think we have the team, group and coaches, everything to win the Champions League.'

Michael Carrick agreed that the Reds were in perfect shape going in to the knockout stages, but maintained that they will need to prove their true quality when the competition resumes in February.

'A 100 per cent record is something to be proud of,' declared the midfielder. 'We set out to top the group and have managed to achieve that, but the hard work really starts in the spring.

'Obviously, we will now have to wait and see how the draw goes, but we realise the biggest tests are still to come and we will need to be at our best when the competition starts again after Christmas.'

As December approached, Sir Alex moved to dismiss tabloid rumours that Gary Neville's career could come to a premature end.

'That's the extreme fear, but we're not at that point with Gary at all,' insisted the boss. 'I look at his training performances and he has been very good. The problem is he has had setbacks. He had one recently, which was a disappointment. He was on the verge of coming back and I was considering him for the game against Dynamo Kyiv. He probably needs two or three reserves' matches and then he'll be back in the frame.'

Having cemented their place in the latter stages of the Champions League, the Reds were aiming to get back on track in the league with a Monday night game with Fulham at Old Trafford next on the agenda.

Chapter Six

DECEMBER – CHARGE GATHERS MOMENTUM

In a season where everything was seemingly going right for Cristiano Ronaldo, the Portuguese winger started the final month of 2007 with a rare dose of bad news. Having been nominated for the prestigious Ballon D'Or award, which recognises the best player in world football, Ronaldo finished ahead of Barcelona's Lionel Messi, but behind AC Milan playmaker Kaka in the stakes for the coveted prize.

The award was decided by a panel of world football journalists, who were swayed by the Brazilian's superb performances in the 2006/07 Champions League campaign – which Milan won, defeating United in the semi-finals.

With Fulham due at Old Trafford the following day, Lawrie Sanchez's Cottagers would provide Ronaldo with the perfect platform upon which he could vent his frustration.

Monday, 3 December 2007, Old Trafford

Attendance: 75,055

FA Barclays Premier League
United 2 **Fulham** 0

Having missed the Reds' previous league outing at Bolton, Cristiano Ronaldo hit a brace at Old Trafford to take his personal haul to 11 goals in his last eight starts, and send United back to second spot in the Premier League table.

Quite how United – and Ronaldo in particular – only scored twice will remain a mystery, after a devastating attacking display threatened to humiliate the visitors, who were indebted to goalkeeper Antti Niemi for keeping the scoreline as respectable.

Carlos Tevez could have bagged a hat-trick inside the opening eight minutes, but he was left to rue a header that inched wide of the post, a fine reflex save from Niemi and a superb last-ditch challenge from Aaron Hughes. Fulham were creaking from the very first whistle, and it was no surprise when Ronaldo smashed United into the lead after ten minutes.

The visitors failed to clear a corner properly – midfielder Steven Davis headed needlessly back towards his own goal rather than away to safety – Nemanja Vidic flicked the ball on and Ronaldo crashed an unstoppable first-time volley into the top corner of Niemi's goal. There may have been a touch of fortune in the build-up to the goal, but it was one of the sweetest finishes of the season.

Now the floodgates could open. Wayne Rooney, back from a three-week spell on the sidelines, Tevez and Ronaldo tormented the visiting defence with their repertoire of neat flicks and tricks, and only a superb reaction save from Niemi prevented Tevez from converting Giggs' cross at the near post.

In Danny Murphy, however, Fulham were in possession of an Old Trafford talisman. Three times a match-winner in Manchester during his Liverpool days, the midfielder came within a whisker of an undeserved equaliser twice in as many minutes. First, Edwin van der Sar was equal to his low drive; then, from the subsequent corner, the Dutchman was beaten as Murphy curled an effort just past the top corner.

With United rattled, Shefki Kuqi squandered a gilt-edged opportunity just before the interval, heading Simon Davies' cross well over the bar, despite being unmarked and only six yards out.

After that let-off, United took just 13 minutes of the second period to make the game safe. Substitute John O'Shea, on for Patrice Evra, made the most of generous marking on the left wing to curl in a superb cross, which Ronaldo headed powerfully home. It was game over.

Evra's departure was enforced by a bug that had affected a few members of staff at Carrington, and Rio Ferdinand was the next to depart as he sprinted down the tunnel. He was replaced by Michael Carrick. Four minutes later, Ronaldo burst clear, nudged the ball past Niemi and was brought down. A clear penalty, and probably a red card for the Finnish goalkeeper, so everyone expected ... not so. Referee Rob Styles ruled that Ronaldo had deliberately gone to ground and booked him for simulation.

It was a frustrating end to the evening for Ronaldo, but he could still reflect on yet another two-goal haul that secured the points for United.

UNITED: Van der Sar; Brown, Ferdinand (Carrick 75), Vidic, Evra (O'Shea 46); Ronaldo, Anderson, Hargreaves, Giggs; Tevez, Rooney (Saha 72)
Subs not used: Kuszczak, Fletcher

Goals: Ronaldo (10, 58)

FULHAM: Niemi; Konchesky, Stefanovic, Omozusi, Hughes; Davies, Davis, Murphy, Bouazza (Ki-Hyeon 72); Dempsey (Healy 65), Kuqi
Subs not used: Bocanegra, Warner, Baird

Despite the victory, Sir Alex Ferguson was left fuming by Rob Styles' decision not to award Ronaldo a blatant penalty and the chance to notch the first hat-trick of his career.

'The penalty incident is a result of the referee's perceived idea that Ronaldo dives,' said Sir Alex. 'There's no question about that. Why would he want to dive? He was going full pelt, he was past the goalkeeper, he's on a hat-trick ... it was a ridiculous decision.'

'The ref took the decision and, although I respect it, I don't have the same opinion,' Ronaldo later said. 'It was a penalty. If he watches the replay, he'll see that the keeper doesn't touch the ball.

'It's frustrating to get a yellow card for it, but that's the way football goes and sometimes referees make mistakes. I don't think he did a great job tonight, but the most important thing is the three points.'

Ronaldo's two-goal haul was the 12th brace of his United career. Although he continued to covet a first Reds' hat-trick, he conceded that he would be happy just to prolong his rich goalscoring form.

'My mum sometimes says to me, "Why do you never score a hat-trick?" But I always tell her I'm happy to keep scoring two goals,' he joked. 'I'm a winger, not a striker, but my mentality is always to try and help the team, whether it is by making a goal or scoring one.'

While Ronaldo took the plaudits yet again for his goalscoring heroics, the performance of Anderson – the latest in a long line of impressive outings – was the one that set tongues wagging. There was no doubt that United had unearthed a gem in signing the Brazilian midfielder, and Sir Alex was delighted with his infant Reds career.

'He's been absolutely superb; the boy's definitely got something special,' enthused the manager. 'There was an urgency to get him once we'd scouted him. Even though he'd broken his leg and had been out for four or five months, we had to move because the reports were saying he was the best young player in the world. At the time I was saying, "For god's sake, let's calm down a bit here." I knew he had real potential, but I didn't want to put labels like that on him.

'We've been delighted with him. He's proven himself to be a true central midfield player. But there is some luck attached to it because, before Paul Scholes got his injury, I could have had a dilemma. Paul prefers to play on the left side in midfield and Anderson's position is the same. But since he's come into the team he's just taken off. He can tackle, he's lightning quick, he's brave and he can pass the ball. What he's got to prove is his goalscoring ability, because that's something Scholesy's always given us.'

Anderson was arguably the surprise package of United's four summer signings. The most familiar, England midfielder Owen Hargreaves, had only been at the club since July, but already felt completely at home.

'I feel like I've been at the club for years,' he said. 'I've known a lot of the players for a long time through the England set-up and, of course, the national team has trained at Carrington on numerous occasions and also played at Old Trafford. So it's always been familiar to me.

'Being a United player is everything I expected and more. I've been really impressed with the club as an organisation, the people, the way everyone has taken to me. The quality of the players, the staff, the fans and also the style of football this team plays is brilliant.'

United's quest to overhaul league leaders Arsenal would pit them next against Derby County at Old Trafford. Having sprinted off with a virus against Fulham, Rio Ferdinand confirmed that he would be fit for the Rams' visit, after narrowly avoiding a catastrophe against the Cottagers.

'I don't know where the bug originated from,' revealed the England defender. 'Patrice had it as well. I felt a bit funny before the game, but thought I'd just be able to play through. I had a bit of a problem at half-time, but thought I'd be able to get through the second 45 minutes. Then it got worse and I had a tablet during the game, but it kept getting worse and I thought, "If I don't go now then it could be embarrassing for everyone," so I sprinted off.'

United fans everywhere were similarly hoping to avoid embarrassment when the rock-bottom Rams came to Old Trafford.

Saturday, 8 December 2007, Old Trafford

Attendance: 75,725

FA Barclays Premier League
United 4 **Derby County** 1

It was never quite the goal avalanche many had anticipated but, in swirling winds and teeming rain, United still coasted to a handsome victory over Paul Jewell's Rams.

Ryan Giggs notched his 100th league goal for the club, Carlos Tevez hit a brace and Cristiano Ronaldo wrapped up proceedings with an injury-time penalty, while Steve Howard scored Derby's first away goal of the season to salvage some cheer for the saturated visitors.

For long periods of the first half, frustration reigned in the rain for United. Wayne Rooney and Cristiano Ronaldo both narrowly missed the target in the opening exchanges, but Derby were holding surprisingly firm for a side already odds-on for an immediate relegation back to the Championship.

Derby's physical approach and the conditions hardly helped United's cause, although Rooney did manage to beat goalkeeper Stephen Bywater, only for defender James McEveley somehow to contrive to clear the ball off the line. It was very much a case of when the dam breaks ... and after 40 minutes it duly did.

Ronaldo cut in from the left and fired a skidding shot goalwards. Bywater could only parry it out, and Giggs was on hand to fire home clinically, bringing up his long-awaited league century. Moments later the Welsh veteran angled a superb crossfield pass to Rooney, who bore down on goal, chipped Bywater and watched in agony as the ball bounced off the post and away.

It was a huge let-off for the Rams, but they ended up going into the interval two goals down after an almighty goalmouth scramble. Tevez swung at and missed a loose ball, but the saturated turf held it in place for him to have another, this time more successful effort at lashing home.

The Argentine doubled his tally in more aesthetically pleasing circumstances after an hour. Just two minutes after Giggs had struck a post, Tevez manoeuvred space for himself inside the Derby area and arrowed a powerful 15-yard shot into the far bottom corner.

Howard pulled a scrappy goal back for the visitors, as Tyrone Mears' cross rebounded off the striker and trickled over the line, for only the second league goal scored by an opposing team at Old Trafford in the 2007/08 campaign.

Typically, Ronaldo had the final say. Having won a penalty at the expense of Mears in the final minute of injury time, the winger waved away hat-trick hunting Tevez, before firing home his 14th goal of the season. The season of goodwill it may have been, but Ronaldo and United were not in a charitable mood.

UNITED: Van der Sar; Brown, Ferdinand (O'Shea 71), Vidic, Evra; Ronaldo, Carrick, Anderson (Fletcher 63), Giggs (Saha 65); Tevez, Rooney. Subs not used: Kuszczak, Nani

Goals: Giggs (40), Tevez (45, 60), Ronaldo (90, pen)

DERBY COUNTY: Bywater; Griffin, Davis, Moore, McEveley (Mears 46); Leacock, Oakley, Pearson, Barnes (Teale 61), Fagan (Howard 46); Miller. Subs not used: Price, Earnshaw

Goal: Howard (76)

Perhaps fittingly for one of the greatest No. 11s in United's history, Ryan Giggs became the 11th player to score 100 league goals for the club after his strike against Derby.

'Obviously I'm really pleased to have done it,' beamed Ryan. 'It's a great achievement and I'm pleased that I eventually got there.'

While Giggs remained his ever-modest self, Sir Alex Ferguson was more than happy to salute the winger's feat. 'I'm amazed that there hasn't been more made of it,' he said. 'I think we should be making a big deal of it because it's a fantastic achievement. Not many players have scored 100 league goals for this club.'

The United manager was also quick to back Cristiano Ronaldo for converting the Reds' late penalty, rather than handing Carlos Tevez the chance to notch a first United hat-trick.

Sir Alex said: 'Cristiano is the regular penalty taker and I can understand him wanting to take it. It would have been great for Carlos to get his hat-trick, but it's also important for Ronaldo to keep his goalscoring run going. When you're on a run like Cristiano is [12 goals in nine games] you want him to carry on. It's the same for any player, it helps to keep your confidence high.'

After taking six points in as many days and with a trip to Liverpool looming large on the horizon, confidence was certainly sky high in the United camp. First up, though, the Reds needed to put the seal on a successful Champions League group campaign that had already yielded five straight wins.

A youthful squad was named for the trip to Italy to take on Roma, with several old heads remaining at Carrington to prepare for the visit to Anfield. Ryan Giggs was among those who skipped the trip, giving him the chance to travel to Buckingham Palace to collect an OBE for services to football.

With Gary Neville still injured, Giggs meeting the Queen and Rio Ferdinand also rested, Sir Alex Ferguson would have to select a one-off captain for the Roma clash. Step forward, Mr Rooney.

'Wayne has been pestering me for ages, so now he gets his chance,' revealed the manager. 'I have no qualms about the decision. Wayne is a player with great determination and spirit. They are qualities similar to those of two or three of our captains of the past, such as Steve Bruce, Bryan Robson and Roy Keane. These are qualities that can help the team.'

Although it would be a youthful United side in Rome, Sir Alex refused to compromise the demands he would be placing on his side. 'We don't want to send a team out to get humiliated or embarrassed, that's for sure,' he said. 'We expect any Manchester United team we field to be 100 per cent committed, and I'm sure you'll see that on Wednesday night.'

Wednesday, 12 December 2007, Stadio Olimpico

Attendance: 29,490
UEFA Champions League Group F
AS Roma 1 **United** 1

United's crop of promising youngsters restored their damaged pride with an impressive draw against a strong Roma side in the Stadio Olimpico.

With qualification and top spot already secure, Sir Alex Ferguson gave starts to seven players who had featured in September's Carling Cup humiliation against Coventry.

And redemption was the order of the day for United's young guns, who, with a little more composure in front of goal – and but for a fine late equaliser from Mancini – could easily have embarrassed their more illustrious opponents.

The Brazilian curled home a leveller 20 minutes from time to cancel out Gerard Piqué's thumping first-half header for United. In other positive news, Wayne Rooney skippered the side for 70 minutes to build his match-fitness ahead of the trip to Anfield.

The powerhouse striker had two speculative early efforts as the hosts sat back, but Polish goalkeeper Tomasz Kuszczak was called into action to palm away a goalbound Antunes cross and a 20-yard strike from David Pizarro.

Those scares aside, United's youngsters visibly grew in confidence, and their poise was aided no end when Piqué steamed onto a Nani corner to power a header past home goalkeeper Doni on 34 minutes. The Spanish defender raced over to the small, jubilant section of United fans who occupied a lonely corner of the Stadio Olimpico – it was a far cry from the violent scenes that overshadowed the teams' last meeting in Rome some eight months earlier.

Mancini was twice denied before the break, once by the bar, once by Kuszczak, as United went into the interval with a deserved lead. *Giallorossi* boss Luciano Spalletti brought on Ludovic Giuly and Mirko Vucinic after an hour, but the Reds continued to pepper Roma's goal. Carrick and Eagles both shot wide from distance, before Doni thwarted Louis Saha after an exquisite one-two between Rooney and the Frenchman.

Rooney was replaced by Dong Fangzhuo moments after Mancini had levelled matters against the run of play with a fine curling shot in the 71st minute. Shortly afterwards Vucinic struck the upright as the home side stepped up the tempo.

Both sides spurned decent chances to take three points right at the death. First Nani raced through on goal, but could only chip his shot straight at Doni. Then, after hesitant defending from United, Vucinic blazed a shot over the bar from two yards.

Defeat would have been cruel on United's youngsters, who showed that they could indeed handle life on the big stage.

AS ROMA: Doni; Cicinho, Ferrari, Mexes, Barusso (Giuly 62); Esposito (Vucinic 62), Antunes, Taddei, Pizarro, Mancini; Totti.
Subs not used: Julio Sergio, Panucci, Juan, De Rossi, Pit

Goal: Mancini (71)

UNITED: Kuszczak; Simpson, Piqué, Evans, O'Shea (Brown 54); Eagles, Fletcher, Carrick, Nani; Rooney (Dong 72), Saha.
Subs not used: Heaton, Lee, Hewson, Brandy, R Eckersley

Goal: Piqué (34)

'It was fantastic to captain the team,' proclaimed a proud Wayne Rooney afterwards. 'I think it was a good result and a good performance. It's a great experience for the young lads to get Champions League football under their belts. I'm sure it will have helped them a lot. Piqué, [Jonny] Evans and Simmo [Danny Simpson] did really well. They have great ability and bright futures ahead.'

Sir Alex Ferguson was similarly satisfied with his young charges' exertions. 'I was pleased with a lot of it,' he said. 'I think in the second half we gave the ball away too much, which is perhaps understandable with our inexperience. But it was compensated for by their ability on the ball. We played some good football against the strongest Roma side. I think we can be pleased with that.

'It [the experience] helps them. The sudden bursts of play from Roma can catch you off guard at times. The explosion of noise from their fans is exactly the same thing, and that's the European game for you. It will do them the world of good.'

With United already safely through to the knockout stages, it was a case of hurrying home and beginning the planning for Liverpool. As ever, the threat of Steven Gerrard would need to be combated, and so too would that of Fernando Torres. Long linked with a move to Old Trafford, the Spaniard had excelled since his summer transfer to Anfield and was intent on prolonging his run of fine form against

United. He certainly provided cause for concern for the Reds' coaching staff.

'Torres is doing really well and I'm impressed with him,' said assistant manager Carlos Queiroz ahead of the game. 'He is already going some way to making the difference for Liverpool this season. He's a good finisher and gives Liverpool something completely different. Certainly we will have to be careful of him because he is dangerous. We are always confident in what we can do and will not worry too much. But we do recognise his quality.'

The day before United's trip to Anfield, Sir Alex Ferguson received a two-match touchline ban for his outspoken views on referee Mark Clattenburg's performance in United's defeat at Bolton, ensuring that the Scot would be in the stands against West Ham and Birmingham.

It was water off a duck's back in some respects, for nothing could halt Sir Alex's anticipation of his favourite fixture – Liverpool at Anfield.

'This is a game separate from everything, it has different tendencies to any other game,' he smiled, at the pre-match press conference. 'I think we look upon each other as our main rivals in English football.

'You have the geography, the history of the clubs, the ability of the players, the competition, the passion and fervour of the fans. Liverpool's support is a big component of that club, particularly against United. You have to be a man to handle that atmosphere. If you are a lamb, you are dead.'

Sunday, 16 December 2007, Anfield

Attendance: 44,459

FA Barclays Premier League
Liverpool 0 **United** 1

Carlos Tevez may have struck the vital winner, but Rio Ferdinand and his defensive cohorts were the stars of the show as United executed a perfect contain-and-counter performance to notch a fifth win at Anfield in six years.

The Reds totally blunted any attacking threat posed by Rafa Benitez's side and, but for a pot-shot from Ryan Babel and two first-half mistakes from Edwin van der Sar, the hosts offered nothing in attack.

Wary of the impending pressure his side would face in the opening exchanges, against a side hell-bent on overcoming their United hoodoo, Sir Alex Ferguson deployed Anderson and Owen Hargreaves as midfield destroyers. The move worked a treat. Steven Gerrard, so often Liverpool's heartbeat, barely had a kick all afternoon.

With their title challenge already floundering, the pressure was on the Merseysiders to make all the early running. They offered little, but two rare slips from van der Sar both ended with United defenders hacking the ball off their own goal-line.

Those errors aside, United remained cool under pressure and, having deliberately soaked up their host's pressure, the Reds moved ahead just before the interval. Ryan Giggs slid a corner to Wayne Rooney, whose slightly scuffed shot was probably drifting wide until the lurking Tevez quickly adjusted his feet to clip the ball into the roof of the net.

Just as had been the case the previous season, a set-piece had ended with a United player stabbing the ball into the top of the Kop net. This time, however, there were still another 45 minutes to play.

The Reds saw out the first 30 of those minutes in total comfort, as Liverpool's attacking impotence saw them resort to hoofing long balls into the United area, where van der Sar, Ferdinand or Nemanja Vidic duly dealt with them. The trio were helpless as Babel smashed a low shot just past the post on 75 minutes, but that was Liverpool's final effort of note.

Wayne Rooney should have made the game safe three minutes later, but he could only divert Ronaldo's left-wing cross wide of Pepe Reina's goal. It was a bad miss, but not a costly one, as United ran down the clock in cruise control, bringing victory for Sir Alex Ferguson in his 50th match against Liverpool. Surely few of them can have been as routine as this one.

LIVERPOOL: Reina; Arbeloa, Hyypia, Carragher, Riise (Aurelio 80); Benayoun, Gerrard, Mascherano, Kewell (Babel 66); Kuyt (Crouch 73), Torres. Subs not used: Itandje, Lucas

UNITED: Van der Sar; Brown, Ferdinand, Vidic, Evra; Ronaldo, Hargreaves, Anderson (O'Shea, 90), Giggs; Rooney, Tevez (Carrick, 83). Subs not used: Kuszczak, Fletcher, Saha

---

Goal: Tevez (43)

Sir Alex Ferguson had warned before the game that lambs would not survive in the Anfield cauldron. Fortunately for him, he had 11 lions on show – and none braver than Rio Ferdinand.

The England centre-back invariably saves his best displays for the biggest games – and Liverpool in particular – but he was keen to focus on the Reds' collective defending after another momentous win on Merseyside.

'These are the best games,' he conceded. 'You enjoy playing football no matter what, but playing against Liverpool at Anfield and getting a good result is something you dream about as a kid. United against Liverpool at Anfield is a fixture you look for on the calendar, and we've been successful here the last couple of years and long may it continue.

'I was happy with the team and I was happy we won the game. My performance comes a long way second to us winning the match. Our fans come here and make themselves heard for the whole 90 minutes, and the satisfaction you get from winning the game is unbelievable. It's one of the best places to come and win.

'Games like this, you don't care who scores, who gets man of the match. Today we had to come here and defend. When you come to Anfield you know you're going to be under immense pressure at times and it's the way you deal with it. We had to clear one off the line in the first half and I think Edwin had just the one save in the second half. They put us under pressure with a few crosses in the first half, but we settled down after that and I think we defended very well.'

Matchwinner Carlos Tevez further endeared himself to United fans with his vital first-half strike, but his burgeoning strike partnership with Wayne Rooney had long since been making headlines. The Argentine-Scouse axis was an unlikely one – given linguistic differences – but Rooney revealed that the pair hardly needed to speak to each other such was their on-field chemistry.

'We don't talk to each other very much because we don't speak the same language, but that doesn't matter when you are playing with a great talent like Carlos,' he explained. 'We do a lot of hard work together on the training pitch, but the understanding between us seems to be very natural anyway.

'It's all about eye contact. It's just a glance here or a nod there and we instinctively know what the other one is going to do and when and where we want the ball to be played. It's a case of playing the game as you see it and when it comes off it looks very good. The goal Carlos scored against Middlesbrough recently was typical of that.

'We've both still got a lot to learn, but the partnership will only get better with the more work we put in on the training ground and the more we play together.'

The pair would have another chance to hone their understanding a week later, when Everton were the next team due to arrive at Old Trafford. Prior to the Toffeemen's visit, however, there was the small matter of discovering who lay in wait in the first knockout round of the Champions League.

At a draw ceremony in Nyon, United could have been handed favourable draws against Celtic, Fenerbahce, Olympiakos or Schalke 04. As it was, the Reds were handed the tough task of overcoming perennial French champions Lyon – a task that defender Nemanja Vidic appreciated would be taxing.

'Lyon have shown in the last couple of years they are a great team in Europe,' said the Serb. 'They tend to do well at home and have good players like Juninho and Sidney Govou. Juninho is especially dangerous – he can score from anywhere. We can't give him too many chances. Lyon will be a tough team, but I think we can deal with them and do enough over these two games.'

On a busy news day, United discovered their Champions League opponents and announced that, after impressing during a trial at Carrington, Angolan striker Manucho had agreed to join the Reds from Petro Athletico of Luanda, pending a work permit, on a three-year contract. A delighted Sir Alex Ferguson said: 'We have had Manucho here for a three-week trial and have been impressed enough to offer him a three-year contract. He is a tall, agile and quick forward and, through Carlos Queiroz's contacts, was brought to our attention around six months ago.'

There was another pleasant surprise to emerge from the manager's pre-Everton press conference – the return of Ji-sung Park from knee-ligament damage. The Korean had been out for almost nine months, and was now ready to feature during the hectic Christmas period.

'Ji has done some excellent training over the last few weeks, absolutely first class and well beyond what we expected,' explained the boss. 'When a player has been out for nine months, you always wonder how quick or slow their recovery will be. But Ji has been terrific. He'll definitely take part in the Christmas games, there's no doubt about that.'

While it was doubtful that Park would return against Everton, United were given a timely boost by the news that Carlos Tevez and Wes Brown would be fit after shaking off the minor niggles they had picked up against Liverpool. Sir Alex appreciated that he would need a fit and ready squad for the visit of David Moyes' side, who had been in fine fettle in the run-up to their trip down the East Lancs.

'Everton have been in great form of late since they lost the derby game to Liverpool [in October],' he said. 'They recovered very well from that and have shown great consistency. They're a young team, but one that's full of confidence and I expect it to be a really good game.'

Sunday, 23 December 2007, Old Trafford

Attendance: 75,749

FA Barclays Premier League
United 2 **Everton** 1

Nerves of steel can decide matches and, ultimately, championships, and Cristiano Ronaldo showed an ice-cool streak a mile long when he converted a dramatic winning penalty against Everton.

The Merseysiders pushed United all the way and looked set to have gained a point after Tim Cahill's powerful header had cancelled out Ronaldo's early opener, but the Portuguese winger fired home after Steven Pienaar had fouled Ryan Giggs two minutes from time.

The result was deserved and hard-fought for a United side bereft of Edwin van der Sar, Rio Ferdinand and Owen Hargreaves through injury – replaced by Tomasz Kuszczak, Danny Simpson and Michael Carrick respectively.

In a fraught opening to the game, referee Howard Webb dealt out four bookings – two per side – but it was United who settled the quicker. Carlos Tevez had an effort deflected just wide, before Ronaldo opened the scoring in storming fashion after 22 minutes.

Former Reds' goalkeeper Tim Howard was afforded a warm reception on his return to Old Trafford, but the American was helpless as Ronaldo cut in from the right flank and drilled a left-footed shot high into the far top corner.

It was the sixth-successive home game in which Ronaldo had struck, but the visitors were level almost immediately. Pienaar was allowed time to pick a cross from the left-wing and Cahill sprung superbly to plant a header past Kuszczak.

It was the Toffees' first effort of note, and their last of the half as United immediately looked to reassert their authority. Joleon Lescott had to be alert to head Wayne Rooney's clever chip off the line with Howard well beaten, then Ronaldo volleyed just over after a slick interchange with Giggs.

United's dominance continued into the second half as Everton seemed to settle for the point they had rather than go in search of all three. Howard had to be on his toes to save well from Anderson and Tevez, while Rooney's shot from the edge of the area clipped the roof of the net with the American comfortably beaten.

Just as frustration looked set to engulf United, Pienaar inexplicably trailed a leg to halt Giggs' winding run, and referee Webb had no choice but to point to the spot. Despite the arduous, nervy delay, Ronaldo kept his nerve and hammered home, ensuring all three points and a merry Christmas for United.

UNITED: Kuszczak; Simpson (O'Shea 45), Brown, Vidic, Evra; Ronaldo, Carrick (Saha 71), Anderson (Fletcher 86), Giggs; Rooney, Tevez.
Subs not used: Heaton, Nani

Goals: Ronaldo (22, 88, pen)

EVERTON: Howard; Hibbert, Yobo, Jagielka, Lescott; Carsley, Cahill (Anichebe 85), P Neville, Pienaar; Yakubu (Gravesen 76), Johnson.
Subs not used: Wessels, McFadden, Nuno Valente

Goal: Cahill (27)

'I think Father Christmas gave me my present early,' joked Cristiano Ronaldo after his double ensured a happy Christmas for the Reds. 'The most important thing is the team. The game was very tough; Everton played well and created a few difficult moments for us, but I think we played very well. In the first half it was not too good, but in the second half I think we played better, created more chances and deserved to win.

'We've got many games coming up now and it's always important to win. At home you need to win. With the next few games, there is not too much time to rest, so a victory was important to stay near the top.'

With Ronaldo in near-unplayable form and tormenting the Everton defence all afternoon, Sir Alex Ferguson could only find one word to describe the winger's display.

'He was perfect,' said the manager. 'I don't think he made a mistake – it was a marvellous performance from him. The first goal was fantastic. The boy really has got everything and we're expecting goals from him all the time.

'The temperament and confidence he's always shown as a kid surfaces at times like that [when he stepped up to take the penalty]. He composed himself and took the spot-kick very well. Of course, others played their part and you could see what a great team spirit we have by the way we never stopped going. It's a very important result.'

So United's players and staff could disband very briefly to celebrate Christmas with their families, safe in the knowledge that they were in a rich vein of form and well in the hunt to retain their league title. Not that they would be able to slacken off for yuletide, of course.

'I'm used to having three weeks off and being on the beach in Miami or Hawaii at this time of year, but I'm glad I won't be there this time because I want to play my part to help the team be success-ful,' confided Owen Hargreaves, accustomed to a winter break during his Bayern Munich career.

'It's a new experience for me and it's a very difficult period from what the lads have told me. This is my first time of experiencing it and I'm looking forward to being involved. We all know how impor-tant this period is in terms of the title race. So our goal over Christ-mas is to win every game.'

The festive season in English football is most certainly a difficult one. The fixtures come thick and fast at a time when others are spending richly deserved time with their families. United's players couldn't even fully indulge in Christmas dinner.

'You can have a small bit, but not too much,' revealed John O'Shea. 'The manager makes sure the players look after themselves and prepare for the Boxing Day match in a professional manner. So we can't enjoy Christmas Day perhaps as much as other people, but that's a small price to pay for playing at a club like United.'

'You couldn't have as big a portion as everybody else but, apart from that, it's still a normal Christmas dinner with your family,' added Wayne Rooney. 'Then you have to leave for the hotel. I imagine that's harder for the older players with kids. But at the moment, it's fine for me personally – I'm just going out to play football, which I love doing, so I've no problem with being away at Christmas.'

Good job really, as Boxing Day wouldn't be about sleeping off Christmas excesses. There were three more points up for grabs, this time at the Stadium of Light.

Wednesday, 26 December 2007, Stadium of Light

Attendance: 47,360

FA Barclays Premier League
Sunderland 0 **United** 4

In his playing days, Roy Keane was a warrior on the field. He will have been far from enamoured, then, to see his side surrender so meekly against a rampant United side on Boxing Day.

Goals from Wayne Rooney, Louis Saha and Cristiano Ronaldo had the game sewn up by half-time, before Saha added late gloss to the scoreline from the penalty spot. Ji-sung Park also returned after knee surgery, posting half an hour as a substitute and bringing further seasonal cheer to United fans everywhere.

Sir Alex Ferguson's side were intent on attacking their hosts from the first whistle. Ronaldo stung Craig Gordon's palms with a vicious dipping free-kick, while compatriot Nani brought a fine low save from the Scotland international. Saha also miscued a volley, but not before Kenwyne Jones and Dickson Etuhu had passed up half-chances for the hosts.

There was always a danger that United's profligacy in front of goal could prove costly, but they soon had the insurance of an opener after some dreadful Sunderland defending. Wes Brown spotted Rooney in an unfathomable amount of space, and the striker coolly advanced and slotted past Gordon for his first league goal since October.

Just ten minutes later, a breakneck United counter-attack saw Ronaldo release Rooney down the left, and his inswinging cross was met by Saha, who directed a first-time volley inside the post. Simple but devastating, and United were almost home and hosed.

There was a slight scare when Tomasz Kuszczak was forced into a finger-tip save to deny Ross Wallace, but Ronaldo brought the first half, and the contest, to a close with a stunning free-kick. Slightly left of centre and 25 yards out, the Portuguese star fizzed his shot over the wall and into the top corner.

It was game over. United essentially went through the motions during the second half, aware of the need to conserve energy in one of the season's most hectic periods. Park's arrival gave the travelling Reds plenty to cheer about, and the Korean almost immediately laid on a goal for Nani, but the Portuguese winger's shot flew just wide.

Nani was involved in the Reds' fourth goal. As he sprinted into the area, the 20-year-old was pulled back by Danny Collins and, having survived an earlier shout for handball by Dwight Yorke, there was no way the Black Cats' luck would see them survive a second penalty shout.

Saha slotted home the spot-kick in comfortable, languid style – not dissimilar to United's display as a whole. A fifth successive league victory had answered the questions posed by the defeat at Bolton. Next, the Reds faced an always-tricky trip to West Ham.

SUNDERLAND: Gordon; Whitehead, McShane, Higginbotham, Collins; Chopra (O'Donovan 87), Yorke (Richardson 61), Etuhu, Wallace (Leadbitter 46); Jones, Waghorn
Subs not used: Ward, Cole

UNITED: Kuszczak; Brown, Ferdinand, Vidic (Piqué 74), O'Shea; Ronaldo (Park 57), Fletcher, Carrick, Nani; Rooney, Saha
Subs not used: Heaton, Evra, Tevez

Goals: Rooney (20), Saha (30, 86, pen), Ronaldo (45)

Relief reigned for Louis Saha, who found the net for the first time since September, against the Black Cats. With goals three and four of the season chalked up, the Frenchman admitted his confidence had received a timely boost – although he attributed much of that to the form of strike partner Wayne Rooney.

'I needed to get back to the basics as a striker, which is obviously scoring goals,' admitted Saha. 'I had a couple of chances today and it's good to be on the scoresheet. Wayne was unbelievable with his movement and the way he controlled the game for us. It was a winning performance.

'Going into an atmosphere like the one you can have at Sunderland's stadium, it was very important to make a good start. That's what we did and I think we scored at good moments. We were very professional.'

Sir Alex Ferguson was delighted with the contribution both his front men made, believing that their displays augured well for the immediate future and the remainder of the season – as did the return of Ji-sung Park.

'The goals will do Louis' confidence the world of good, as will completing the full 90 minutes,' said the manager. 'I thought he and Wayne linked well. Our front players were a real threat today. I have said before that strikers do go on little runs like that. It was Wayne's first goal for six games, but his goals have come in waves. When he got his recent injury, he was out for nearly a month and, since then, he has been gradually getting towards what we have seen of him against Sunderland.

'I was delighted with Ji-sung's performance, too. It was an important day for him. He came on and got more than half an hour under his belt. He's a natural mover. When the team passes the ball he moves – he's always had a great talent for that and today was another great example of that. He kept moving, passing and running behind the Sunderland defence. He gave us a lot of energy and it was good to see.'

The manager's mood, already upbeat, was enlivened further when Arsenal could only notch a goalless draw against Portsmouth at Fratton Park. United were now back on top of the Premier League, and were boosted by a bulging squad for the trip to West Ham.

Not that Sir Alex would be counting his chickens, of course. He was all too aware of the need for strength in depth, particularly at a time of year where sickness can suddenly appear and spread.

'We're taking a big squad down for West Ham,' the manager said at the pre-match press conference. 'We're taking 20 players and keeping them all together, because you never know at this time of year. Utilising the squad is important. We freshened up the other day by leaving Ryan [Giggs], [Carlos] Tevez and Anderson out against Sunderland. Against West Ham we'll make some more changes. Hopefully that brings the right freshness and gets us the right result.'

Unfortunately for the United manager, he would prove thankful for having an enlarged squad, as Wayne Rooney went down with exactly the kind of sudden sickness that was feared. It was a blow, particularly as Rooney had missed every one of United's defeats so far in the 2007/08 season.

Saturday, 29 December 2007, Upton Park

Attendance: 34,966

FA Barclays Premier League
West Ham United 2 **United** 1

A fired-up performance and a late double from West Ham ensured a miserable end to what had been an exceptional 2007 for United.

Cristiano Ronaldo headed an off-colour Reds into the lead, then missed a penalty, before Anton Ferdinand and Matthew Upson headed late goals for the Hammers, who registered a third-successive victory over Sir Alex Ferguson's side.

Little went right in a tepid United display, as Sir Alex began the first of a two-game touchline ban from an unfamiliarly lofty perch high up in the stands. West Ham took the early initiative and should have gone ahead after ten minutes as Hayden Mullins' shot hit the bar and rebounded to Mark Noble, but the England U21 midfielder sidefooted wastefully over the bar.

A massive miss for the Hammers, and one that was punished shortly afterwards. Carlos Tevez – who received a standing ovation on his return to Upton Park – found Louis Saha, who fed Ryan Giggs on the left wing. The veteran winger advanced and curled in a perfect cross for Ronaldo to nod powerfully beyond Robert Green.

The goal did little to lift United from their lethargy, however, and West Ham could easily have drawn level through Nolberto Solano's lob – well saved by Tomasz Kuszczak – or Carlton Cole's close-range header, which went over the bar. The Hammers retained the momentum going into the second half, but struggled to forge as many openings.

United were handed a glorious chance to put the game to bed with 24 minutes remaining, when former Reds defender Jonathan Spector handled the ball inside his own area. Up stepped Ronaldo, but surprisingly fired his spot-kick a yard wide. He is human after all.

West Ham were buoyed by their reprieve and, after a flurry of corners, they finally drew level. Substitute Anton Ferdinand rose highest to power his header past Kuszczak with just over ten minutes remaining. The home side could smell blood. Five minutes later, Noble whipped in a right-wing free-kick for Matthew Upson to loop a header into the top corner.

Upton Park erupted as the hosts quite deservedly moved into a late lead, which they retained in relative comfort until the final whistle. It may have been a sour end to 2007 for United, but the feeling remained that 2008 could be a very big year indeed.

WEST HAM UNITED: Green; Neill, Spector, Upson, McCartney; Solano (Pantsil 49), Parker (A Ferdinand 55), Noble, Mullins, Ljungberg (Ashton 70); Cole.
Subs not used: Wright, Camara

Goals: Ferdinand (77), Upson (82)

UNITED: Kuszczak; Brown (O'Shea 88), Ferdinand, Vidic, Evra; Ronaldo, Hargreaves (Nani 81), Fletcher, Giggs; Saha, Tevez (Anderson 65).
Subs not used: Heaton, Piqué

Goal: Ronaldo (14)

The media had a field day. Finally there was a chink in Cristiano Ronaldo's armour, as his missed penalty passed up the chance to bury West Ham and allowed them back into the match. The winger's team-mates were not in finger-pointing mood, however, and offered unanimous backing for the Portuguese star.

'Ronaldo missed his penalty, but that can happen,' reasoned Darren Fletcher. 'We were still in a comfortable position at 1-0 up and then it came down to set-pieces. He's not to blame. He's been fantastic for us and won us many games and many points. We were still in a winning position, so the penalty did not lose us the game. It was individual errors at set-pieces that have cost us.'

'If we had scored from the penalty then we would have been 2-0 up,' added Wes Brown. 'Unfortunately Ronny missed it, but we were still winning 1-0 and were still in control. We possibly dropped too deep after that, which put pressure on us. We got the lead and we've conceded from two set-pieces that we should have dealt with. We've let ourselves down.'

Having dropped points for the first time in December, United's players were already itching for the next match. Fortunately, given the frantic nature of the festive fixtures, they would only have to wait three days for Birmingham's visit to Old Trafford.

'Every time you drop points or lose, you have to pick yourself up and go on another winning run,' said Fletcher. 'We wanted to get through the Christmas period with maximum points and put pressure on the teams below us, but unfortunately that's not happened. We've got to pick ourselves up for Birmingham now and get three points and go on another winning run. We can't wait for that game to come now.'

For Sir Alex, the Blues' visit would provide the chance to pit his managerial wits against another of his former players – Alex McLeish, one of his defensive generals from his time at Aberdeen.

'Alec was one of my great stalwarts at Aberdeen,' admitted Sir Alex. 'He and Willie Miller were without doubt the mainstay of that great Aberdeen team. I always felt Alec was going to be a manager, because he was always a great student of the game.

'Even in his early years as a manager at Motherwell and Hibs, he was always phoning me and asking me why I made certain changes, asking about training programmes, and he would come down to games here all the time. He was always a certainty to become a good manager. He's a very intelligent boy and I'm pleased for him.'

Friendships would have to be put to one side, however. Twenty-four hours after celebrating his 66th birthday, Sir Alex was chasing a win to get United back on track in the title race, and start 2008 as he meant to go on.

Chapter Seven

JANUARY – RONALDO RUNS RIOT

United's last game of 2007 may not have ended as planned, but in his programme notes for the New Year's Day clash with Birmingham, Sir Alex reflected on what he described as a 'pleasing' opening half to the campaign.

'At this point I'm very happy with how things are going. When you win the Premier League you wonder if you can carry on where you left off and one of the things we spoke about was the necessity for a good start,' explained the boss. 'We hit a hiccup straight away because it just didn't happen, but I stayed calm because there were reasons for our slow opening. Cristiano [Ronaldo] was suspended, we had injuries and our new players were still settling in. Once they returned, though, we quickly picked up and motored on to fight our way back into contention and now head for the New Year in good shape.'

The United manager also highlighted the importance of stability off the pitch to aid what happens on it.

'I'm very optimistic. We have been playing some great football and United are solid as a club, too. At a number of clubs there have been problems with friction between managers and owners, but you can see how smoothly the United ship is running as far as that's concerned, despite early hostility over the Glazer family's ownership,' he said. 'Those protests were unfair because they [the Glazer family] weren't given a chance, but the Glazers kept their cool and have been nothing but supportive. Good teamwork starts at the top, and I am happy to say that is what we have at Old Trafford.'

A United front was exactly what was needed to help get over the disappointment at Upton Park.

Tuesday, 1 January 2008, Old Trafford

Attendance: 75,459

FA Barclays Premier League
United 1 **Birmingham City** 0

United fans have become accustomed to free-flowing football at Old Trafford, but winning ugly gets you just as many points, as the Reds proved with a battling display against a stubborn Birmingham side.

Carlos Tevez netted the crucial goal in the Reds' opening game of 2008 and produced a baby's dummy to celebrate. He later explained that the unusual routine was dedicated to his daughter Florencia, who had flown home to Buenos Aires for the holiday period.

The Reds went into their New Year's Day clash on the back of a disappointing 2-1 defeat at West Ham. Only a victory would do and Sir Alex's men certainly began the match with a far greater purpose than had been on display at Upton Park.

A virus forced Wayne Rooney to sit out proceedings once again, meaning that Cristiano Ronaldo was asked to partner Tevez up front. And it was the Portuguese star who registered United's first effort on goal after just three minutes, firing in a low shot that visiting goalkeeper Maik Taylor had to be alert to.

Tevez was next to be denied, this time by the woodwork. Nice play between Anderson and Patrice Evra down the left allowed the Frenchman to cross towards the Argentine striker, whose glancing header beat Taylor, but struck the post.

Ronaldo and Nani went close soon after, before Tevez made the breakthrough thanks to a rare moment of delectable attacking football with Ronaldo, inevitably, involved. Tevez played a one-two with the winger, whose delightful backheel glided straight into his team-mate's path and Tevez duly applied the finishing touch. Cue the dummy.

Birmingham, while dogged in their approach, never really threatened and offered little going forward. Their lack of ambition seemed to dull United's own sense of purpose, but the Reds still had chances to make the game safe.

First, Taylor parried Ronaldo's point-blank header from Ji-sung Park's corner, before a posse of Birmingham defenders blocked Ronaldo's rebound effort after Tevez's initial shot had smacked against the post.

The football on display wasn't exactly what the doctor ordered in terms of hangover cures, but three more valuable points certainly proved to be a good antidote.

UNITED: Kuszczak; O'Shea, Ferdinand, Vidic, Evra (Brown 85); Park (Hargreaves 76), Carrick, Anderson, Nani; Ronaldo, Tevez (Saha 72).
Subs not used: Heaton, Piqué

Goal: Tevez (25)

BIRMINGHAM CITY: Taylor; Kelly, Ridgewell, Jaidi, Queudrue; Muamba, McSheffrey (De Ridder 67), Larsson, Nafti (Palacios 82); O'Connor, Jerome (Forssell 67).
Subs not used: Doyle, Parnaby

Sir Alex Ferguson was pleased to see his side get back to winning ways, but admitted the combination of United's profligacy in front of goal and a quiet Old Trafford crowd prevented the Reds from making the 1-0 victory more convincing.

'I don't think it was a suitable game for us in many ways. The crowd was dead. That was the quietest I've heard our crowd. We need the supporters to create a good atmosphere here because the players respond to that,' he declared. 'It's all very well saying the players need to play to get the crowd going for them to respond, but in situations like today we need the fans to get behind us. At times it was like a funeral. It was so quiet. I don't think that helped us.'

Although United failed to hit top gear against Alex McLeish's men, Rio Ferdinand felt the Reds' dogged display was more than deserving of the three points.

'At home, in particular, you always like to try and get a cushion of two or three goals, but it's not always meant to be and you can't win every game in style. Therefore you have to grind out results and, thankfully, we managed to do that.

'Losing at West Ham ruined the Christmas period for me, especially as my brother scored as well!' he joked. 'But you've got to take results on the chin sometimes and make sure you don't drop any more points in the next match. We didn't get the exact response we wanted against Birmingham [in terms of the performance] but, most importantly, we got the result we needed. We're still there or thereabouts in the title race and we'd have taken this position at the start of the season.'

Unfortunately for United the victory wasn't enough to take them above Arsenal, who maintained their two-point advantage at the top of the table with a 2-0 home win over West Ham. Elsewhere, Chelsea came from behind at Craven Cottage to beat Fulham 2-1, ensuring they remained within touching distance of the top two.

The frenetic run of four festive games in ten days left Sir Alex with no choice but to utilise his squad. One player who benefited from the scenario was Ji-sung Park, who made his first appearance at Old Trafford for nine months against Birmingham following his recovery from knee-ligament damage.

'It's nice to be back. I played for 75 minutes, so that will give me confidence. My knee feels 100 per cent and after the game I felt no reaction, so I am not afraid of getting injured again,' he said. 'It was difficult being out for so long, but the lads have done a great job in the league during that time, so I am pleased. This squad is even better than last season. We have a lot of very good players at this club and that will definitely help us for the rest of the campaign.'

There was even more reason to be positive on the injury front with the news that Gary Neville and Paul Scholes were both recovering well from their long-term injuries.

'Gary's training with the team,' revealed Sir Alex when asked about the skipper's recuperation from an ankle injury. 'What we need to do now is get him a game. The reserves league is closed down during the Christmas period, but once that starts up again that's one avenue to go down. We have to look at practice matches or that sort of thing to get some more intensity into his training. Game situations will bring him on a good bit. We're happy with his progress, we're assured he's okay now and it's just a matter of getting him games.'

Scholes, meanwhile, looked set to return within the next few weeks following knee surgery. 'Paul's doing nice, easy running now,' continued the United boss. 'That was the plan. He's out of the cast he was in and the time we set for him was around February, and I don't think we'll be far off. Probably the middle of February to be on the safe side, but he's certainly doing very well.'

Not doing so well was Carlos Tevez. Despite having netted the winner in United's opening game of 2008, the Argentine finished the match on the treatment table having been carried off after a heavy challenge on his ankle.

'Carlos got a bad tackle on his ankle in the first half and the longer he played the worse it got,' explained Sir Alex, who was also without the services of groin-injury victim Edwin van der Sar for the fourth-consecutive game. 'We had to bring Carlos off and will assess him on Wednesday morning to see what damage there is. Obviously, he is doubtful for Saturday now.'

Thankfully, after a full assessment by United's medical team, any fears of a break were allayed, with severe bruising being the main concern. Tevez remained a major doubt for the Reds' FA Cup third-round trip to Villa Park, but the return of Wayne Rooney from a virus provided timely compensation for the Argentine's absence.

Saturday, 5 January 2008, Villa Park

Attendance: 33,630

FA Cup Third Round
Aston Villa 0 **United** 2

Wayne Rooney had occupied many roles already this season, be it as part of a front pairing, a lone striker or left- or right-sided midfielder in a three-pronged attack. Following United's FA Cup victory over Aston Villa, the role of super-sub could now be added to the ever-growing list.

The Reds striker, a constant bundle of energy and enthusiasm, roared off the bench to galvanise United to victory when a dour cup-tie seemed destined for a replay.

Clear-cut chances were few and far between prior to Rooney's introduction. Ryan Giggs wasted the Reds' two best opportunities of the opening period, first heading Patrice Evra's cross wide and, then, with the goal gaping, he failed to connect cleanly with a rebound after Villans goalkeeper Scott Carson had parried Cristiano Ronaldo's initial effort.

After the break, Carson needed two attempts to clutch Anderson's rifled effort, while at the other end Stilian Petrov and John Carew both had glimpses of goal that amounted to nothing.

Sir Alex had seen enough as the clock hit the 70-minute mark and brought Rooney on for Ji-sung Park. The striker's impact was immediate, linking up via a long one-two with Ronaldo, before firing a fine shot just over the bar.

The dynamic duo were involved soon after as the Reds made a vital breakthrough nine minutes from time. Rooney found Giggs wide on the left and his cross was duly stabbed home by Ronaldo three yards out.

A minute from time Rooney confirmed United's place in the fourth round, blasting a low shot past Carson after Ronaldo's blocked effort had rebounded to the edge of the area.

Villa striker John Carew labelled Rooney 'a golden player' after the game, and he looks set to be part of a golden generation at Old Trafford if he and the team keep up this kind of form.

ASTON VILLA: Carson; Mellberg, Laursen, Davies, Bouma (Gardner 83); Petrov (Maloney 75), Reo-Coker, Barry, Young; Agbonlahor, Carew (Moore 64).
Subs not used: Taylor, Knight

UNITED: Van der Sar; Brown, Ferdinand, Vidic, Evra; Ronaldo, Carrick, Anderson, Park (Rooney 70); Giggs (O'Shea 90), Saha (Hargreaves 79).
Subs: Heaton, Nani

Goals: Ronaldo (81), Rooney (89)

United's star man was his ever-modest self afterwards, choosing to focus on the team's never-say-die attitude and the support of United's travelling faithful rather than on his own contribution. But his manager and team-mates were unequivocal in their appraisal of the striker's 20-minute cameo.

'He changed the game,' declared Sir Alex Ferguson. 'He brought a sudden thrust of enthusiasm and direct play through the way he attacked their defenders. We've been looking for a new Solskjaer to come off the bench for a few years now! Seriously, though, he made a heck of a difference when he came on.'

'Wayne is a fantastic footballer with bundles of energy. He may have missed the last couple of games, but he looked very fresh when he came on and I think he was the difference,' added Rio Ferdinand.

'We always knew it was going to be a tough game, but I thought we were grinding them down gradually in the second half and we had a lot of possession. When Wayne came on, the openings started to come and, thankfully, we managed to stick the ball in the back of the net.'

A home tie against either Tottenham Hotspur or Reading (who were due to contest a replay at the Madejski Stadium on 15 January) awaited the Reds in the next round, to be played on Sunday, 27 January. Incredibly, it meant United had been drawn with Premier League opposition in each of their last nine FA Cup ties (including two replays).

As is always the case when the January transfer window opens for business, the Reds found themselves linked with a glut of players, both domestic and Europe-based. Hertha Berlin defender Gilberto, Spurs striker Dimitar Berbatov, Lyon front man Karim Benzema and Ajax forward Klaas-Jan Huntelaar were the most notable names to crop up in the media at the start of 2008.

After over 21 years in the Old Trafford hot-seat, Sir Alex has become more than accustomed to idle gossip fuelled by mischievous scribes, but he was more than a little irked by ongoing reports linking Cristiano Ronaldo with a multi-million pound switch to Real Madrid ahead of the Reds' Premier League clash with Newcastle United at Old Trafford.

'I anticipated this,' Sir Alex said somewhat wearily. 'In the New Year you almost expect it. The thing about this story is that it has been claimed that David Gill has been speaking to them. That is a complete lie. We have never spoken to them. The story depends on agents and their imaginations. At best it's mischievous, but I just dismiss it because it's nonsense. But who wouldn't be interested in Ronaldo? That's why we bought him.'

While categorically slamming the door shut on Madrid, the boss also declared that, bar potential loan deals for some of the Reds' younger players, he expected to be saving his pennies for the summer months. 'It's unlikely we will be making any moves,' he said, before revealing that the Reds had turned down an offer for Wes Brown from Newcastle.

With just a few months left to run on his contract and negotiations between player and club at a standstill, it remained unclear as to whether Brown would still be on United's books come the start of next season.

'The matter rests with Wes and his agent,' explained Sir Alex. 'We'll just wait and see what happens. Our offer is still there – it's now up to Wes.'

One defender who would definitely not figure in the manager's plans for the remainder of the campaign was youngster Jonny Evans, who returned to Sunderland for a second spell on loan at the beginning of January until the season's climax. Evans became the fifth

Reds youngster to make a loan switch since the turn of the year following Kieran Lee's move to QPR, Michael Barnes' to Chesterfield, Lee Martin's to Sheffield United and Febian Brandy's to Swansea. Darron Gibson and Fraizer Campbell, meanwhile, opted to extend their running loan deals with Wolverhampton Wanderers and Hull City respectively.

One man certain to be sticking around Old Trafford for a while longer was Edwin van der Sar after he agreed a new one-year deal until the end of the 2008/09 campaign.

'As we did last year, we said we'd evaluate things in December and both parties were very happy with things so there was no reason for me to quit,' revealed the Dutch stopper, who joined in June 2005. 'I'm still feeling very good [about my fitness] and with the way the team plays and everything about the club it's a delight to be here.'

Sir Alex was equally pleased to have secured van der Sar's services for a further 12 months, saying: 'Edwin's consistency and experience have been a great help to this club and I'm delighted he's staying on.'

There was good news for the Reds in the lead-up to their league clash with Newcastle. Skipper Gary Neville enjoyed a 45-minute run-out in the reserves' 2-2 draw with Everton and capped his return with a goal, while Mikael Silvestre revealed he was progressing well with his gruelling rehabilitation from cruciate knee-ligament damage.

'I know if I come back to my best then I will be able to play again because there are so many games. You always get an opportunity to play,' said the French defender. 'I have been doing five, six hours a day of rehab since I got injured. It is a bit boring and very tiring because I only stay in the gym and don't get to go on the field. It's a long process, but I feel good and hope I'll be back soon.'

Just 48 hours before the Reds entertained Newcastle, it was announced that the Toon Army would arrive at Old Trafford manager-less after Sam Allardyce's eight-month reign at St James' Park came was brought to an abrupt end by a run of poor results. Assistant boss Nigel Pearson was handed temporary charge of team arrangements.

Sir Alex gave his reaction to the news at the pre-match press conference, and admitted he found it hard to believe he was discussing yet another managerial casualty just six months into the season.

'Eight times this season I've had to talk about a Premier League manager leaving their jobs and every time I say there's a lack of patience from clubs,' explained the manager, himself a good friend of Allardyce. 'I think it's a modern-day trend – people today have not got the patience and the unfortunate thing for Sam was he was appointed by a different chairman [Freddy Shepherd] to the one that's there now. That was probably the most dangerous part about the situation he found himself in.

'I don't really know what to make of the game itself,' he added. 'Sometimes when a team loses a manager and appoints a new one it can be difficult, as we found when we played West Ham last season [after Alan Curbishley took over]. But in Newcastle's case they don't have a new manager yet. Hopefully, we can do what we have to do and get the win.'

In terms of team news, the Reds looked set to be shorn of the services of Owen Hargreaves and Gary Neville, but Louis Saha was given an outside chance of playing.

One other matter on Sir Alex's pre-match agenda was a tribute to goalkeeping coach Tony Coton (affectionately known as TC), who had been forced into retirement after an operation failed to repair his ongoing knee problems. Although disappointed to see him leave, Sir Alex was quick to pay tribute to a hugely popular member of his staff.

'He's been a fantastic servant for the club, not just as a coach, but he's also a fantastic personality. He's always looked after all of our keepers. We're all really going to miss him and we're very sad to see him go after ten years.'

United's No.2 stopper Tomasz Kuszczak echoed those sentiments, adding: 'TC was one of the guys who gave me the chance to join United. He watched me and provided good reports to the club and they decided to sign me after that. So I'll always be grateful to him.

He always gave me a lot of encouragement and helped me improve. He'll be missed around the club by all the players, especially the goalkeepers. He was, and still will be, a good friend to us all.'

Saturday, 12 January 2008, Old Trafford

Attendance: 75,965

FA Barclays Premier League
United 6 **Newcastle United** 0

After falling one goal short on 13 previous occasions, Cristiano Ronaldo finally netted his first ever hat-trick for the Reds, who hit a manager-less and somewhat spiritless Newcastle side for six.

Buoyed by the news of Arsenal's 1-1 draw at home to Birmingham earlier in the day, the Reds were in no mood to take mercy on the visitors. And with top spot in the league up for grabs, the Reds started at a tempo Newcastle struggled to cope with.

United should have taken the lead with just two minutes on the clock, but Wayne Rooney blazed an effort just over the bar. Rooney was then left frustrated by alert goalkeeping from Shay Given, who prevented the Reds' No.10 from opening the scoring for a second time.

As the clock ticked towards the half-hour mark, both sides were left more than a little aggrieved by the officials. First, Ronaldo was denied a clear penalty after Steven Taylor's body-check on the winger went unpunished, and soon after Newcastle, who offered very little attacking threat all day, had a perfectly good goal chalked off when Michael Owen was wrongly flagged for offside.

United continued to pepper Given's goal, but to no avail. Four minutes after the restart, however, Ronaldo made the vital breakthrough as he fired a free-kick under the Newcastle wall and past Given.

The Reds doubled their advantage six minutes later thanks to some woeful defending from the visitors. A poor Given clearance struck Claudio Cacapa, allowing Ryan Giggs to square a pass across goal for Carlos Tevez to steer home at the far post.

United's dominance continued and Ronaldo notched up his second goal of the game on 70 minutes after some incisive build-up play. Carrick, Rooney and Tevez all swapped passes before the Argentine found Ronaldo, who finished emphatically past Given.

Rio Ferdinand volleyed home at the far post five minutes from time to make it four, before Ronaldo completed his hat-trick with a deflected shot and Tevez fired home United's sixth of the afternoon via the underside of the bar. Newcastle's misery was compounded by the late dismissal of former Red Alan Smith for dissent, but by that point the match was already well and truly over.

UNITED: Van der Sar; O'Shea, Ferdinand, Vidic, Evra (Simpson 67); Ronaldo, Carrick, Anderson (Fletcher 72), Giggs (Nani 72); Tevez, Rooney. Subs not used: Kuszczak, Park

Goals: Ronaldo (49, 70, 88), Tevez (55, 90), Ferdinand (85)

NEWCASTLE UNITED: Given; Carr, Taylor, Cacapa, Enrique; Milner (Viduka 64), Butt, Smith, N'Zogbia; Duff, Owen (Rozehnal 82). Subs not used: Harper, Emre, LuaLua

A beaming Cristiano Ronaldo, match ball in tow, strode up the players' tunnel to face the cameras afterwards and spoke of his pride at finally netting his first Reds treble.

'I've said before, that if I score two goals in every game then I'm very happy, but I've looked for a few years to score three goals for this massive club and I'm very proud. It's a special day. I'm happy, of course, to win the game and to go top of the league – I think this is most important thing. It is also important to score, to help my team and today I'm very proud.'

His manager was equally buoyant, describing Ronaldo's goalscoring feat as 'fantastic and incredible' after the winger took his tally to 22 for the campaign, just one behind his total figure for the 2006/07 season.

'We wondered at the start of last season whether he could match his tally of 23. You had to say "why not?"' said Sir Alex. 'I expected him to score more this season because he works so hard. That's why there were no bets this season, all bets are off with Ronaldo! His first hat-trick was always coming. He's been close on a number of occasions, but today he capped a really fine display with three goals. We're all delighted for him.'

Having seen Arsenal and Liverpool once again drop points, Sir Alex predicted that the final points tally for top spot could be lower than in recent years.

'It's a hard league. You saw the results with Arsenal and Liverpool drawing, teams are taking points off one another,' he reasoned. 'We expected it to be tough. Teams well below the top four are spending a lot of money on their squads. There is a drive for teams to improve themselves and stay in the Premier League. The winning points total could be lower this year.'

It seemed as though things couldn't be going much better on the pitch, and events were mirrored off it as United announced a record turnover and profits for the year ended 30 June 2007. Independent research also indicated that the club's global fan base had risen to a colossal 333 million followers. Chief executive David Gill was understandably delighted by such figures.

'This is a remarkable, record-breaking set of results,' he declared. 'The expansion of Old Trafford, allied with the ability of Alex's team to continue to attract full houses at every game, and the increase in media and sponsorship revenues have all combined with team success to produce a substantial financial improvement.

'Group turnover was £210m, positioning the club as a true leader in world sports, underpinned by a near doubling in pre-tax profits of £59.6m. I am confident that the uplift in the Premier League television deal, together with our new sponsorship sales structure will enable the club to continue to increase its revenues and profitability to provide support to the team's quest for further on-field success.'

The Reds' chief also confirmed that the team would be heading to South Africa in the summer of 2008 as part of their pre-season preparations for the upcoming campaign.

Before that, however, the Reds would embark on a mid-season break to Saudi Arabia, once a trip to Reading had been safely negotiated.

Saturday, 19 January 2008, Madejski Stadium

Attendance: 24,135

FA Barclays Premier League
Reading 0 **United** 2

It was no surprise the Reds trudged off the pitch proclaiming this the 'hardest match of the season'. Steve Coppell's side ground out a 0-0 opening-day draw at Old Trafford, and very nearly made it a double whammy on their own patch, until the late intervention of Wayne Rooney and Cristiano Ronaldo.

The ever-exuberant and skilful pair produced when it really mattered and ensured United consolidated their position at the top of the table.

In an entertaining first period, the Reds picked up where they had left off against Newcastle, creating chance after chance. Inside the opening minute, Ronaldo fired a shot just wide. But Reading were eager to give as good as they got, and looked to play United at their own game.

After ten minutes Leroy Lita found himself in behind Rio Ferdinand, but was denied by Edwin van der Sar. And only a superbly timed tackle from Nemanja Vidic – a rock at the back all afternoon – prevented Dave Kitson from slotting the rebound into an empty net.

Ronaldo went close soon after, as did Carlos Tevez, while Owen Hargreaves saw his free-kick brilliantly turned behind for a corner by Marcus Hahnemann.

At the other end, Kitson returned van der Sar's poor clearance goalwards, but Ferdinand was on hand to head the striker's 40-yard lob off the line.

Two minutes after the restart, Kitson nearly scored at the wrong end, but he had Hahnemann to thank after the American goalkeeper averted the danger. United's frustrations continued as Ronaldo blasted over just after the hour, but the Reds finally got their reward 13 minutes from time thanks to a moment of sheer brilliance from Rooney.

Tevez picked up possession 35 yards from goal and lofted a pass to Rooney, who defied the difficult flight of the ball by expertly guiding it into the far corner with the outside of his right boot.

Ronaldo made sure of the points in injury time, running the full length of the pitch to dispatch his 23rd goal of the season with a low shot across Hahnemann. Job done, but certainly not the easy way.

READING: Hahnemann; Murty, Cisse, Ingimarsson, Shorey; Doyle, Harper, Hunt, Convey (Matejovsky 79); Lita (Long 83), Kitson. Subs not used: Federici, De la Cruz, Rosenior

UNITED: Van der Sar; Brown, Ferdinand, Vidic, Evra; Ronaldo, Hargreaves (Nani 70), Carrick, Park (Giggs 46); Tevez (Fletcher 79), Rooney. Subs not used: Kuszczak, O'Shea

Goals: Rooney (77), Ronaldo (90)

There was an element of relief in the United camp after their narrow victory, but Rio Ferdinand insisted he was always confident the Reds would strike the killer blow thanks to the squad's abundance of attacking talent.

'You start wondering [whether you'll score], but in the last 15 minutes we always knew we'd get three or four more chances,' said the defender. 'With the talent we've got, you keep thinking "We'll score the next one". And thankfully Rooney and Ronaldo, who have been doing so well for us lately, managed to put the ball in the back of the net.

'Getting a clean sheet is important, because if we do that then we know we're going to have the chance to win the game. That was one of the main things for us today, keeping a clean sheet. We had a lot of opportunities in the first half, but we didn't put them away. In the second half it followed a similar pattern, but we managed to get two goals late in the game.'

With both Arsenal and Chelsea earning hard-fought away wins at Fulham and Birmingham respectively, a victory for United was vital.

'All three of us could have dropped points,' reasoned Rio, 'but we've all won. So things are still very tight and it's all to play for. We're just pleased with our result. We've not conceded a goal and we've won the game.'

Ahead of their FA Cup fourth-round tie against Tottenham Hotspur eight days later, the Reds headed for the Middle East for some much deserved R&R, which included a friendly against Al Hilal Club for former Saudi international striker Sami Al-Jaber's testimonial.

'It'll be a good opportunity for the players to have a little break away with some peace and quiet. And hopefully they'll get a bit of sun on their backs, too,' explained Sir Alex. 'It's always nice to get all the squad together and the players who joined this season, like [Carlos] Tevez, Nani and Anderson, will enjoy the camaraderie and get to know their team-mates even more. So it'll do us good. We return home on Thursday afternoon and hopefully we will come back refreshed and ready to continue the challenge for honours, starting with the FA Cup game with Tottenham on Sunday.'

The Reds may have lost out 3-2 in their friendly game in Saudi, but they returned to Manchester fully refreshed and prepared for the cup clash against Juande Ramos' side. A day of relaxation allowed players to work on their golf, cut loose on dune buggies or ride camels, and made for plenty of banter and high spirits before the trip back to Manchester.

In the build-up to the Spurs tie, the club confirmed that defender Phil Bardsley would be making a permanent move to Sunderland, while another player insisted that, despite a lack of first-team opportunities, he was more than content with life at Old Trafford.

'I am still happy playing for Manchester United and I am not thinking of going elsewhere,' confirmed midfielder Darren Fletcher after reports suggested his former international boss Alex McLeish was keen to take him to Birmingham City. 'I've never heard anything about Birmingham being interested, I just know I want to be here for a long time. My only focus is on being ready when the manager needs me and being able to perform for the club when asked.

'The last few months have been frustrating, because any player wants to play. But it has been down to the form of the midfield. Fair play to Anderson, when Paul Scholes got injured, he came in and did great. The manager has stuck by him, which is what he does when you perform well. We will see how things pan out at the end of the season in terms of games played and what you have contributed to the squad. But I am not thinking about that just now. I'm looking short term, and I'd like to win a few trophies and hopefully go a few steps further than last year.'

As it turned out, Fletcher found himself watching from the stands once more as the Reds welcomed Spurs to Old Trafford.

Sunday, 27 January 2008, Old Trafford

Attendance: 75,369

FA Cup Fourth Round
United 3 **Tottenham Hotspur** 1

For the second game running, United were made to fight tooth and nail for victory after a brave and adventurous Tottenham side threatened to cause an FA Cup upset at Old Trafford.

Robbie Keane gave the visitors a deserved lead on 24 minutes, but United fought their way back into the tie thanks to Carlos Tevez's equaliser, before yet another Cristiano Ronaldo double ensured safe progression to round five.

Spurs were far from favourites going into the game, having failed to record a win at Old Trafford since December 1989, but, buoyed by their 5-1 Carling Cup thrashing of Arsenal five days earlier, Robbie Keane gave them hope of breaking that particular hoodoo when he converted Aaron Lennon's teasing low cross.

United prodded and probed in search of an equaliser, but too often mislaid passes in vital areas of the pitch. Nevertheless, 60 seconds after Ryan Giggs had seen Radek Cerny tip his rasping half-volley over the bar on 36 minutes, Carlos Tevez drew the Reds level, clinically despatching Giggs' knockdown in the area.

Ex-Spurs midfielder Michael Carrick blasted over soon after as the Reds appeared to gain a foothold on the game, but Spurs still posed a real threat in an end-to-end match, and Jermaine Jenas forced Edwin van der Sar into a fine finger-tip save as half-time approached.

The introduction of Paul Scholes, after three months on the sidelines, on 65 minutes brought a renewed energy to United's play and their second goal duly arrived four minutes later, once again thanks to Ronaldo.

Eagle-eyed referee Peter Walton spotted Michael Dawson's deliberate handball in the area as Wayne Rooney was about to shoot, which led to both the defender's dismissal and a spot-kick for the Reds. Having missed his last penalty at West Ham, Ronaldo made no mistake this time round and produced an emphatic finish.

Jermaine Defoe was introduced with ten minutes left as Spurs went for broke. Their enterprise very nearly paid off when Wes Brown turned a cross onto his own post, while under pressure from Dimitar Berbatov.

The Stretford End breathed a sigh of relief and, seconds later, they were celebrating once more as Ronaldo's shot squeezed underneath the body of Cerny to put the result beyond doubt.

UNITED: Van der Sar; O'Shea, Brown, Ferdinand, Evra (Simpson 90); Ronaldo, Hargreaves, Carrick (Scholes 65), Giggs; Rooney, Tevez (Anderson 81).
Subs not used: Kuszczak, Nani

Goals: Tevez (38), Ronaldo (69 pen, 88)

TOTTENHAM HOTSPUR: Cerny; Pyo-Lee (Gunter 59), Huddlestone, Dawson, O'Hara; Lennon (Boateng 72), Tainio (Defore 81), Jenas, Malbranque; Berbatov, Keane.
Subs not used: Robinson, Kaboul

Goal: Keane (24)

While delighted to see his side book their place in the fifth round for a gargantuan tussle with Arsenal, Sir Alex couldn't conceal his elation at seeing Paul Scholes make a successful return to action, believing his experience – together with that of Ryan Giggs – would reinforce United's hopes of silverware.

'I am more confident now that Scholes is coming back, because he brings a bit of class at important times in games,' explained the boss. 'That's what he is probably best at – producing moments that turn games – so it's a big bonus for us having him back.

'What I've come to realise with Paul and Ryan is that I can no longer see an end to their careers. In fact, I don't expect to see an end. There must come a day when it will end but, the way it's looking now, I can't see that end coming. I think I'll be away from the club before them!

'Bearing in mind their longevity, they must be the best two players I've ever had. Giggs was here from 13 and Scholes was the same, so they have both been here almost as long as I have. Scholes is 33 now, but I regard him just as highly as I did when he was 23.

'Players like him and Giggs, who look after themselves, give themselves extra years. Look at Giggs, he's flying this season. He came on at Reading last Saturday and the stats show that he made 45 sprints in the second half. That's incredible for a player of his age.'

The Welshman was handed a well-earned rest for the Reds' Premier League clash with Portsmouth three days later, with Nani filling the left-wing position, but, not for the first time, it was another Portuguese star who invariably grabbed the headlines.

Wednesday, 30 January 2008, Old Trafford

Attendance: 75,415

FA Barclays Premier League
United 2 **Portsmouth** 0

David James' dumbfounded expression and a shrug of the shoulders said it all. He had just been beaten by another of Ronny's rockets, but this one was arguably the greatest he's ever scored and, according to some pundits, the best free-kick ever witnessed in Premier League history.

Some 25 yards out, Cristiano Ronaldo set himself, cheeks puffed, gunslinger stance, before arrowing an unstoppable strike past the helpless James, who remained rooted to the spot.

Just three minutes earlier the winger had set the Reds on their way to victory. Paul Scholes, an imperious figure throughout his hour-long run-out, won possession in midfield and found Ronaldo. The Portuguese man chested the ball to Nani before turning to run onto his countryman's lofted return. Despite finding himself at an acute angle on goal, Ronaldo calmly threaded the ball inside James' near post.

United could have easily tripled the final scoreline after half-time. First, James saved Rio Ferdinand's powerful header from Nani's corner, and the Pompey stopper was alert enough to run back and divert Wayne Rooney's lofted effort after Sol Campbell's wayward header had left James in no-man's land.

Harry Redknapp's deployment of a midfield quintet to smother United's attacking threat may have stemmed the Reds' first-half attacking tide, but it also blunted Pompey's own ability to penetrate up front. David James was easily the busier of the two stoppers and was on hand to deny Ji-sung Park and Nani in quick succession.

The game dropped to walking pace in the final ten minutes, with Rooney, Ronaldo and Scholes afforded a chance to put their feet up on the bench some time earlier.

Substitute Anderson had the Reds' final chance, but saw his shot trickle past the post after an inspired burst forward that took out two Pompey defenders. As two-goal victories go, this was one of the most emphatic you could hope to see.

UNITED: Van der Sar; Brown, Ferdinand, Vidic, Evra; Park, Carrick, Scholes (Anderson 63), Nani; Ronaldo (Tevez 74), Rooney (Hargreaves 74).
Subs not used: Kuszczak, O'Shea

Goals: Ronaldo (10, 13)

PORTSMOUTH: James; Johnson, Distin (Hreidarrsson 46), Campbell, Pamarot; Lauren (Mvuemba 46), Diarra, Davis, Kranjcar; Baros (Hughes 79), Benjani.
Subs not used: Pedro Mendes, Begovic

At the final whistle, Sir Alex admitted to being in awe at some of the penetrating football his side produced, but remained baffled that the scoreline was only 2-0.

'It was a fantastic performance from us – one of the best of the season. I just can't believe it was only 2-0,' he said. 'We opened them up so many times. There was a bit of misfortune, shots were blocked and the goalkeeper made a few saves, but we missed some chances. Nevertheless, the energy we put in was tremendous and the movement and penetration was very good. So I'm very pleased.'

Also bubbling with delight was matchwinner Cristiano Ronaldo, who labelled his humdinger of a free-kick as the best goal of his career to date.

'It's difficult to say, but maybe this one is the best,' he said. 'It's my style to shoot like that – sometimes it's a goal, sometimes not. I'm very proud to help my team.'

Manager and team-mates alike concurred with Ronaldo's assessment.

'That must be the best free-kick ever in the Premier League,' declared Sir Alex. 'It was a marvellous hit. It was within two inches of the junction of the crossbar and the post. No goalkeeper in the world could possibly save it.'

'I was in the wall, trying to block David James' view,' explained Michael Carrick. 'I just turned around and saw it go in the top corner. It was a fantastic free-kick, probably the best one he's scored.'

Reds defender Nemanja Vidic added: 'It was unbelievable. I think it's the best goal I've seen in a game I have played in.'

With the resumption of the Champions League, an FA Cup tie with Arsenal and, of course, the 50th anniversary of the Munich air crash all looming large, February promised to be both a challenging and an extremely poignant month for the Reds.

Chapter Eight

FEBRUARY – EMOTION TAKES ITS TOLL

With United on top of the Premier League going into February, there was plenty of cause for optimism around Carrington.

One player who could only gain a brief taste of the feel-good factor, though, was Angolan striker Manucho. Less than a month after joining the club, the powerful 23-year-old was farmed out on loan to Panathinaikos for the remainder of the season.

'The set-up at Panathinaikos is Portuguese, the coach there is Portuguese and Manucho speaks their language, so he will feel comfortable there,' explained Sir Alex Ferguson, who confirmed that the club would be applying for the striker's work permit again at the end of the season.

'We knew Manucho wasn't going to come to us straightaway because he didn't have the criteria,' he said. 'But we'll apply for his work permit in the summer and I'm sure we'll have a good chance. We gambled on him having a good Africa Nations Cup and he's been terrific.'

Manucho ended the competition with four goals from as many games, and he was still out in Ghana when United took on Tottenham for the second time in six days.

On the back of the demolition of Portsmouth, the Reds were basking in confidence, but Sir Alex Ferguson had seen enough in Spurs' FA Cup display at Old Trafford to know that his side would face a tough challenge at White Hart Lane.

'The performance level the other night [against Portsmouth] was unbelievable,' said the United manager. 'But Tottenham away is a very different game. We saw last Sunday [in the FA Cup clash against Spurs] that there is a wind of change at Tottenham, no question. The tie was terrifically open and for the first time in a few years at our ground there were some goals in the game.

'The games at Old Trafford have generally been one-goal affairs with more goals being reserved for White Hart Lane. So goodness knows what's going to happen on Saturday. Hopefully we can get the result we want, but I'm expecting a very tough, but open game.'

Saturday, 2 February 2008, White Hart Lane

Attendance: 36,075

FA Barclays Premier League

Tottenham Hotspur 1 **United** 1

Carlos Tevez snared United a priceless point with the final kick of the game at White Hart Lane, getting the Reds out of jail after an outstanding display from Tottenham.

The Argentine striker volleyed Nani's corner inside the near post in the last of four added minutes, to cancel out Dimitar Berbatov's early strike for Juande Ramos' side.

The Bulgarian striker ran United ragged at times and could have doubled his tally, while Robbie Keane wasted a glorious chance to bury the Reds halfway through the second period.

United only got going in the final 20 minutes, having been on the back foot for almost the entire game. Owen Hargreaves turned away a Berbatov cross on virtually his own goal-line after 15 minutes, but the England international was unable to prevent Spurs taking the lead five minutes later.

Jermaine Jenas raced into the area and toppled under Hargreaves' attention. Although he brushed the ball with his arm as he fell, knocking the ball into Aaron Lennon's path, Jenas escaped censure and, after Edwin van der Sar had parried out Lennon's cross, Berbatov was able to slot the ball into the empty net.

The Reds' goalkeeper was booked for his vehement protests, but the goal was the least Tottenham deserved for such an enterprising start. It took United 34 minutes to fashion their first opening, as Cristiano Ronaldo headed wide from 15 yards.

Berbatov then volleyed another Lennon cross over the bar from inside the area, but Lennon was fortunate not to concede a penalty for a needless shove on Patrice Evra in the final moments of the first half.

Sir Alex Ferguson introduced Michael Carrick, Nani and Anderson in the opening 15 minutes of the second period as he sought to build on an improved spell of attacking intent from his side.

A slip from Nemanja Vidic almost allowed Spurs to end the contest, however, as the imperious Berbatov slipped a pass to Keane, but the Tottenham skipper could only sidefoot tamely at van der Sar from the edge of the area.

Anderson registered United's first meaningful effort on target with 15 minutes remaining, stinging Radek Cerny's palms from 25 yards, while only a last-ditch challenge from Pascal Chimbonda prevented Tevez from converting Rooney's centre.

Rooney was then booked for diving under a challenge from Michael Dawson – a caution that ensured he would miss the visit of Manchester City eight days later – before the Reds forced a corner with the game deep into injury time.

So desperate were the circumstances, that van der Sar saw fit to join the pack of players jostling for a telling touch on the ball. He failed to make one, but Tevez didn't and he steered the ball home under pressure from Dawson, snatching a scarcely deserved point for the Reds.

TOTTENHAM HOTSPUR: Cerny; Hutton, Woodgate, Dawson, Chimbonda; Lennon (Boateng 78), Huddlestone, Jenas, Malbranque; Berbatov, Keane (O'Hara 90).
Subs not used: Robinson, Taarabt, Lee

Goal: Berbatov (21)

UNITED: Van der Sar; Brown, Vidic, Ferdinand, Evra; Ronaldo, Hargreaves (Carrick 46), Scholes (Anderson 60), Giggs (Nani 60); Rooney, Tevez. Subs not used: Kuszczak, O'Shea

Goal: Tevez (90)

'We deserved a point, but just,' a relieved Sir Alex Ferguson said afterwards. 'It could be massive. We don't stop trying. When we're 1-0 down we'll throw everything at a game, we've always done that. All things being equal, a point's a good point for us, bearing in mind we were 1-0 down at half-time.

'If we'd have got the goal earlier, we'd have won the match. I think in the last 25 minutes we've absolutely battered them. Under Juande Ramos, Tottenham are on the upswing, there's no question about that. It was a really difficult game for us. Maybe we've gained a point.'

Arsenal's victory at Manchester City had usurped the Reds from top spot, but Sir Alex still expected points to be dropped by United's rivals in the coming weeks.

'Okay, Arsenal are two points ahead of us, so there are those two points to claw back sometime, but you've also got to look at the fact that there are some difficult games coming up,' he said. 'It's a hard league, teams will drop points.'

Rio Ferdinand was adamant that, although United had been some way off top form at White Hart Lane, Tottenham's opener should have been ruled out for handball by Jermaine Jenas in the build-up.

'I think they were a bit fortunate with their goal,' said the defender. 'I was behind it and I could see Jenas lying on the floor handling it. That's why I remonstrated with the linesman – how he didn't see it, I'll never know.

'We knew we had to come here and work hard. You need spirit if you want to win things and we showed that.'

Just four days after the White Hart Lane draw, United were moved to remember the 23 passengers who had lost their lives 50 years earlier in the Munich air disaster.

After a European Cup tie in Belgrade, players Geoff Bent, Roger Byrne, Eddie Colman, Mark Jones, David Pegg, Tommy Taylor and Liam Whelan, together with club club staff Walter Crickmer, Bert Whalley and Tom Curry all perished after their plane crashed on its third attempt to leave a slush-covered runway in Munich. United and England star Duncan Edwards died days later in hospital, while manager Sir Matt Busby was read the last rites twice but recovered to eventually lead United back from the disaster.

Not that the tragedy was confined to United's staff, as journalists Alf Clarke, Don Davies, George Follows, Tom Jackson, Archie Ledbrooke, Henry Rose, Frank Swift and Eric Thompson, together with crew members and fellow passengers Captain Kenneth Rayment, Tom Cable, Bela Miklos and Willie Satinoff also passed away.

In a bid to educate his players on an event that still resonates within Old Trafford, Sir Alex Ferguson called a squad meeting to show a documentary of the disaster. The results, he revealed, were staggering.

'We showed the players a film concerning events of 6 February and you could have heard a pin drop,' said the United manager. 'I know what players are usually like when they're called into the classroom, it's a bit of a giggle, a laugh, the usual carry-on. But it was an absolutely fantastic atmosphere, so silent.

'Bobby Charlton did a piece on the club and what it was like for him and the players and friends he lost. Foreign lads like Anderson, Nani and Carlos Tevez may not know about Manchester United in the same way Ryan Giggs, Paul Scholes and Gary Neville do, but I think it was terrific to get that response: it was quite a solemn moment.

'There is no need for us to repeat it to them continually; they will gradually learn about it, because it is indelibly printed in our history.'

On such a significant anniversary, an event of Munich's seismic impact demanded a fitting tribute. Months of detailed planning came to fruition on 6 February 2008, when a special memorial service took place at Old Trafford, led by club chaplain Reverend

John Boyers. Furthermore, the South Stand tunnel was renamed the Munich tunnel, where a free, permanent exhibition of the Busby Babes was unveiled.

'We've tried to make sure we deal with things around the anniversary appropriately and compassionately,' explained chief executive David Gill. 'We spoke to those who were directly affected by the crash, such as Sir Bobby, as well as people who know the club and its history intimately like [club secretary] Ken Ramsden and [former United correspondent for the *Manchester Evening News*] David Meek.

'We formed a committee and debated various ideas, taking into account everyone's thoughts and feelings about what the disaster meant to people at the time and also what it means to the club today.'

Outside the newly renamed tunnel, United fans gathered in their thousands to pay tribute to the Busby Babes. The crowd sang in eulogy, fell silent for the minute's silence at 3:04pm, then sang again. Heard amid the fervour was 'The Flowers of Manchester', the song traditionally sung every year under the Munich clock on the Old Trafford forecourt. Over in Germany, hundreds of Reds attended a service at the crash site in Trudering, near Munich, while flowers were laid at a commemorative plaque.

The commemorations weren't just restricted to the exact anniversary of Munich. Both United and Manchester City were to wear special 1950s-style, sponsor and manufacturer-free kits during the looming Manchester derby, which would be preceded by a minute's silence, while fans of each side would be handed a special dedicatory scarf.

For Sir Alex Ferguson, the chance to voice his respect for another great Scot, Sir Matt Busby, was long awaited. He paid tribute to the man whose legacy he continually honours by practising the values Busby brought to the club over half a century ago.

'Obviously the crash had a huge impact on everyone – and Scottish people particularly, with Matt Busby being such a respected figure,' recalled Sir Alex. 'Matt had gathered a great affection for the way his United side were playing, but the esteem in which he was held in Scotland wasn't just down to that alone – it was also because of how he'd built his teams. I'd gone to see them as a teenager in 1953 play in the Coronation Cup against Rangers and Celtic – but United were the main attraction.

'What we see at United today has its foundations back in that era – in particular the way it was done with young players. And that's really the saddest part of all; that these young men lost their lives almost before they'd really started to enjoy their football: Duncan Edwards, Eddie Colman, David Pegg, just young lads at the start of their careers; such a terrible tragedy. I was lucky enough to see Duncan play for England U23s against Scotland – he scored a hat-trick. I trust Bobby Charlton's opinion without question, and when he says Duncan, at just 21, was the best he ever played with, that tells you everything.

'I recall reading that it took Matt a long time to deal with how he would face the players again; of how he'd lain there in hospital knowing he'd lost all these young lads, but had to go back to those who had survived. He felt commitment to do something about it, which gave him the drive and purpose to rebuild. But it takes special people to do what he did, to come through that and carry on. I think if he'd retired there and then, people would have understood.

'It tells you something about the man's character and the steel he had. It's about having a foundation you can rely on – and I think Matt had that: the concept of loyalty, a work ethic and the trust of and in those around him. I think you bring these things to your job; be it sport, business, or whatever – and I think it's an asset, because you've got something to fall back on during trying times. And that's what ultimately saw him through. If I'd have been there that day, I'd have had a bet on him doing it, because he had the will.

'Of course, Matt lovingly rebuilt his team to win the European Cup in 1968 – again in all the right ways – with all but a handful of that side homegrown. It was a staggering achievement: one that, in part, has helped to create the romance associated with United today; an affection across the world engendered by playing the game in the right way, with entertaining and attacking footballers.

'Manchester United was the perfect club for me, particularly as Bobby Charlton was desperately keen to have a rebirth in developing the young players. He, along with [former chairman] Martin Edwards, saw the right way in terms of rebuilding, and I needed that support because, like them, I felt this wasn't so much a football team as a football club.'

And with the football world watching, United had the perfect opportunity to pay a lasting tribute to Busby and his pioneering side by overcoming Sven-Goran Eriksson's Manchester City.

'Like any game we play at Old Trafford it's important we win, but this one is particularly significant,' admitted club captain Gary Neville. 'As a group of players we wouldn't want to come away from this game with anything other than a victory and hopefully a fantastic performance as well.

'As a United player you're always reminded of the club's history. Therefore, we have got to mark this occasion in the best way possible, because we owe the lads that died an awful lot.

'As players we're always under pressure at this club,' he added. 'We've just got to go out there and do our job. City will try and play on the fact that we might be distracted, but we know that won't be the case.

'We'll be really up for it, it's a game that any footballer would want to play in and the atmosphere will be unbelievable. We've just got to make sure we go out there and do it, simple as that.'

With form and logic invariably counting for little in derby matches, Wes Brown, who continued to do a sterling job at right-back in Neville's ongoing absence, was all too aware of the threat posed by the visiting Blues.

'Both teams always step up for the occasion,' he said. 'It doesn't matter where they are in the league. It's 50-50 and down to whoever wants it most. We've got to show we want it more. They are a good team and we know what they can do. They've got some good new players who are capable of punishing us if we give them too much time and space on the ball.'

Sadly for United, Brown's words would prove prophetic.

Sunday, 10 February 2008, Old Trafford

Attendance: 75,970

FA Barclays Premier League
United 1 **Manchester City** 2

The plaudits and the points went to the Blue half of Manchester as City gatecrashed United's remembrance ceremony and registered a first win at Old Trafford since 1974.

Perhaps weighed down by the history and significance of the occasion, United never hit their stride and were caught cold by a City side who were first to every ball.

First-half strikes from Darius Vassell and Benjani Mwaruwari rendered Michael Carrick's late strike inconsequential, ensuring a first derby double for the Blues in almost four decades.

The match was preceded by an impeccable minute's silence. Despite concerns that the visiting contingent might spoil the occasion, both home and away fans were united in perfect respect.

A deafening roar greeted the commencement of the game itself, and United started strongly in the opening exchanges. Ryan Giggs volleyed narrowly over Joe Hart's near post, before Richard Dunne made a superb challenge to deny Carlos Tevez a shot. It wouldn't be the Irishman's last telling intervention, as he turned in a flawless performance alongside Micah Richards.

City grew in stature as the game progressed and, 24 minutes in, they drew first blood. Martin Petrov slipped in Stephen Ireland and, although Edwin van der Sar was equal to the midfielder's shot and Vassell's initial follow-up, the ball fell invitingly for the former England striker to hammer the visitors ahead.

Although clearly some way short of top form, United continued to push for a route back into the game and forged plenty of chances. Tevez's long-range volley was brilliantly turned away by Hart, Ronaldo arrowed a free-kick narrowly over the bar and Nemanja Vidic stabbed wide from a half-cleared corner. For all those chances, however, it was City who struck next, just before half-time.

Having forced a succession of corners, Petrov picked the ball up on the right flank and fizzed in a superb cross. Debutant Benjani, back at Old Trafford just 11 days after lining up there for Portsmouth, got the faintest of touches on the cross and took it beyond the despairing van der Sar.

City fans rejoiced. Not only were their side ahead in clinical fashion, but they also deserved it. Having established a two-goal lead, the Blues could sit back and soak up the host's pressure during the second period.

That they duly did, with Richards and Dunne equal to everything United threw at them. When Tevez did find the net, ten minutes after the restart, he was flagged offside.

Michael Carrick, Owen Hargreaves and Ji-sung Park were all introduced in a bid to engineer a route back into the match, and the former gave United a glimmer of hope in injury-time, steering home a superb low shot from 20 yards.

Unfortunately, though, there would be no fairytale comeback. On the day, United failed to meet their own high standards and those demanded by the occasion. Once again the Reds would have to triumph against adversity and a more fitting tribute to Busby's Babes would have to wait.

UNITED: Van der Sar; Brown, Ferdinand, Vidic, O'Shea (Carrick 73); Ronaldo, Scholes, Anderson (Hargreaves 73), Nani (Park 65); Giggs, Tevez.
Subs not used: Kuszczak, Simpson

Goal: Carrick (90)

MANCHESTER CITY: Hart; Onuoha, Richards, Dunne, Ball; Ireland, Fernandes, Hamann (Sun Jihai 84), Petrov (Garrido 88); Benjani (Caceido 76), Vassell.
Subs not used: Isaksson, Geovanni.

Goals: Vassell (24), Benjani (45)

Unsurprisingly, United's players were devastated in the aftermath of the shattering defeat. All were at a loss to explain such a poor performance on such an historic occasion.

For Michael Carrick, getting off the mark with his first goal of the season counted for nothing – he was stunned by the off-colour nature of the Reds' performance.

'Scoring doesn't really mean much because we lost, we're all desperately disappointed,' he admitted. 'We never got going and didn't create the chances we normally do. That's not like us. It was good to see that the minute's silence was well observed. But in terms of the game we're not going home happy.

'Once City got the two goals it was hard to come back from it. They set out their game plan and it worked for them. One goal down, you always believe you've got a chance of coming back, but two is difficult. We needed to score right after half-time to give us momentum, but when we did score it was too little, too late.'

There are very few firsts left for Ryan Giggs but, after sampling defeat to City at Old Trafford for the first time in his glittering career, the veteran winger was gracious towards Sven-Goran Eriksson's side.

'It was probably the result that City deserved really. They played better than us,' he said. 'They scored at important times in the game and we didn't recover. City could just sit back then and try to catch us on the counter-attack. Defensively we didn't play well. Attacking-wise, we just didn't turn up.

'There were a lot of players that didn't look as sharp and [international duty] may be the reason. But there was enough motivation for us – a massive game for the club, a derby and an important three points. We probably can't afford to drop any more points now. We've got to make sure we don't produce any more performances like that.'

With Arsenal entertaining Blackburn the following evening, the likelihood was that United would have to overcome a five-point deficit in order to retain the Premier League title. Despite the disappointment of defeat to City, Carrick denied that the Blues had sounded a death knell on the Reds' title hopes.

'There are still games to play,' he said. 'I don't think Arsenal will go the rest of the season without dropping points. If they did, then fair play to them. There are still going to be ups and downs in the title race and, hopefully, there will be more ups for us and we can overtake them.'

The Gunners did indeed establish a five-point advantage over the Reds, courtesy of a 2-0 victory over Mark Hughes' side. Sir Alex Ferguson conceded that Arsenal had clocked up a valuable lead, but warned that the race was far from done and dusted.

'It was an important weekend for Arsenal in that ourselves and Chelsea [who drew 0-0 with Liverpool] dropped points,' he said. 'But points will be dropped by the top teams. There is a long way to go and it makes it interesting now. It's going to be a really good, tight finish.

'The neutrals will all be enthralled by it. We know the job we've got to do. Arsenal still have to come to Old Trafford and go to Chelsea. I think it will go to the wire.'

By quirk of fate and fixtures, the Gunners would be United's next opponents. No Premier League points were on offer, but the Reds could lay down a marker and regain some damaged dignity by overcoming the league leaders in the FA Cup fifth round.

Having suffered in the aftermath of the defeat to City, Rio Ferdinand could hardly wait to exact revenge on the Gunners.

'It was a very bad weekend,' said the defender. 'We've all been thinking about the reasons why it happened and how we want to pull ourselves together and get the result out of our minds. The best thing you can do is to come into training and just get focused on winning the next game, and that's what we're doing.'

The absence of Wayne Rooney was put forward as a chief reason for the Reds' limp surrender against City and, with the firebrand striker due back from suspension, John O'Shea expected Rooney to show Arsenal what had been missing in the derby.

'Wayne can lift players around him,' said the Irishman. 'His work-rate is infectious. He gets the crowd buzzing. We're all just waiting for the next game to come around. We're still in a great position in three competitions. We can't just forget a disappointing result, especially against our local rivals, but we do have a lot to be positive about. We've got to make sure we bounce back straight away and go on a long winning run.'

With Rooney and Patrice Evra back from suspension, plus Louis Saha unscathed after a week's training, Sir Alex Ferguson had a wealth of options for his head-to-head with Arsene Wenger. With both sides casting one eye forward to the following midweek's Champions League resumption, Sir Alex expected to shuffle his pack accordingly.

'I don't think either side will play the team that everyone expects,' he said. 'We'll make a couple of changes. My view is that with massive games like Arsenal and then Lyon next Wednesday, you have to give a lot of consideration to how you balance out your teams. Hopefully I get it right.'

With the derby defeat still fresh in everyone's minds, the United manager admitted his side had been affected by the embarrassing setback. The key, he insisted, was how they would respond to that.

'It's been a quiet training field this week,' he told the pre-match press conference. 'There has been a deep impact on the team. I think they really felt it.

'The only thing I can offer is that the emotion of the occasion perhaps got to the players. The minute's silence was very moving, it certainly got to me. It was certainly one of the worst performances you can expect from Manchester United. But we have to put that behind us. It's a test for us now, just as it was for the club back in 1958.

'They are genuine players, and they have a desire to do better. It's an uphill fight to win the league, but it's certainly not beyond them. Points will be dropped and won. We have to ensure we don't drop many. That's the challenge for us.'

And as for the spectre of another United-Arsenal battle in the FA Cup? 'Fasten your seatbelts,' smiled the United manager. 'It will be a typical United-Arsenal game, full of great commitment, with competitive football, but good play as well.'

Saturday, 16 February 2008, Old Trafford

Attendance: 75,550

FA Cup Fifth Round
United 4 **Arsenal** 0

Guts, fire, vigour, steel ... all that had been missing six days earlier returned to United's game in style, as Arsenal were comprehensively outclassed at Old Trafford.

The Reds reached the quarter-finals of the FA Cup in style, with first-half goals from Wayne Rooney, Darren Fletcher and Nani ending the contest inside 45 minutes, while a second Fletcher goal and the second-half sending-off of Emmanuel Eboue ensured a smooth passage for Sir Alex Ferguson's side.

At the heart of it were Rooney, who shone as a lone striker, Fletcher and Anderson, who both provided sterling attacking support while Michael Carrick anchored the midfield. Arsenal had no answer to a pulsating performance from the hosts, who swarmed about the league leaders from the very first whistle.

Anderson almost opened the scoring after nine minutes, but recalled Arsenal goalkeeper Jens Lehmann saved well down to his right. It took another seven minutes for the Reds to draw first blood.

Nani's left-wing corner was not properly cleared by the Gunners, giving Anderson ample opportunity to head back goalwards. He duly did, and Rooney was on hand to flick another header past Lehmann from inside the six-yard box.

Rooney's absence six days earlier had been cited as a huge factor behind the Reds' defeat to City and, at times, this performance seemed like a one-man crusade to right those wrongs, and the striker played a role in doubling United's lead on 20 minutes.

He found Anderson, who in turn fed Nani down the left wing. The Portuguese youngster had started in irresistible fashion, and he fashioned space brilliantly before clipping in a cross for Fletcher to steam in and power home a header, via a slight deflection off William Gallas.

Rooney twice dragged half-chances wide as the Reds sought to further their advantage, but it was Nani who did just that shortly before the interval. Latching onto Carrick's brilliant lofted pass, the winger took a touch with his right foot and lashed a left-footed strike past Lehmann into the bottom corner.

The game was essentially over, but United refused to let up. Moments after the start of the second half, Rooney saw a powerful shot parried away by Lehmann, before the German clutched a deflected free-kick from the insatiable striker.

Arsenal's job became one of damage limitation when Eboue was dismissed for a high tackle on Evra, although Rooney was again thwarted by Lehmann in a one-on-one. Arsenal's attacking threat was virtually nil, save a looping header from Eduardo that never looked remotely goalbound.

Fletcher showed the Croatian striker how to do it with 16 minutes remaining. Again Nani was involved, as he floated a cross to the back post where Fletcher was ready and waiting to head powerfully past Lehmann.

That goal marked the close of the scoring, an FA Cup quarter-final berth, a potentially damaging psychological blow to Arsenal's title hopes and, most importantly, a timely return to devastating form for the Reds.

UNITED: Van der Sar; Brown, Ferdinand, Vidic, Evra; Nani, Fletcher, Carrick, Park; Anderson (Scholes 71), Rooney (Saha 71).
Subs not used: Kuszczak, O'Shea, Tevez

Goals: Rooney (16), Fletcher (20, 74), Nani (38)

ARSENAL: Lehmann; Hoyte, Gallas, Toure, Traore; Eboue, Gilberto, Fabregas (Flamini 70); Hleb (Senderos 70), Bendtner, Eduardo (Adebayor 70).
Subs not used: Fabianski, Clichy

For two-goal hero Darren Fletcher, patience had paid off. The softly-spoken Scot turned in a stunning performance on only his seventh start of the season, and plaudits were the least he deserved after waiting so long for a chance to showcase his talents.

'It's a squad game and you have to be patient,' reasoned the midfielder. 'We have a talented squad with a lot of players in it and against Arsenal I was called upon to do a job. I always go out there and do my best in every game, whether that's as a substitute or from the start. Everyone wants to play all the time. It's no different whatever level you play at. When you're not playing regularly you just have to keep yourself fit, train hard and your chances will come.'

The Reds set about their visitors like wild dogs, and Fletcher admitted they were inspired by a desire to atone for the previous weekend's humiliation against Manchester City.

'It was the perfect response to last week's defeat,' he said. 'We were all hurt by that performance and we wanted to put things right today. Our attitude, tempo and work-rate were top-class and we got our just rewards. We created some great chances and it could have been even more. But the important thing is we're in the next round of the FA Cup after a terrific team performance.

'At times it was a bit feisty out there, but you expect that in a cup game against Arsenal. It's part of the game and we enjoy that. Sometimes it boiled over a little bit, but I think it was all right. We try to tackle hard and fair and we enjoy it that way.'

Arsenal certainly didn't enjoy themselves. Already trailing by three goals and a man down, the Gunners didn't react favourably when Nani indulged in a spot of ball juggling inside his own half. A pack of visiting players chased the Portuguese winger down and clattered him to the ground, but the youngster later insisted that he had never tried to wind up Arsene Wenger's side.

'The ball came to me quite high and what I did was just a natural thing,' said Nani. 'I didn't do it to wind up the Arsenal players or please the supporters, even though I know fans like to see players do things like this. Football is a show and these things sometimes happen naturally. Other players do similar things and they enjoy themselves and that's what I did.

'I had no intention of upsetting anyone, it just happened naturally. I did not do it to take the mickey. Some Arsenal people were

Tottenham's Michael Dawson nudges the ball away from Wayne Rooney with his arm, prompting a red card and a penalty, which Cristiano Ronaldo converts as the Reds reach the FA Cup fifth round.

Cristiano Ronaldo hits a stunning free-kick into the top corner of David James' goal to register a strike which is ultimately named United's Goal of the Season.

Spurs manager Juande Ramos ruefully eyes Sir Alex Ferguson, just moments after Carlos Tevez's last-gasp equaliser for the Reds at White Hart Lane.

On an emotional day at Old Trafford, fans, staff and players from both sides of Manchester unite to pay tribute to those who perished in the Munich air disaster 50 years before.

Darren Fletcher powers home his second and United's fourth goal against Arsenal, as memories of the derby day humiliation are well and truly banished.

Having dominated Cesc Fabregas at the Emirates in November, Anderson again terrorises the young Spaniard in Arsenal's FA Cup thumping at Old Trafford.

Spirits are high in Lyon, as squad members crack up during a pre-match training session at Stade Gerland.

Cristiano Ronaldo cements his status as the scourge of Newcastle, rounding Steve Harper to slot in his fifth goal against the Magpies in six weeks, as the Reds run riot in a 5–1 win at St James' Park.

Owen Hargreaves is mobbed by his team-mates after opening his United goalscoring account in the Reds' 3–0 stroll at Fulham at the beginning of March.

On a nervy Champions League night against French champions Lyon, Cristiano Ronaldo hits the only goal of the game to book a quarter-final clash with Roma.

Stand-in goalkeeper Rio Ferdinand lies beaten after Sulley Muntari's penalty secures a smash-and-grab victory for Harry Redknapp's Pompey in the quarter-final of the FA Cup.

Having passed up a hatful of chances, Ronny finally finds a way past Roy Carroll to give United an unexpectedly tight 1–0 win at rock-bottom Derby County.

For the first time in his Old Trafford career, Cristiano Ronaldo captains United – and scores two more goals to overtake George Best's record of 32 goals in a season for a winger.

(top) In a match laced with attacking talent, it's unlikely lad Wes Brown who opens the scoring between United and Liverpool, setting the Reds on the road to a 3–0 stroll.

(centre) For the second time during 2007/08, Fernando Torres endures a frustrating afternoon against United's miserly central defensive partnership of Nemanja Vidic and Rio Ferdinand.

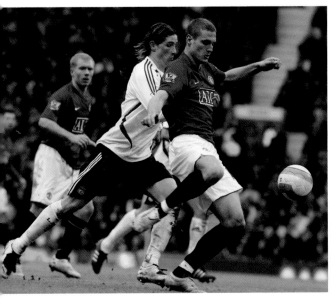

(bottom) Wayne Rooney slots home his first of two goals against Aston Villa, ending a six-game goalless run and ensuring yet another Old Trafford defeat for Martin O'Neill's side.

Goalscorers Cristiano Ronaldo and Wayne Rooney wheel away in delight after reducing Roma to ruins in the Stadio Olimpico.

Rio Ferdinand and defensive cohorts Patrice Evra and Edwin van der Sar celebrate a colossal backline performance against Roma in Italy.

furious for other reasons and this incident gave them the chance to let off steam.'

While the riled Gunners would have to switch their attentions to the visit of AC Milan in the Champions League, United could prepare for the tricky trip to French champions Lyon after a welcome return to form.

Alain Perrin's side were undoubtedly the toughest opponents the Reds could have been paired with, and Sir Alex Ferguson fully anticipated a stern test from a side who had ruled France for six successive seasons.

'We got the hardest draw in terms of the teams we could have faced, but I think we can navigate it successfully,' said the United manager. 'Lyon have won their league for the last six years and they're top again this year, so I expect it to be a tough game.

'We want to do well this year in the Champions League. Losing to Milan last year really hurt us. We just didn't have the legs. We had a bad injury spell in March, which killed us. We were well short of being full-strength, whereas Milan had rested players and were primed for that game. We were unlucky. This year, if we stay fit, we'll have a better chance.'

The travelling squad was slightly late to depart for France after traffic had delayed Argentine striker Carlos Tevez en route to the airport. After hurriedly arriving at the team HQ, Sir Alex and Patrice Evra set about addressing the world's media.

'We haven't discussed the Arsenal match with the players because we have a big match tomorrow,' said Sir Alex, focused entirely on looking forward rather than savouring the thumping of the Gunners. 'It's normal. We don't look back, we look forward. Today's the day, tomorrow's the big day.'

'Just because we put in a beautiful performance against Arsenal last weekend doesn't mean that it's going to be the same against Lyon,' concurred Evra. 'They have won their championship for the last six years on the run and they're in the last 16, so clearly they're a major team.

'We must show them serious respect. We don't want to fall into the trap of not respecting them and end up struggling to qualify. But, at such a big club like United, with Sir Alex at the helm, it's very difficult to actually lose concentration.'

Wednesday, 20 February 2008, Stade Gerland

Attendance: 39,230

UEFA Champions League Last 16, first leg
Olympique Lyonnais 1 **United** 1

Once again United left it late, and once again Carlos Tevez was the hero, stabbing home a priceless equaliser three minutes from full-time as the Reds overcame a strenuous examination from Lyon.

The Argentine striker popped up to convert a deserved leveller for Sir Alex Ferguson's side, but not before Karim Benzema had given the French champions a second-half lead with a stunning goal.

The young powerhouse striker terrorised the Reds defence all evening, doing little to quell rumours that a host of Europe's top clubs – United included – were weighing up a big-money move for him.

At the other end of football's experience scale, Ryan Giggs returned to the Reds' starting line-up to make his 100th European appearance for the club, over 14 years after making his non-domestic debut.

Giggs almost laid on the opening goal for Wayne Rooney after 25 minutes, flicking through a lovely ball to the rampaging striker. Rooney touched the ball past Sebastien Squillaci, but found goalkeeper Gregory Coupet equal to his low shot.

Benzema then blazed over the bar at the other end before Paul Scholes – the killer ball again provided by Giggs – was denied by a last-ditch block from former Newcastle defender Jean-Alain Boumsong.

Ronaldo fizzed a couple of free-kicks off target, but Benzema continued to threaten the Reds defence, pulling Rio Ferdinand and

Nemanja Vidic out of position and generally menacing the entire backline.

Although it came against the run of play, it was little surprise that Lyon's opener came through Benzema ten minutes into the second half. The youngster received the ball 30 yards from goal, advanced and shrugged off the attentions of three United defenders to hammer an unstoppable low shot in off Edwin van der Sar's post.

United's response was to dominate the remainder of the game. Tevez and Nani were introduced for Paul Scholes and Giggs respectively, and chances began to come. First Coupet spectacularly turned away Ronaldo's inswinging free-kick, before Michael Carrick saw a shot blocked on the Lyon line.

In the same passage of play, however, the Reds drew level. Lyon failed to clear Nani's right-wing cross, and Tevez was on hand to sidefoot the loose ball into the roof of the net and give United a slender, but priceless, advantage for the second leg.

OLYMPIQUE LYONNAIS: Coupet; Reveillere, Squillaci, Boumsong, Grosso; Clerc (Ben Arfa 78), Juninho (Bodmer 74), Toulalan, Govou, Kallstrom; Benzema (Fred 83).
Subs not used: Vercoutre, Cris, Delgado, Keita

Goal: Benzema (54)

UNITED: Van der Sar; Brown, Ferdinand, Vidic, Evra; Ronaldo, Anderson, Hargreaves (Carrick 78), Scholes (Tevez 65), Giggs (Nani 65); Rooney
Subs not used: Kuszczak, Saha, O'Shea, Fletcher

Goal: Tevez (87)

'Scoring near the end makes it feel a little bit like a victory,' admitted a delighted Nemanja Vidic. 'Nani and Tevez made a big difference when they came on. We are capable of finishing games strongly because we have so much strength on the bench.'

'First and foremost you have to get results,' added defensive cohort Rio Ferdinand. 'Performances come second. Ideally, you would like the performances, but that's not always possible.

'Against Lyon I thought we played well in parts. After the break we performed well for about 10 to 15 minutes until they scored. Then we upped the tempo again. They sat back and we managed to get the vital away goal. At this stage we need to concentrate on results. To score an away goal is important. We did that and that's going to be a big advantage to take back to Old Trafford.'

That advantage was established thanks to Tevez's late intervention, and fellow striker Wayne Rooney was full of praise for the Argentine's dramatic leveller.

'Carlos came on and did what he does best – getting on the ball and creating chances, and thankfully he took one of them,' said the striker. 'It's always crucial to get an away goal, and 1-1 is a lot better than losing 1-0 or even 0-0.

'I felt we controlled the game overall. They had a few chances and scored a good goal, but we showed good courage to fight back. Lyon are a good team and we know we have to concentrate 100 per cent to beat them at Old Trafford.'

With two of Sir Alex Ferguson's summer signings playing such a prominent role in the crucial goal, the United manager took time out to salute the impact all four of his new arrivals had had to date.

'We're very pleased with their progress,' Sir Alex said of the quartet. 'The evidence of their development is there to see on the pitch. With Anderson, he has exploded onto the scene, whereas Nani is taking his time. But he is gradually getting better and better. They're different players, of course, so that makes a difference. But all of them are doing really well.'

With United now back in the groove, a tantalising trip to face Newcastle at St James' Park beckoned. Just over a month after hitting the Magpies for six at Old Trafford, the Reds would travel to Tyneside to face a side still chasing a first victory under Kevin Keegan – back at the Newcastle helm for the second time.

The tabloids, naturally, played up the reunion between Sir Alex and Keegan, who famously embarked on a rant against the United manager on live TV during the climax to the 1995/96 season. Both managers sought to play down the incident in the run-up to this latest clash, with Newcastle in search of a morale-boosting first victory and United looking to close the gap on Arsenal, who dropped two points at Birmingham earlier in the day.

Saturday, 23 February 2008, St James' Park

Attendance: 52,291

FA Barclays Premier League
Newcastle United 1 **United** 5

Never a team to go big on sympathy, United ran riot at St James' Park to inflict another heavy defeat on a struggling Newcastle United side, with Cristiano Ronaldo and Wayne Rooney each bagging a brace.

Louis Saha also struck in added time against his former side, taking United's haul to six points and 11 goals against the Magpies in the space of just six weeks.

Sir Alex Ferguson, mindful of the need to keep rotating his squad in the ongoing quest for three trophies, brought in Nani, Darren Fletcher, Michael Carrick and Carlos Tevez for Anderson, Paul Scholes, Owen Hargreaves and Ryan Giggs, with the latter two not even on the bench.

Just as United had taken a while to warm up in January's six-goal romp against the Magpies, the Reds looked far from their clinical best in the opening exchanges and, but for a superb interception from Rio Ferdinand in the 24th minute, Michael Owen would almost certainly have given the hosts the lead.

The importance of the centre-back's intervention was underlined just a minute later as United went 1-0 up. Ronaldo teased Habib Beye down the left flank, cut inside and delivered a pinpoint cross to the back post. Rooney, who had escaped the attentions of makeshift defender Charles N'Zogbia, had the simple task of sidefooting a volley inside the near post.

That goal marked a step up in United's attacking incision, and Carlos Tevez should have doubled the Reds' advantage shortly before half-time, only to head wastefully wide from Nani's right-wing cross. It mattered little, though, as Ronaldo converted a second goal moments later.

Carrick strode unchallenged through the midfield, slipped a perfect pass into the Portuguese winger, and Ronaldo took a touch at high speed before instantly slipping a low shot inside the far post. Game over.

Steve Harper replaced beleaguered Magpies goalkeeper Shay Given at the interval, but that change had no effect on Newcastle's misfortunes. More haphazard defending, this time from Steven Taylor, gave Ronaldo a clear run on goal five minutes into the second half. The winger rounded Harper and slotted in comfortably, registering his fifth goal of the season against the Magpies.

Ronaldo's hopes of a second hat-trick in as many months were dashed when Saha replaced him after 67 minutes. Although United continued to make all the running and chances, the aim was now to close out the game with a clean sheet.

When Abdoulaye Faye smashed home a loose corner ten minutes from time, that simply served to anger the Reds, who once more upped the ante and began surging forward in numbers. Just a minute later, Rooney collected a half-cleared corner 20 yards from goal and curled a delightful shot inside Harper's far post.

But that wasn't the end of the humiliation for the hosts, as United continued to pile forward. Harper brilliantly turned away close-range efforts from Paul Scholes and Saha, but the French striker did poke home a fifth goal from 15 yards in injury time.

The result poured more salt onto the Magpies' wounds and served as a warning to Arsenal that United were very much back in the hunt to retain their title.

NEWCASTLE UNITED: Given (Harper 46); Beye, Taylor, Faye, N'Zogbia; Milner (Geremi 84), Butt, Barton (Carroll 61), Duff; Smith, Owen.
Subs not used: Cacapa, Ameobi

Goal: Faye (79)

UNITED: Van der Sar; Brown, Vidic (Scholes 74), Ferdinand, Evra (O'Shea 46); Ronaldo (Saha 67), Carrick, Fletcher, Nani; Rooney, Tevez.
Subs not used: Kuszczak, Anderson

Goals: Rooney (25, 80), Ronaldo (45, 56), Saha (90)

Sir Alex Ferguson was delighted to see his side's voracious approach in swatting aside Newcastle, and was buoyed by the sprightly nature of the display.

'It was a good performance,' he said. 'We could have scored more goals, but the important thing is that we look really fresh. Coming to Newcastle is never easy. The crowd here are fantastic, they urge their team on and it's a volatile place. The first job is to try and quieten them. It's not easy, but I think we did that for the most part of the game.

'We freshened up the centre of midfield, because that's an area in which we have a lot of strength. But the match was decided by the ability of our front players, they were all absolutely fantastic. Obviously with Ronaldo and Rooney scoring two goals apiece, they're going to get all the headlines, but the movement of Tevez and the penetration of Nani contributed to that.'

A half-time substitute against the Magpies, John O'Shea was excited by the strength in depth of United's swelling squad. With countless options in each position, the Reds' reinforcements augured well for the remainder of a busy campaign.

'It's a dream situation,' said the Irishman. 'About this time last season we picked up a few injuries and the squad was quite bare, but this year it's been fantastic.

'The manager can keep his side fresh, changing one or two things around without really affecting how the team is playing, which is ideal because there are games coming up thick and fast in the league and Champions League. The manager has faith in the quality of his squad and we have to repay that by winning trophies.'

Although a boyhood Newcastle fan, midfielder Michael Carrick revelled in the Reds' destruction of the Magpies, and insisted that his side's attacking incision could make the difference at the business end of the season.

'It's very satisfying when it all comes together like this because that's the standard we set ourselves,' he said after the game. 'We're finishing strongly at the moment. We have so much pace and when we attack with speed, we cause any team problems.

'With Arsenal drawing with Birmingham, we knew before kick-off it would be a big three points for us. There are bound to be ups and downs before the end of the season, but in the end it was a good day for us, closing the gap on them and doing our goal difference the power of good.'

Arsenal's surprise slip at St Andrews was their third game in a row without a victory, and the unexpected sight of Gunners skipper William Gallas staging an on-field protest at Birmingham's equaliser began to raise questions about the Londoners' collective temperament. Were they beginning to bottle it? For Darren Fletcher, the Gunners' FA Cup hammering at Old Trafford had stunned Arsene Wenger's side.

'The title race was open even before today,' insisted Fletcher. 'We know Arsenal have still got to come to Old Trafford [in the league], but that result last week maybe gave us a little psychological edge. We went out there, played fantastically and managed to win convincingly, and they've not won since.

'It's getting to the nitty-gritty now. We've been there before and know what it's about. We're hoping to push on and keep winning every game now until the end of the season – that's the target.'

Chapter Nine

MARCH – ON COURSE FOR GLORY

Having cut Arsenal's lead to three points a week earlier with a 5-1 thrashing of Newcastle at St James' Park, the Reds set about closing the gap even further as they prepared to face Fulham at Craven Cottage on 1 March.

United would be without the services of calf-strain victims Ryan Giggs and Nemanja Vidic for the clash, but there was positive news on long-term absentees Gary Neville, Ben Foster and Mikael Silvestre.

'Gary is training well and suffered no effects from his run-out for the reserves [against Liverpool, three days earlier],' confirmed Sir Alex Ferguson at the pre-match press conference. 'He will continue his fitness programme over the weekend rather than travel with the team to London.

'Mikael may join the first team in full training at the end of next week, while Ben is in contention for the reserves' game with Middlesbrough the day after the Lyon match,' added the boss. 'So hopefully, by the end of March, we should have a complete and fully fit squad.'

Saturday, 1 March 2008, Craven Cottage

Attendance: 25,314

FA Barclays Premier League
Fulham 0 **United** 3

A comfortable 3-0 victory at Craven Cottage, allied to Arsenal's home draw with Aston Villa, saw United move to within a point of the top of the Premier League table.

With the second leg of the Champions League clash against Olympique Lyonnais looming, Sir Alex opted to stick Wayne Rooney, Cristiano Ronaldo and Anderson on the bench.

Michael Carrick and Darren Fletcher, both of whom had impressed in United's midfield engine room in the recent wins over Arsenal and Newcastle, were left out of the squad altogether. In came Owen Hargreaves and Ji-sung Park in their place, while Louis Saha faced his former side as the Reds cruised to victory.

It wasn't quite one-way traffic from the first whistle, but United soaked up what little pressure Fulham could muster. A rasping Danny Murphy volley drew a smart plunging save from Edwin van der Sar, but otherwise the Dutchman had little else to do against his former employers.

Saha and Tevez went close for the Reds, before the Argentine won a free-kick on the edge of the box on the quarter-hour mark. With Ronaldo watching from the bench, Owen Hargreaves leapt to the head of the queue, took aim and fired his first goal in a red shirt with a lovely, curling effort.

Soon after, Nani unleashed a powerful effort just wide, before Antti Niemi brilliantly turned Paul Scholes' goal-bound header round the post. United's ginger wizard, a constant thorn in the Cottagers' side, made one of his famous dashes into the box as half-time approached, overlapping Nani who fed the ball into his path on the right edge of the area. Scholes clipped a first time cross into the centre, where Ji-sung Park was waiting to crash home a header via the underside of the bar.

Rooney and Ronaldo entered the fray on 69 minutes, but they were barely needed. Two minutes later, the luckless Simon Davies blasted John O'Shea's right-wing cut-back into his own net to seal a three-goal stroll for the Reds.

FULHAM: Niemi; Stalteri, Hangeland, Hughes, Konchesky; Volz (Kamara 89), Johnson (Nevland 89), Bullard, Murphy (Smertin 64), Davies; McBride.
Subs not used: Keller, Bocanegra

UNITED: Van der Sar; O'Shea, Ferdinand, Brown, Evra; Park, Scholes, Hargreaves, Nani (Anderson 75); Tevez (Ronaldo 69), Saha (Rooney 69)
Subs not used: Kuszczak, Piqué

Goals: Hargreaves (15), Park (44), Davies o.g. (72)

Across London, Chelsea waltzed to a 4-0 victory over West Ham at Upton Park to keep themselves well and truly in the title hunt, but Arsenal's slip against Villa ensured another good day for United.

'The title race has been like a see-saw of late,' observed Sir Alex after the Craven Cottage cakewalk. 'We were ahead, then Arsenal went five points clear, now the gap is back to one. And, of course, we're both looking over our shoulders at Chelsea. So it looks as if it's going to be a fantastic run-in. The important thing for us is to keep our momentum going. The players are showing a great appetite to play and the team spirit is very good.'

Goalscorer Hargreaves was delighted to set the ball rolling on another United victory, and was naturally relieved to get off the mark in a red shirt.

'Sometimes you feel good about a free-kick and other times you don't,' he admitted. 'I decided to take it because I thought I'd have a chance to score and, thankfully, it went in.

'It was a good performance from everyone in the team against Fulham after a great display at Newcastle last weekend. A different team played that game, so I think the balance of the squad is very good at the moment.

'We are all part of the jigsaw puzzle. Nobody is going to play in all the games at United. You trust the boss with all the experience he has. So far this season, as far as I'm concerned, he has picked the right team pretty much every time.

'I think all our players have something different to bring to the table. So, depending on how we want to play, we can perform in different formations. You only need to look at the win at Fulham – to have Rooney, Ronaldo and Anderson all coming on late from the bench is quite remarkable. And I think the depth and balance in our squad could make the difference in the end.'

Whether or not Hargreaves would still be part of the starting XI to face Lyon the following Tuesday was debatable, such was the wealth of options, particularly in midfield, at Sir Alex's disposal.

'Picking my team to play Lyon is a real headache. I had one in mind before the Fulham victory, but I changed my mind at half-time,' the United boss wryly admitted in the build-up to the Champions League clash. 'The one thing all the players realise is it's a massive game for the club and we simply have to win.'

The Reds would again have to try and do so without Ryan Giggs, who had failed to recover from a calf strain he sustained in the first leg. United held a slender yet crucial advantage in the tie thanks to Carlos Tevez's late leveller but, during the pre-match press conference, Sir Alex was quick to dismiss claims that his side already had one foot in the quarter-finals.

'There is still work to do,' he insisted. 'Lyon have to score and they will try and play attacking football. But we have the bonus of an away goal and we played better in the first leg than was suggested.'

The away goal had certainly given Sir Alex's men the upper hand and, in the Old Trafford faithful, the boss felt the Reds had another trump card up their sleeve.

'Our home record in European football has been the foundation of our group-stage successes,' he explained. 'The atmosphere at Old Trafford helps. There is a big stimulant for the fans to come to European nights.'

Victory over Lyon would equal Juventus' record of ten straight home wins and defender Patrice Evra, like his manager, believed the 'Old Trafford effect' would send the French champions running scared.

'The stadium is known as the Theatre of Dreams – but that's only for United, not for any other team,' he insisted. 'It's a big stadium, the pitch is wide, and we play with pace. Teams don't like that. It can be hard for them to cope.

'The atmosphere at Old Trafford is not the same as anywhere else on a European night. The fans really lift the team from the first minute until the final whistle. When I play here I feel I have more power, more energy in my legs, more character. It's strange, but teams can be scared when they come here. We shouldn't underestimate the effect it can have.'

Sir Alex has commented many times on the fact that United should have won more European Cups than the two triumphs of 1968 and '99. In the build-up to the Lyon clash, Rio Ferdinand admitted that helping the Reds clinch a third title would be the 'stuff of dreams', but insisted it isn't the only criteria when determining a team's greatness.

'I think teams who are considered great ones have normally won the European Cup, but I don't think it's the be all and end all,' he declared. 'Some that have won the Champions League are not considered great teams, but if you do well domestically and then go on to win it, then obviously that adds to you being a good side.

'Before I came to this club, I watched many a time when I expected United to win the Champions League, but they didn't, and the same thing has happened a couple of times while I've been here. Last season, for example, we had a great opportunity to go on and at least be part of the final, but for whatever reason that didn't happen again.

'We'd like to change that. This club has a great history domestically and in Europe, but obviously we'd like to be a bit more fruitful in this competition because we've got the talent, we've got the numbers and we've got the desire to do well in it. When you are a United player you have to want to win every competition you play in or you shouldn't be here. Not many people have the opportunity to win the European Cup, or even play in the final, and we dream like everybody else.'

Tuesday, 4 March 2008, Old Trafford

Attendance: 75,521

UEFA Champions League, last 16, second leg
United 1 **Olympique Lyonnais** 0 (United win 2–1 on aggregate)

United may not have put on their most dynamic display of the season, but Cristiano Ronaldo's 30th goal of the season ensured a 2-1 aggregate victory over Lyon and a place in the Champions League quarter-finals.

United understandably did not go full pelt at the French side, safe in the knowledge that they had a valuable away goal in their possession. While Lyon, knowing they had to score at least once to avoid elimination, proved stubborn opposition throughout, their deployment of a cautious approach was, in the end, to their detriment.

The big debate in the build-up to this match was who would get the nod in United's midfield engine room? As it turned out, Sir Alex Ferguson opted for Darren Fletcher, Michael Carrick and Anderson, while Paul Scholes and Owen Hargreaves took up places on the bench.

Karim Benzema, who had so impressed in the first leg, looked lively once more for the visitors, and Juninho had a few early free-kicks to test United's backline. But the Reds never wobbled.

A tight contest of few chances was decided four minutes before the break. Lyon failed to clear Anderson's effort, allowing Ronaldo to pick up possession. The winger cleverly found space in the box, before sneaking his strike inside Gregory Coupet's near post.

Lyon stuck to their original gameplan after the break and had their best sight of goal 20 minutes from time when substitute Kader Keita crashed his shot against the post. United had chances to put the game out of reach soon after: first Rooney was unable to convert Hatem Ben Arfa's baffling back pass; and then Nani opted to cross rather than shoot when he found himself within sight of Coupet's goal.

It was a tenth-consecutive Champions League victory for the

Reds at Old Trafford and although it may not have been one of the more memorable wins, it was certainly an important one.

UNITED: Van der Sar; Brown, Ferdinand, Vidic, Evra; Ronaldo (Hargreaves 90), Fletcher, Carrick, Anderson (Tevez 70), Nani; Rooney. Subs not used: Kuszczak, Saha, Park, Scholes, O'Shea.

Goal: Ronaldo (41)

OLYMPIQUE LYONNAIS: Coupet; Clerc, Squillaci, Cris, Grosso; Ben Arfa, Juninho, Toulalan, Kallstrom (Fred 79), Govou (Keita 67); Benzema. Subs not used: Vercoutre, Bodmer, Cesar Delgado, Mounier, Boumsong

Sir Alex was brimming with a combination of relief and delight after the match and he had special praise for Ronaldo following his 30th strike (in as many games) of another outstanding season.

'It's a fantastic record,' enthused the boss. 'For a wide player to do that is incredible. He drifts into the middle at times, as he did tonight. He took the goal very well. We're very pleased, it's a great contribution.'

The Reds' manager was also keen to highlight the role played by Darren Fletcher, who had been given the nod ahead of Paul Scholes following a string of impressive performances on the big stage.

'Darren emerged from the Arsenal [FA Cup] game with great credit and since then he's come into the frame,' explained Sir Alex. 'It's a great credit to the lad and the patience he's shown.

'He shows something we always admire at this club: true professionalism. That's why you give players good contracts. You hope they get the first part right and obey the laws of being a professional. He is a very good example of that.

'It was a big decision to leave out Paul [Scholes] because his performance against Fulham was vintage,' added the boss. 'If the game had been on Wednesday I would have played him. But I had to ask the question with it being three days after the Fulham game, especially given the time he has been out injured and his age.

'Darren came in to do a job, which he did very effectively. He's not easy to play against. I wouldn't like to play against him. He has such a long stretch, which means he can close players down quickly and he wins possession without conceding many fouls.'

Scholes himself was professional enough to admit that the young Scot had indeed deserved his chance.

'All the players know what a quality player Fletch is. He was unfortunate not to play during the first part of the season, but you have to give him credit for sticking at it,' explained Scholes. 'He never moaned, he just continued to train well every day and deserved his shot more than anyone. Whenever he plays he's fantastic for the team and he showed that against Arsenal. It was unbelievable to see the way he ran about, despite not having really played for a couple of months. He scored two great goals and deservedly kept his place in the team after that.'

Having secured a spot in the quarter-finals, talk immediately turned to who the Reds would face in the last eight. Another English club perhaps?

'It'd be nice if all the English teams could stay apart,' insisted Wayne Rooney afterwards. 'It would be better for English football if we all progress.'

Sir Alex remained philosophical about the scenario, insisting a meeting with a fellow Premier League side was inevitable somewhere down the line.

'Once the format changed and three or four teams from each country were allowed into the competition, it was bound to happen that they would face each other at some point, so I'm always geared to playing against an English team.'

United were one of four Premier League sides – along with Arsenal, Chelsea and Liverpool – in the hat for the draw, along with one side each from Spain, Germany, Italy and Turkey. And, according to Sir Alex, such a ratio demonstrated the quality of English football.

'I think the Premier League is the strongest in Europe,' he insisted two days before the draw. 'For a spell it was the Spanish league, but I think the English game has now reached that level. You expect three of the four English teams to be in the semi-finals this year, unless they are drawn against each other [in the quarter-finals]. We now have a 40 per cent chance of being drawn against an English team, which is a measure of the quality of this division.'

The opening week of March was one in which the Reds were fighting on all three fronts. Having got the job done in the league (at Fulham) and Europe (against Lyon), the players ended the week with their attention firmly focused on ensuring a safe passage to the FA Cup semi-finals. Harry Redknapp's Portsmouth stood between the Reds and a place at Wembley – the new location for both last-four clashes. Redknapp had already masterminded two famous Cup victories over United during his days at Bournemouth and West Ham and, despite having seen his side soundly beaten in the league clash back in January, Pompey arrived at Old Trafford with nothing to lose.

In the build-up to the tie, talk of a potential date for Sir Alex's retirement resurfaced in the media, with the *Daily Mirror* attributing quotes to the United manager that claimed he would finish in three years' time. But during the pre-match press conference, Sir Alex, who went back on his decision to retire in 2002, stressed his desire not to put a timescale on the remainder of his United tenure.

'I'm not putting a time limit on it, it's impossible,' he told reporters. 'You never know what happens in life. It's something I have said for quite a while. If you are fit and healthy and enjoying your job, then who knows? Two, three, maybe four years, it's difficult to pigeon-hole myself on that one.'

The manager, who is on a one-year rolling contract, also reiterated his intentions to bring more success to the club during his final years and provided a glimpse of the legacy he hopes to leave behind.

'When I make the decision I will be satisfied that the club is in good hands,' he insisted. 'We have made good decisions in the last few years in terms of the future of the club and the team. The youth policy is reasonably strong, and I think the youth at the club will be here for a few years. There is a good balance and strong prospects for Manchester United.'

When he was asked what he had left to achieve, he added: 'The thing to strive for is maintaining the standards and the level of success. It's not a matter of adding anything more to what I have done, it's maintaining the level we have been at. The past won't really matter at that point, it's the future. Today is the day. Tomorrow's the big day.'

Unfortunately, it didn't turn out to be United's day 24 hours later when Pompey arrived at Old Trafford.

Saturday, 8 March 2008, Old Trafford

Attendance: 75,463

FA Cup, Sixth Round
United 0 **Portsmouth** 1

Sometimes things just aren't meant to be. Despite dominating possession, creating chance after chance and being denied a clear penalty, United crashed out of the FA Cup quarter-finals and saw their Treble dream left in tatters.

Pompey snatched victory with a 78th-minute penalty, despatched by Sulley Muntari past makeshift goalkeeper Rio Ferdinand, who found himself between the sticks after Tomasz Kuszczak was red-carded for the concession of the spot-kick. The fact that it was the visitors' only meaningful attempt of the afternoon, married to an outstanding display from Pompey's defensive unit, merely compounded United's frustration.

Sir Alex Ferguson and his assistant Carlos Queiroz were further irked by the denial of an arguably clearer-cut penalty for United, after Cristiano Ronaldo was cynically barged to the ground by Sylvain Distin inside the area. Television replays backed up the disbelief that wafted round the ground but, in truth, the hosts had countless opportunities after that incident to put the tie to bed.

United enjoyed the lion's share of possession during the first period, but their final pass wasn't quite up to scratch. Kuszczak replaced groin injury victim Edwin van der Sar at the break, but all the action was down at the other end.

First, Nani stung the palms of goalkeeper David James, before the winger's corner led to an almighty scramble in the box, but neither Vidic, Tevez nor Scholes could force the ball over the line. Substitute Michael Carrick was next to be denied, this time by a last-ditch tackle from Distin after rounding James. The Pompey stopper then brilliantly touched Patrice Evra's stinging shot onto the post – all the signs said it wasn't United's day.

That proved the case 12 minutes from time when the visitors struck a killer blow. A Pompey breakaway saw Niko Kranjcar beat both Anderson and Rooney to a long punt upfield from James, before sending substitute Milan Baros clear on goal. The Czech tumbled under a challenge from Kuszczak, who was promptly – perhaps harshly – dismissed, and moments later Harry Redknapp's men were in front after Muntari slotted home past stand-in stopper Ferdinand.

There was no denying Pompey's unwavering work-rate and resolute defending during the 90 minutes, but how United lost the match remains a mystery.

UNITED: Van der Sar (Kuszczak 46); Brown, Ferdinand, Vidic, Evra; Ronaldo, Hargreaves (Carrick 69), Scholes, Nani; Tevez (Anderson 68), Rooney.
Subs not used: O'Shea, Park

PORTSMOUTH: James; Johnson, Campbell, Distin, Hreidarsson; Utaka (Lauren 74), Diarra, Diop, Kranjcar (Hughes 81), Muntari; Kanu (Baros 54).
Subs not used: Ashdown, Mvuemba

Goal: Muntari (78, pen)

The aftermath of United's Cup exit was dominated by the decisions that had gone against the Reds. Ronaldo was astonished at the lack of protection he had been afforded throughout the 90 minutes, in which he had been peppered by persistent fouls. He even admitted afterwards that he was considering altering his style of play for fear of picking up a serious injury.

'It's very frustrating, the referee was unbelievable,' said the bemused Portuguese star. 'He didn't want to give the penalty, he didn't want to give yellow cards – I'm very disappointed. Refs don't protect skilful players. I think about [Arsenal striker] Eduardo and I'm scared sometimes to do skills because some players do unbeliev-able fouls and the ref protects the defender, not the skilled player! It's very disappointing and I'm thinking a lot about changing my game. When referees don't give penalties, yellow cards or reds, it's difficult to play.'

Team-mate Wayne Rooney admitted he too was becoming increasingly concerned by the lack of consistency on a weekly basis from match officials.

'You get frustrated by certain decisions, particularly when a foul is committed and the referee doesn't give it,' he said. 'I think some players in some teams get away with more fouls than others. There has been a lot of talk about it recently and I think that's down to the lack of consistency from referees. Some players make a few fouls and get away with it, whereas others make one tackle and are booked straight away. It's difficult to take sometimes.'

Despite the incredulity surrounding the result, Sir Alex Ferguson urged his players to regroup and ready themselves for the challenges that lay ahead in the league and Europe.

'This result has to have an impact,' he insisted. 'The impact is that we're going to do something about it. There is a determination and energy from our team that will show itself now.'

The first opportunity they had to do so would come seven days later at Pride Park. Before that, however, there was the small matter of the Champions League quarter-final draw.

The rehearsal (a UEFA formality) had kept the four English teams apart, but come the real thing, it didn't. Fortunately, as Sir Alex and the majority of his players had hoped, United avoided their Premier League rivals, but they did find themselves pitted against familiar opposition in AS Roma. United had already met the *giallorossi* in the group stages and, for the second-consecutive season, the two would now go head-to-head at the last-eight stage.

'It's incredible,' said Sir Alex after the draw. 'I had a strong feeling that we would draw an English side. It's amazing to think that we will have played Roma six times in a year. That makes it an intriguing tie because we know a lot about them, but they also know a lot about us.'

In the other half of the draw, Liverpool found themselves up against Arsenal, with the winners facing either Chelsea or Turkish outfit Fenerbahce in the semis. Should United progress to the last four, they would meet either Schalke of Germany or Catalan giants Barcelona.

Back on the domestic front, the Reds travelled to bottom-placed Derby County for a rare Saturday 3pm kick-off. Sir Alex confirmed that goalkeeper Ben Foster would make his competitive debut for United – almost three years after signing for the club – in the absence of Edwin van der Sar and Tomasz Kuszczak.

Just a week earlier, the Reds boss had discussed the possibility of sending Foster, now fully recovered from knee-ligament damage, out on loan for the remainder of the campaign. However, the groin strain that had forced van der Sar off at half-time against Portsmouth and Kuszczak's subsequent sending-off had left Sir Alex with little option but to blood the England stopper at Pride Park.

'Having been out for the best part of a year and with only one reserves game behind him, it's a big challenge for Ben,' admitted the manager at the pre-match press conference. 'But I have no fears. He will be okay. What encourages me is that he has got fantastic presence, speed and agility.

'His rehabilitation went completely as planned and he's been in full training for about a month, so there are no question marks over his fitness. What we can't tell is how match sharp he is. He's only had one game. But his assets give me confidence he'll do well.'

Saturday, 15 March 2008, Pride Park

Attendance: 33,072

FA Barclays Premier League
Derby County 0 **United** 1

It's virtually become a club motto around Old Trafford: 'United must always make things difficult for themselves.' They certainly made heavy weather of their first visit to Pride Park in six years, only for 'you know who' to pop up in the nick of time and secure all three points.

Paul Jewell's bottom-placed Rams – and former Reds goalkeeper Roy Carroll in particular – may have frustrated United all afternoon, but it was the visitors who had the last laugh as Cristiano Ronaldo stabbed home from close range 14 minutes from time.

The Reds had started brightly enough, with Ryan Giggs going close with a header just seconds after the kick-off. Former United stopper Roy Carroll dived to his left to avert the danger, setting the tone for an inspired afternoon as he waged an enthralling one-on-one battle with Ronaldo – making save after save from the Portuguese winger.

Having been made to suffer for profligacy a week earlier against Portsmouth, it was almost a quick-fire dose of déjà vu for the Reds when Derby striker Kenny Miller twice found himself in sight of goal. Thankfully for United, debutant stopper Ben Foster was on hand to repel the striker's stinging volley and low shot in two madcap minutes just before the interval.

As time ebbed away after the break, chances were few and far between. When they came, Carroll continued to look unbeatable. But his and the Rams' resistance was finally broken on 76 minutes. Rooney, released down the left wing by John O'Shea, clipped in a cross to the onrushing Ronaldo, who expertly dealt with an awkward bounce and guided the ball home – much to his, and United's, utter relief.

The Reds held out for three crucial points and went top of the table in the process. They may not have hit Derby with the avalanche of goals everyone expected but, at such a vital stage of the season, the bottom line is victory, regardless of how it is achieved.

DERBY COUNTY: Carroll; Edworthy (Todd 55), Leacock, Moore, McEveley; Sterjovski (Robert 83), Savage, Jones, Lewis; Miller, Earnshaw (Villa 77). Subs not used: Price, Ghaly

UNITED: Foster; O'Shea, Brown, Vidic, Evra; Park (Saha 62), Scholes (Carrick 62), Anderson (Fletcher 74), Giggs; Ronaldo, Rooney. Subs not used: Heaton, Hargreaves

Goal: Ronaldo (76)

The result temporarily moved United a point clear of Arsenal, who dropped two more points later that afternoon against Middlesbrough at the Emirates. Kolo Toure's late strike equalised Jeremie Aliadiere's early goal for the visitors, but it wasn't enough to take the Gunners back above United, who retained top spot on goal difference. Chelsea, meanwhile, continued their pursuit of the top two and moved to within three points of the pair with a 1-0 victory at Sunderland, thanks to John Terry's first goal in 19 months.

Though relieved to see the Reds grind out an unexpectedly tight victory over Paul Jewell's men, Sir Alex admitted afterwards that his side's charity in front of goal was becoming a concern.

'Last Saturday, of course, missing chances knocked us out of the cup, and today we made it hard for ourselves because we missed so many opportunities. We were really charitable. Maybe it's a little sticky spell, but we want to get over that. We've got big games coming up, Bolton at home on Wednesday and then Liverpool on Sunday, and we want to start taking chances. We are making them, and I suppose that's the biggest bonus of all. If we keep making them, you know at some point someone's going to suffer. We just have to keep going with that.'

Sir Alex also took time out to salute the performance of debutant

Ben Foster, who produced two vital saves to ensure a clean sheet on his first competitive appearance for the Reds.

'It was an excellent performance from Ben and he showed what England are going to enjoy for the next ten years,' said the United manager. 'I think he'll be England's goalkeeper without question. He's not had a lot of football, but he produced two great saves and his distribution and speed off the line were fantastic. It was really a first-class performance.'

Whether or not Foster would keep his place between the sticks for United's next game – at home to Bolton – four days later was unclear. Edwin van der Sar seemed set to be rested ahead of the Easter Sunday clash with Liverpool, while Tomasz Kuszczak was available again after serving a one-match suspension.

Wednesday, 19 March 2008, Old Trafford

Attendance: 75,476

FA Barclays Premier League
United 2 **Bolton Wanderers** 0

It's little wonder Sir Alex Ferguson wants Cristiano Ronaldo protected. He is a rare species indeed. Tricky winger, stand-in striker, leading goalscorer and now inspirational captain – there appears to be no end to his talents. And it was the Portuguese marvel who single-handedly blew Bolton Wanderers away and secured a 2-0 victory in United's game in hand over Arsenal.

Ronaldo skippered a side featuring seven changes from the one that won at Pride Park, with only John O'Shea, Nemanja Vidic, Anderson and Ronaldo retaining their spots in the starting XI. Despite speculation that Ben Foster would continue in goal after his impressive debut, the manager opted for Tomasz Kuszczak between the sticks and the Pole was magnificent throughout. The same could be said of Ronaldo, who opened the scoring on nine minutes, sweeping home on the half volley after Bolton failed to clear Nani's corner.

The visitors, fighting for their Premier League lives, went close to nicking an equaliser on 18 minutes through Kevin Davies, but Kuszczak reacted brilliantly to avert the danger.

A minute later Ronaldo doubled the Reds' advantage with another of his dead-ball specialities. Having dusted himself down after being felled 30 yards out by Abdoulaye Meite, he duly lashed home an unstoppable dipping, swerving 'Ronny rocket'. It was his 33rd goal of an incredible season – and the strike that broke George Best's record haul of 32 goals in a season for a winger.

Nani forced a smart save from Bolton stopper Ali Al Habsi just after the restart, while Kuszczak did well to clutch a twice-taken El-Hadji Diouf free-kick. He was beaten by the first kick, only for referee Alan Wiley to rule that it had been taken too quickly. That was the only effort to find a way past the Pole all evening, as he acrobatically tipped Nicky Hunt's well-struck volley over the bar and turned Gavin McCann's low effort around the post.

At the other end, Louis Saha, Nani and Tevez all had chances to extend United's lead but, in keeping with recent form, the Reds failed to show their clinical streak in front of goal. Thankfully, it mattered little – the Madeiran magician had already conjured up another vital three points for United.

UNITED: Kuszczak; Hargreaves, Piqué, Vidic (Brown 58), O'Shea; Ronaldo, Fletcher, Anderson (Scholes 70), Nani; Saha (Rooney 70), Tevez.
Subs not used: Foster, Evra

Goals: Ronaldo (9, 19)

BOLTON WANDERERS: Al Habsi; Steinsson, Meite (Hunt 46), A O'Brien, Gardner; Diouf, McCann, Guthrie (Giannakopoulos 82), J O'Brien, Taylor; Davies.
Subs not used: Walker, Campo, Rasiak

Ronaldo, the toast of Old Trafford once again having broken George Best's 40-year-old goalscoring record, was beaming with pride after captaining the Reds for the first time in his career.

'It's always good to be captain at this massive club,' he insisted.

'For me it's an honour and a pleasure. But my responsibilities are the same. I do not change my game or personality just because I'm captain. I very much enjoyed the role.'

It turned out to be a perfect evening all round for United after Chelsea were pegged back by Tottenham in a thrilling game at White Hart Lane. Chelsea, who like the Reds were playing their game in hand on Arsenal, seemed set to gain revenge for their Carling Cup final defeat to Spurs after going 3-1 up just after half-time. Spurs clawed their way back into the game through Dimitar Berbatov and Tom Huddlestone, before Joe Cole restored the visitors' advantage on 80 minutes with his second goal of the game. But a superb curling effort from Robbie Keane two minutes from time incredibly made it 4-4 on the night and ensured Chelsea dropped two valuable points, leaving them five behind United and two behind Arsenal.

'I think Chelsea hold the key to the title race,' admitted Sir Alex afterwards. 'They have ourselves and Arsenal at home, and their home record is very good, so that, to my mind, is going to make it a really tight finish.

'The important thing was that we had the opportunity and incentive to go three points clear of Arsenal, our nearest pursuer, and we've done that. It's a lead, that's important. It's not a significant lead, but it's a lead nonetheless. The team that is the most consistent will win the league and I'm confident in my squad. We've got proven winners here and the enthusiasm to succeed. If we can keep our consistency we have a chance.'

United had a tremendous opportunity to put some daylight between themselves and their two closest rivals on Easter Sunday, or 'Grand Slam Sunday' as the media were dubbing it, with the 'big four' set to go head-to-head. Liverpool were the visitors to Old Trafford, while Chelsea hosted Arsenal at Stamford Bridge.

Before they welcomed Rafa Benitez's side to Old Trafford, the Reds squad was slightly weakened by the loan departure of Danny Simpson to Ipswich, but two timely reinforcements were racing to be ready for the clash. Having missed United's last two matches with a groin strain, Edwin van der Sar – yet to concede a league goal against Liverpool as a United player – was rated as 'hopeful' to make the game by Sir Alex, while Rio Ferdinand was still a doubt for the eagerly anticipated lunchtime clash.

'I love the Liverpool games, I must admit,' revealed Sir Alex at the pre-match press conference. 'There's nothing better for me and my players, particularly the older ones, who have experienced it many times. It brings out a certain anticipation in our players and they'll be anticipating a difficult game. We have to do our preparation tactically, but if we play to our form we'll have a good chance.'

Sunday, 23 March 2008, Old Trafford

Attendance: 76,000

FA Barclays Premier League
United 3 **Liverpool** 0

Some observers would have you believe that Javier Mascherano's decision to press the self-destruct button cost Liverpool three points at Old Trafford. Don't be fooled.

The midfielder's sending-off certainly aided United's cause, but the Reds' thorough domination of the 90 minutes more than warranted another crucial victory.

United forged chances with promising regularity prior to the Argentine's ill-advised outburst, while the visitors' best effort by far was a Steven Gerrard attempt that deflected over off Nemanja Vidic.

Only six minutes had elapsed when Anderson played Wayne Rooney through, only for Pepe Reina to block his close-range effort. The Liverpool stopper found himself beaten on 24 minutes, but the post spared his blushes when Ronaldo guided Ryan Giggs' free-kick against the woodwork.

While Reina's shot-stopping was exemplary, he never looked comfortable on crosses and almost turned Giggs' centre into his own net after half an hour. After that let-off, the Spaniard was made to pay for his uncertainty in the air when Wes Brown – in a rare foray into enemy territory – leapt highest to head home Rooney's left-wing cross.

Two minutes before the break, Liverpool's task of restoring parity was made all the more tricky following the dismissal, for two yellow cards, of Mascherano. Having earlier been cautioned for scything down Paul Scholes, the Argentine inexplicably continued to question referee Steve Bennett's decision to book team-mate Fernando Torres.

Having been repeatedly subjected to the midfielder's dissent all afternoon, Bennett wasted little time in producing another yellow and a subsequent red card. A seething Mascherano had to be restrained by both his team-mates and his manager before he eventually headed down the tunnel.

United remained in control after the break, but their failure to finish off the visitors made for a somewhat nervy final period. Reina, to his credit, kept Liverpool in it, denying Rooney, substitute Carlos Tevez and Ronaldo with brilliant reaction stops. The save from the Portuguese winger was the best of the lot, as the Spaniard somehow managed to parry his point-blank effort onto the bar and out for a corner. Ronaldo gained revenge from the resulting set-piece, however, heading home substitute Nani's in-swinging centre as Old Trafford erupted with relief.

Nani himself then added the gloss to a fine display from the Reds, cutting inside from Rooney's clever pass and bypassing the visitors' usually sturdy defence before lashing a venomous drive past Reina.

Victory, bragging rights and three points towards another title charge. Days are rarely as satisfying.

UNITED: Van der Sar; Brown, Ferdinand, Vidic, Evra; Ronaldo, Scholes, Carrick, Anderson (Tevez 73), Giggs; (Nani 73); Rooney.
Subs not used: Kuszczak, Hargreaves, O'Shea

Goals: Brown (34), Ronaldo (79), Nani (81)

LIVERPOOL: Reina; Arbeloa, Carragher, Skrtel, Aurelio; Mascherano, Alonso, Kuyt, Gerrard; Babel (Benayoun 66), Torres (Riise 82).
Subs not used: Itandje, Hyypia, Crouch

Though visibly brimming with delight after the final whistle, midfielder Michael Carrick insisted the Reds would not rest on their laurels, even though the victory sealed United's status as strong title favourites.

'We're playing well at the moment, but we've still got a tough run-in and it's not going to be easy,' he maintained. 'We're not getting carried away by any means, but we're happy with our position. Three or four weeks ago we were a few points behind Arsenal and aware that we needed to get points on the board fairly quickly. We've managed to do that, and obviously Arsenal have slipped up a little bit and opened the door for us.'

Many pointed to Mascherano's first-half sending-off as the pivotal moment in the game, and although Sir Alex agreed that it put the Reds in the ascendancy, he was quick to point out United's earlier dominance.

'The sending-off gave us complete control of the match, but I think we had reasonable control up until that point anyway,' he insisted. 'The 3-0 scoreline wasn't flattering; both Wayne Rooney and Cristiano Ronaldo could have had hat-tricks. We certainly had the better chances and the better penetration. I was disappointed we didn't finish them off earlier. We've done our job, but we're not getting carried away. Now I hope both Chelsea and Arsenal lose!'

Sir Alex had part of his wish granted as Chelsea ran out 2-1 winners and edged to within five points of United, leapfrogging Arsenal into second place in the process. The Gunners, who hadn't won in the league since 11 February, took the lead on 59 minutes through Bacary Sagna, only for two late Didier Drogba strikes to turn the game on its head and hand the Blues victory.

With just seven games to go and the destiny of the title in their hands, Patrice Evra admitted United would be treating every remaining fixture as a one-off cup final.

'Psychologically the win over Liverpool was very good for us,' said the Frenchman. 'It was a massive game, an important one for the fans and for the club. But we have seven games left to play and we need to win them too. They are like seven finals. We have the destiny of the title in our hands and I hope we continue to win.'

The race for the title was put on the backburner for a few days after the Liverpool win as the vast majority of the squad headed off on international duty for a host of friendly games. However, both Cristiano Ronaldo and Nani remained in Manchester for treatment on slight leg injuries sustained during the victory over Rafa Benitez's side.

There were mixed results for United's international contingent. Rio Ferdinand lived the dream of leading England out as captain against France, but there was no fairytale ending as the Three Lions slumped to a 1-0 defeat in Paris. A first-half Frank Ribery penalty was enough to hand the home side victory in a match that also saw former Red David Beckham win his 100th England cap. Ferdinand and Owen Hargreaves completed 90 minutes, while Wayne Rooney and Wes Brown also turned out for England. Patrice Evra was an unused substitute for the French side.

In London, Reds midfielder Anderson came on for the last half-hour as Brazil beat Sweden 1-0 at the Emirates Stadium. Darren Fletcher helped Scotland come from behind to earn a 1-1 draw with Croatia at Hampden Park, but worryingly the midfielder limped off seconds before the final whistle. Elsewhere, Tomasz Kuszczak was an unused substitute as the USA ran out 3-0 winners in Poland, while Nemanja Vidic played 74 minutes in Serbia's 2-0 defeat at the hands of Ukraine. Ji-sung Park played in South Korea's World Cup Qualifier against Korea DPR, which ended 0-0.

Away from matters on the pitch, United confirmed they had appointed former captain Bryan Robson as an ambassador for the club. Robson, nicknamed Captain Marvel during his illustrious 13-year Reds career, would help promote the club's name, charity and community work around the world, working alongside United director Sir Bobby Charlton.

'I'm delighted to have the chance to work alongside Sir Bobby and to be such a central part of United's future,' said the 51-year-old former Middlesbrough, West Brom and Sheffield United manager. 'Since signing for the club in 1981, it's always been special to me. I enjoyed the happiest and most memorable times of my career at Old

Trafford and it will be great to play a role in making the club even more successful.'

Maintaining supremacy in the title race was uppermost in Sir Alex's mind as he looked ahead to the Reds' third home game in ten days against Aston Villa. But the United boss would be without the services of Darren Fletcher for the game and the foreseeable future as news emerged that the knee injury he had sustained against Croatia would lead to a lengthy absence. Once again it raised question marks over the arrangement of international friendlies at such a crucial stage of the season.

'It's a bad blow that emphasises the futility of these games,' insisted an unimpressed Sir Alex. 'Darren was recovering from a bad chest cold, which is why we rested him against Liverpool. He should have only played for 45 minutes, 60 at most, but he played the full game for Scotland. Now we've lost him for six weeks.'

Villa's visit was a tea-time clash for television coverage. Having earlier seen Arsenal come from two goals down at Bolton to win 3-2 with ten men, the Reds knew they had to win to maintain their advantage at the top of the table.

Saturday, 29 March 2008, Old Trafford

Attendance: 75,932

FA Barclays Premier League
United 4 **Aston Villa** 0

'I think the football we play is similar to the way Brazil play,' declared a delighted Wayne Rooney after helping his side to a stunning 4-0 victory over Aston Villa. On this evidence few would disagree.

It was a mesmerising performance from United, with a wide range of flicks and tricks served up alongside four sumptuous goals – and Rooney was at the heart of Villa's torment alongside partner-in-crime Cristiano Ronaldo.

So impressive were the Reds' deadly duo that even Villa boss

Martin O'Neill took time out to eulogise over their display, suggesting to his young players that they watch a DVD of the thrashing that was kicked-off in sublime style by Ronaldo after 17 minutes.

Gareth Barry and Wilfred Bouma's failure to clear a United corner allowed the ball to fall to the Portuguese winger who, with his back to goal, guided a deft backheel through Martin Laursen's legs and past goalkeeper Scott Carson.

Ronaldo turned provider on 33 minutes as Carlos Tevez, an ever-willing runner all afternoon, capped off an excellent flowing move involving Rooney and Paul Scholes, diving to meet Ronaldo's pinpoint cross at the far post.

Despite the torrential rain, United's dominance and penetration showed no signs of abating after the break, with Rooney firing a shot agonisingly past the post after a neat one-two with Tevez had put him through on goal. Shaun Maloney followed suit at the other end after a rare defensive mix-up by the Reds. And as the following minutes proved, the visitors' big chance to get back into the game had gone begging.

United continued to press, and the Old Trafford faithful were willing Rooney more than anyone to find the net and end his scoring drought. Eight minutes after the restart the moment arrived. A flicked pass from Ronaldo laid the ball into Rooney's path and he duly rounded Carson and slotted the ball home. Cue a deafening roar from the Stretford End that threatened to lift the roof off Old Trafford.

The woodwork denied Rooney a second on 65 minutes and it also did United a favour at the other end as Tomasz Kuszczak brilliantly turned Maloney's curling effort onto the crossbar and away for a corner.

Rooney made sure the Reds registered at least four goals for the 11th time in 2007/08 with 20 minutes remaining, calmly slotting inside Carson's near post after a delightful nutmeg from Ronaldo.

It was United's sixth league win on the trot and, as Rooney remarked, it really was 'just like watching Brazil'.

In blizzard conditions in early April, Wayne Rooney celebrates his equaliser – teed up by Ji-sung Park – against Middlesbrough on a tough afternoon for the Reds.

Carlos Tevez's diving header sets a new Champions League record for consecutive home victories – 11 – and secures United's semi-final date with Barcelona.

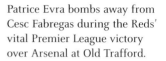

Patrice Evra bombs away from Cesc Fabregas during the Reds' vital Premier League victory over Arsenal at Old Trafford.

Owen Hargreaves celebrates his second successful set-piece of the season, having secured a 2-1 victory over long-time league leaders Arsenal.

Carlos Tevez, the man with the knack for scoring important goals, finally finds a way past Brad Friedel to snare a priceless point for United at Blackburn.

Michael Carrick and company cannot believe the decision to award Chelsea a late penalty at Stamford Bridge. Michael Ballack converts, hauling the Blues level with United on points with just two league games remaining.

United bounce back in style, as Paul Scholes' blistering early strike nudges United past Barcelona and into the Champions League final, on one of the greatest nights Old Trafford has seen.

Despite the trickery of Lionel Messi, Barcelona couldn't find a way past a United defence marshalled brilliantly by Wes Brown and Rio Ferdinand.

The first of three must-win games in May: Michael Carrick's deflected drive puts the seal on an imperious 4–1 win over West Ham at Old Trafford.

Cristiano Ronaldo coolly puts United ahead from the penalty spot at Wigan, putting the Reds on the brink of retaining their title.

Buried under a mass of bodies, Ryan Giggs celebrates scoring on his record-equalling appearance, and clinching the title in doing so.

Sir Alex Ferguson jumps for joy at the JJB Stadium as his side post a 2–0 win at Wigan, sealing a tenth league title for the United manager.

Champions again! The Reds can finally celebrate retaining their title after a nervy end to a breathless Premier League season.

The party starts at the JJB Stadium, with the champagne flowing from virtually the final whistle.

Cristiano Ronaldo rises high above Michael Essien to power United into the lead in the Champions League final. Frank Lampard equalises for Chelsea, however, and the game is eventually decided by penalties.

Edwin van der Sar parries away Nicolas Anelka's spot kick, giving United victory over Chelsea and securing a dream double for the Reds.

After a gruelling campaign and over 120 minutes of nail-biting drama in Moscow, the Reds are crowned champions of Europe for the third time in the club's history.

The players can finally unwind at the after-party, and cut loose they do. Sore heads and bloodshot eyes all round but, with the double secured, nobody cares a jot.

UNITED: Kuszczak; Brown, Ferdinand (Hargreaves 62), Vidic, Evra (O'Shea 62); Ronaldo, Carrick (Anderson 61), Scholes, Giggs; Tevez, Rooney.
Subs not used: Foster, Park

Goals: Ronaldo (17), Tevez (33), Rooney (53, 70)

ASTON VILLA: Carson; Reo-Coker, Mellberg, Laursen, Bouma (Osbourne 80); Petrov, Barry, Young, Harewood (Salifou 69); Agbonlahor, Carew (Maloney 41).
Subs not used: Taylor, Knight

A buoyant Wayne Rooney faced the cameras afterwards having ended a six-game run without a goal, and a five-month wait to find the net in the league at Old Trafford.

'It's been a bit frustrating in the last few weeks, so I'm very pleased,' he beamed. 'It was a good game for us. Coming after international matches, it can be tricky. But we got two goals in the first half that settled us down. It was a good performance all-round and a well-deserved win. With each match we're getting closer, but we have to keep playing our game and picking up the wins. If we do that it will hopefully see us through.'

Sir Alex was equally satisfied with his side's effervescent display, despite the monsoon-like conditions.

'I think we showed fantastic energy. That's very pleasing, considering that some of the players had been away for internationals and the pitch was very heavy. I said last week the players had reached a peak and that continued today. I think they realise now it's a race to the line and we need consistency, we need real focus. They want to play at their very best. There's good evidence of that in the last two games.'

Not so promising were the injury concerns over five members of the squad ahead of the Champions League quarter-final tie with AS Roma three days later. Michael Carrick, Patrice Evra and Rio Ferdinand were all withdrawn because of slight knocks in a triple substitution against Villa, while United were forced to play the last five minutes with ten men after Ryan Giggs limped off the field. The fifth player causing worry was goalkeeper Edwin van der Sar, who was again plagued by a troublesome groin strain. The Dutchman missed the Villa win as a precaution, and Sir Alex confirmed that the veteran stopper's fitness would be assessed over the next 48 hours.

Mikael Silvestre was a surprise inclusion in the 21-man squad that boarded the plane to Rome the day before the game at the Stadio Olimpico. Nani was left behind for treatment on a thigh problem, while 17-year-old striker Danny Welbeck and reserves goalkeeper Tom Heaton also made the trip.

In the previous season's corresponding fixture, Wayne Rooney had ensured the Reds left Rome with a vital away goal and that was once again the prime objective as the squad touched down in the Italian capital.

Chapter Ten

APRIL – SQUEAKY BUM TIME

It may have been 1 April, but only a fool would have predicted anything other than a stern test for United inside the Stadio Olimpico, particularly against a Roma side hell-bent on revenge.

Almost exactly one year earlier, United had slipped to a 2-1 defeat against Luciano Spalletti's side, before roaring back to inflict an infamous 7-1 second-leg obliteration and advance to the semi-finals.

Having shown in the 2007/08 group stages that they had learned valuable lessons from their humiliation at Old Trafford, Roma again awaited United with newfound self-confidence and the urge to exorcise their year-old demons.

Not that Sir Alex Ferguson and his players were overly concerned, however. Two trips to Rome in 12 months had removed any tinge of mystery over what lay before them. A year on from the previous season's defeat, the Reds were confident of securing a telling result in the first leg – particularly with Cristiano Ronaldo in such fine form.

As Sir Alex and Paul Scholes sat themselves down for the routine pre-match press conference, they were both faced with a barrage of questions about the Portuguese youngster, all generally hinting at the same wonderment – can he now deliver on the big stage?

'You have to remember, the boy's not had as much European football as a lot of the top players on the European scene,' countered Sir Alex. 'He's only young – he's just turned 23. I'm sure in two or three years' time the question will not even need to be asked. In domestic football this season he's improved in every department of his game and the more he plays in Europe, the more he'll show his attributes on the European stage.

'I have no concerns about that. All I can say is that a year after we came to Rome last season we're bringing back a player who's shown incredible improvement and is in fine goalscoring form.'

Scholes' assessment of his junior colleague was even more telling. Invariably a man of few words, the veteran midfielder was forced to admit: 'I've played with some top, top players in my time at Old Trafford but, if I'm honest, I think Cristiano must now be at the top.

'To score the amount of goals he has done this season – and from his midfield position – is nothing short of amazing. And it's not only his goals. He's making chances as well. He poses such a big threat to other teams.'

Rome were only too away of that threat.

Tuesday, 1 April 2008, Stadio Olimpico

Attendance: 60,931

UEFA Champions League Quarter-final, first leg
AS Roma 0 **United** 2

If Sir Alex Ferguson has a blueprint for an ideal European away performance, then surely his players followed it to the letter at the Stadio Olimpico. Contain, retain and counter were the three key aspects – contain Roma's fluid attacking style, retain possession and counter at devastating speed when the ball has been recovered – and all three were clinically deployed as United virtually sealed a berth in the Champions League semi-finals for the second season in a row.

Cristiano Ronaldo – he who wilts on the biggest stages, apparently – and Wayne Rooney were the familiar names to inflict the damage on the hosts with goals either side of half-time, but it was United's teamwork that reduced Roma to ruins.

Indeed, after Rooney's second just after the hour-mark, the Reds could have bagged a hatful of goals, but for near-misses and the heroics of home goalkeeper Doni.

The one-sided nature of the match's climax was not in keeping with a tense opening to the game in which both teams were reluctant to make the first move. Roma were aware of the need to build up a first-leg lead; United were happy to sit back and dictate play. If an opportunity to counter-attack arose, so be it. This was not, after all, a Premier League trip to St James' Park or Craven Cottage, this was taking on one of Italy's finest teams in their own backyard. The name of the game in the Champions League is chess, not checkers.

It came as scant surprise, then, that chances were few and far between for both sides, until United took the lead in devastating fashion six minutes before half-time. Rooney released Paul Scholes, travelling away from goal on the right-hand side of the area. The midfield schemer stabbed up a superb hanging cross, which Ronaldo met at high speed to power a header beyond Doni and into the net. The Portuguese winger took an almighty clattering in scoring the goal, but would not have cared a jot when he realised the result of his pluck.

Either side of the interval, Roma fashioned decent chances to draw level through Mirko Vucinic. The Montenegrin striker first toe-poked wide almost immediately after Ronaldo's opener, then drew a stunning one-handed save from Edwin van der Sar with a glancing header just before the hour-mark.

That save, allied to a formational change from Sir Alex Ferguson, would prove to be the game's turning point. Roma had dominated the early exchanges of the second period, leading the United manager to switch to a 4-4-2 formation with Rooney upfront. Less than ten minutes later, the move had been validated in style. Ji-sung Park, a surprise starter, but excellent all evening, headed Wes Brown's deep cross back across goal. Doni floundered amid a crowded six-yard box, and Rooney was able to pounce from close range to hand United a two-goal cushion.

It was game over, and there were chances to put the tie itself beyond doubt. Doni brilliantly tipped Ronaldo's low drive onto a post, Michael Carrick curled an effort just wide and Ronaldo again volleyed over from a superb Carlos Tevez cross.

To bemoan those missed opportunities would be excessive greed, however, and United could look forward to hosting the Romans at Old Trafford eight days later with a massive advantage.

AS ROMA: Doni; Cassetti, Mexes, Panucci, Tonetto (Cicinho 69); Taddei (Giuly 59), De Rossi, Pizarro, Aquilani (Esposito 77), Mancini; Vucinic.
Subs not used: Curci, Antunes, Ferrari, Brighi

UNITED: Van der Sar; Brown, Ferdinand, Vidic (O'Shea 31), Evra; Ronaldo, Carrick, Scholes, Anderson (Hargreaves 55), Park; Rooney (Tevez 84).
Subs not used: Kuszczak, Giggs, Piqué, Silvestre

Goals: Ronaldo (39), Rooney (66)

Striker Wayne Rooney may have scored the all-important second goal in the Stadio Olimpico, but he far preferred to focus on the sterling work of United's defence in securing a vital clean sheet.

'The defence was brilliant,' he enthused. 'All season they've been the same. I thought we defended well as a team. It was important to try to keep a clean sheet and then hopefully nick a goal and we did that just before half-time and it put us in a good position in the second half.

'We knew Roma would come out and attack us and it created a bit of space for us. We had the two counter-attacks and made them count. It was a good professional job to come here and play well and it gives us a good platform.

'But with the Champions League you never know what can happen, so we'll have to go out focused and with a good attitude. If we do that, hopefully we'll see the second leg through.'

Sir Alex Ferguson was similarly delighted by his side's evident maturity and defensive resolve, particularly in the intimidating atmosphere of the Stadio Olimpico.

'It was a very good team we were playing against,' he said. 'I think we had to defend really well at times. It was a good, disciplined performance, we had good possession of the ball and that's not easy in that atmosphere. And we didn't lose a goal, which is really vital.

It's a fantastic scoreline for us, and we're very, very pleased.'

The manager's only cause for concern came through the loss of Nemanja Vidic, who landed awkwardly in the first half and was replaced by John O'Shea. 'We hope it's a nerve,' Sir Alex gravely insisted. 'It's a knee injury anyway, we're just praying it's not anything other than a nerve injury.'

Fortunately, subsequent scans showed only minor damage to the Serbian defender, who would have to miss two weeks of action. Coming two days after the victory in Rome, it was a timely boost for Sir Alex Ferguson and Carlos Queiroz, who were charged for their post-match comments in the wake of the Reds' FA Cup exit against Portsmouth.

It was time to switch attentions back to the small matter of seeing out the Premier League title race, however, and Sir Alex was well aware of the potential pitfalls that lay ahead. Six games stood between the Reds and a 17th league title, and first up were Middlesbrough at the Riverside Stadium.

'All the games are important now,' said Sir Alex. 'We're at the stage of the season where you could class every game as a decider. We've only got two home games left. We've got to go to Middlesbrough, Blackburn, Chelsea and Wigan. So, on the balance of that, we have to make sure our away form stays strong.

'We're approaching the finish line and there's not long to go now. But sometimes it feels like a lifetime away. Nerves and form can play a part. You can get a shock result. We just have to make sure our form remains consistent.'

Sunday, 6 April 2008, Riverside Stadium

Attendance: 33,952

FA Barclays Premier League
Middlesbrough 2 **United** 2

It's almost taken for granted that teams raise the bar when they come up against United – and that selective form seems to apply to

Middlesbrough more than most. Gareth Southgate's side have traditionally been a thorn in the Reds' side and, but for Wayne Rooney's late equaliser, the Teessiders could well have seriously damaged United's title hopes.

Brazilian striker Afonso Alves struck his first goals for Boro either side of half-time, cancelling out Cristiano Ronaldo's early opener and requiring Rooney's late intervention to ensure a share of the spoils at a snow-swept Riverside Stadium.

Bereft of Nemanja Vidic, United's defence looked shaky under pressure from the fired-up hosts, and goalkeeper Edwin van der Sar had to make a number of fine saves to keep Boro at bay.

In the opening exchanges, it had seemed more a case of how many United would score, rather than whether they could rescue a point. Ronaldo put the visitors in front after ten minutes, casually converting Michael Carrick's pull-back after Boro had failed to clear a Ryan Giggs corner.

Giggs then smashed into the side netting, Rooney was denied by a fine goal-saving challenge from Luke Young and Ronaldo failed to cap a brilliant, winding run by missing the target.

United were left to rue those misses when Gary O'Neil hoofed a clearance forward, Jeremie Aliadiere neatly flicked the ball into Alves' path, and the Brazilian striker strode forward before finishing emphatically past van der Sar.

Stunned by the Brazilian's leveller, the Reds were indebted to a fine save by van der Sar to block Stewart Downing's volley. As the hosts' attacking menace continued into the second half, Emmanuel Pogatetz saw his shot blocked by Carrick before Alves shot his side into the lead.

Wes Brown's clearing header ricocheted off the back of Aliadiere's head and fell into the path of the Brazilian, who curled a fine finish outside of van der Sar's reach but inside the post, prompting wild celebrations among the home supporters.

Boro's gloating was heightened when, with 20 minutes remaining, Rio Ferdinand limped off, seemingly having injured himself in blocking another Alves effort on his own goal-line.

He was replaced by Gerard Piqué, but it was another substitute, Ji-sung Park, who made a telling contribution to help United draw level. The Korean cleverly tricked his way into the area and pulled back for Rooney, who fired the ball home via a sizeable deflection.

Both sides continued to pour forward in search of a winner, with both Rooney and Paul Scholes going close for United, but van der Sar's injury-time save from Aliadiere was a final reminder that a point may not have been such a bad return from what had been a stern examination.

MIDDLESBROUGH: Schwarzer; Young, Wheater, Pogatetz, Taylor; O'Neil, Boateng, Arca, Downing; Aliadiere (Johnson 90), Alves (Tuncay 77). Subs not used: Turnbull, Cattermole, Grounds

Goals: Alves (35, 55)

UNITED: Van der Sar; Brown, Ferdinand (Piqué 70), O'Shea (Hargreaves 67), Evra; Ronaldo, Scholes, Carrick, Giggs; Rooney, Tevez (Park 65). Subs not used: Kuszczak, Anderson

Goals: Ronaldo (10), Rooney (74)

United's draw on Teesside gave renewed hope to title chasers Chelsea and Arsenal, who beat Manchester City and drew with Liverpool respectively. Sir Alex Ferguson was far from downbeat, however, as he fully appreciated how close his side had come to defeat against a voracious Boro side.

'We could have lost the game,' admitted Sir Alex afterwards. 'They had some chances and our defending was a bit haphazard at times. But, on the other side of it, we could have won the game. Some of our football was terrific and we looked very strong and in control when we took the lead.

'It was end-to-end and both teams deserve great credit for producing a performance like that at this stage of the season. The nature of our football club is we never give in and that's a great quality to have at this time of year.

'It could turn out to be an important point and our goal difference is very good as well. But we can't take anything for granted. I said some weeks ago that the most consistent team will win it, and hopefully that will turn out to be us.'

A key aspect of United's consistently fine form throughout the season had been the almost inseparable central-defensive duo of Nemanja Vidic and Rio Ferdinand.

Having seen both sustain injuries in successive games, there were fears that the late-season injury jinx of 2006/07 was about to be repeated. Certainly the tabloids were happy to go to town on the potential crisis, but a scan revealed that Ferdinand had not suffered a broken foot, and could even return in time for the quarter-final decider against Roma at Old Trafford.

Gerard Piqué, who replaced Ferdinand at the Riverside, was in contention to continue after proving his worth and maturity, while the return of two old stalwarts ensured there would be plenty of defensive options if Ferdinand was unable to feature.

'Gary Neville and Mikael Silvestre will be involved,' Sir Alex told the pre-match press conference. 'Both won't start, but one may do depending on Rio's situation. I'm hopeful that both players will get part of a game. The good thing is they are back and training very well.

'The best news we've had with Gary is that he has no interruptions. I'm very pleased with his progress and he has the ability to play in a match like Wednesday's. We'll make the decision in the morning, but by that time I could have five different teams!'

With the comfort of a two-goal cushion and Arsenal the next visitors to Old Trafford, it was widely expected that there would be changes made to the Reds' starting line-up against the *giallorossi*. Whatever the team, though, there was never any danger of United sitting back at Old Trafford – particularly with the chance of setting a new record for successive home victories in the Champions League.

Wednesday, 9 April 2008, Old Trafford

Attendance: 74,423

UEFA Champions League Quarter-final, second leg
United 1 **AS Roma** 0 (United win 3-0 on aggregate)

Sir Alex Ferguson demonstrated the benefits of having strength in depth as he chopped, changed and triumphed against Roma to book a mouth-watering semi-final clash with Catalan giants Barcelona.

Carlos Tevez glanced home a fine diving header 20 minutes from full-time to seal the Reds' passage to the final four, but there were hearts in mouths early on as Daniele De Rossi blazed a first-half penalty over the bar for the visitors.

Roma must be particularly sick of United. Just over a year after overcoming the Reds in the 2006/07 quarter-final, first leg, the Italian side slipped to a fourth defeat in five subsequent matches against Sir Alex Ferguson's side.

Given the luxury of a two-goal cushion, Wayne Rooney, Cristiano Ronaldo and Paul Scholes were all handed richly deserved rests. Rio Ferdinand did recover in time to play, lining up alongside Gerard Piqué in the centre of defence, flanked by Wes Brown and Mikael Silvestre, who was making his first appearance since September. There was also a place on the bench for skipper Gary Neville, more than a year after his last first-team outing.

Although the onus was firmly on Roma to overcome United's advantage, it was the hosts who made all the early attacking motions. Ji-sung Park fired wide from a tight angle, Tevez headed narrowly wide and Brown was just off target with a header from a Ryan Giggs corner. Owen Hargreaves became the first United player to hit the target but, after being played through by Giggs, the midfielder's low shot was well turned away by Roma goalkeeper Doni.

The Italians took a quarter of an hour to muster their first meaningful effort, but Edwin van der Sar was equal to a low shot from Mirko Vucinic. United's immediate response was to draw another fine save from Doni, who this time turned away Giggs' half-volley from a low Hargreaves cross.

For all United's dominance, Roma were handed a glorious opportunity to halve their deficit when Brown was adjudged to have fouled Mancini inside the area. The Brazilian winger reacted more than a little dramatically, but the referee had no hesitation awarding a spot-kick.

Amid a shrill cacophony of noise from the home fans, a clearly unnerved De Rossi stepped up and blazed the penalty high into the Stretford End. The miss brought the chorus to its deafening peak.

The end-to-end nature of the game slowed from then on, although Silvestre was forced to make a vital block on 57 minutes when the ball dropped to Taddei in the area.

The Roman resistance was ended, however, with 20 minutes remaining when Tevez fed Hargreaves, raced into the area and met the midfielder's superb cross perfectly, glancing a header low into the far corner.

Relief reigned, and Sir Alex responded by handing Gary Neville a late cameo – in the centre of midfield, of all places – safe in the knowledge that United would record a Champions League record 11th straight home win en route to securing a tantalising semi-final clash with another of world football's most-revered names – FC Barcelona.

UNITED: Van der Sar; Brown, Piqué, Ferdinand, Silvestre; Park, Carrick (O'Shea 74), Hargreaves, Anderson (Neville 81), Giggs (Rooney 74); Tevez.
Subs not used: Kuszczak, Ronaldo, Scholes, Welbeck

Goal: Tevez (70)

AS ROMA: Doni; Panucci, Mexes, Juan, Cassetti (Tonetto 56); De Rossi, Pizarro (Giuly 69), Taddei (Esposito 81), Perrotta; Mancini, Vucinic.
Subs not used: Curci, Cicinho, Aquilani, Brighi

'We have the opportunity now to achieve something really special,' Sir Alex declared after reaching the semi-finals. 'We want to go to

Barcelona and show we're a good team. Barcelona are a wonderful club, but we can't go there and be negative. We have to go there and be really positive. If we do that then we've got a chance.'

'Barcelona will be a difficult challenge,' echoed defender Wes Brown. 'But we're playing well as a team and I can't wait for those two games. A lot of the injured players are coming back now and the squad is in great shape. Last season we played AC Milan [in the semi-final] with loads of players out, but now everyone is back and enjoying their football.'

Brown's reference to the previous season's injury nightmare was particularly poignant for Gary Neville, who had only five weeks before the AC Milan clash suffered the ankle injury that would keep him out of senior action for over a year. After making his long-awaited return to a rapturous reception at Old Trafford, the club captain was predictably delighted to be back.

'Missing the end of last season was bad,' he said in an understated manner. 'I missed the Champions League quarters and semis, the Premier League run-in and the FA Cup final, so it's good to be back to help the team now.

'People kept asking me when I was coming back and it was a bit embarrassing. I'd try and give them a date and then it wouldn't materialise. But the fans have always supported me, and they gave me a good reception when I came on.'

Having Neville back in the fold further reinforced Sir Alex's bulging squad. Having shuffled his pack with great effect against Roma, the United manager conceded that keeping his team fresh was a key element at such a hectic period of the season.

'We have to think about Arsenal on Sunday and you have to look at the big picture at times,' he said. 'We were going into a game at Old Trafford with a two-goal lead and I have to trust the players in that situation.

'I keep saying it's the best squad I've ever had, so if that's the case then why shouldn't I play them? I took out Scholes, Rooney and Ronaldo, but Ji-sung Park, Carlos Tevez and Owen Hargreaves were our three best players.'

While progress to the semi-finals had placed United on the crest of a wave going into the potentially huge visit of Arsenal, the Gunners were still licking their wounds after a heartbreaking, dramatic quarter-final exit against Liverpool at Anfield.

So often the media's favourite foes, Wenger and Sir Alex Ferguson were in rare agreement before the Gunners' visit to Old Trafford – anything but an Arsenal victory would reduce the title race to a straight fight between United and Chelsea.

'A win for us makes it difficult for them. No question,' Sir Alex said at the pre-match press conference. 'Five games to go is not a lot of leeway for them. They can't afford to drop any points. But that doesn't make it any different for us in our preparations for an Arsenal game because they are always very competitive games anyway.'

Sunday, 13 April 2008, Old Trafford

Attendance: 75,985

FA Barclays Premier League
United 2 **Arsenal** 1

Just as heavyweight boxing matches often descend into wanton slugfests, so United and Arsenal served up a see-saw, 'you attack, we attack' feast of football at Old Trafford, with both sides' sights trained all the while on one thing – the Premier League trophy.

Although neither team were at their brilliant best in a game often littered with mistakes, the sheer morbid entertainment of two sides intent solely on victory was hard to rival.

Anything but three points dealt a damaging blow to both sides. United had Chelsea lurking menacingly behind them, waiting for any slips, while Arsenal needed to stay in touch after surrendering the five-point summit lead they held in early February.

The Gunners had registered just two victories from 12 matches since their FA Cup hammering at Old Trafford. For United, victory over the visitors would represent bypassing a major remaining hurdle, and meeting them at such a low ebb had the home contingent in optimistic mood – as did the pre-match award of Barclays Manager and Player of the Month for March, handed to Sir Alex and Cristiano Ronaldo respectively.

The early exchanges did little to prolong the home support's sanguinity, however, as Arsenal oozed the slick passing and fluid movement that had made them frontrunners for such a large portion of the campaign. United were chasing shadows at times and, had Emmanuel Adebayor turned up in the form of three months earlier, the Reds would surely have been behind inside the first half-hour.

There were sparks of inspiration from Sir Alex's side, however, and Wayne Rooney twice found himself in sight of the goal, only to be denied by veteran goalkeeper Jens Lehmann, restored at the expense of the injured Manuel Almunia.

Those openings aside, United could count themselves lucky to be level at half-time, but that merciful parity was ended in controversial fashion just after the restart. Robin van Persie pulled back a fine left-wing cross that bypassed the entire United defence, and Adebayor was on hand – literally – to convert from close range. Although there were few protests at the time, replays showed that the Togolese forward had deflected the ball home with his arm.

Shortly afterwards Edwin van der Sar had to make a fine reaction save to prevent Rio Ferdinand from inadvertently putting through his own goal, and the gravity of the situation clearly dawned on the Reds. They snapped into life, and drew level just six minutes after falling behind. Michael Carrick's flicked pass was clumsily handled inside the area by Gunners skipper William Gallas, and referee Howard Webb immediately pointed to the penalty spot.

Goalkeeper Lehmann did his level best to put off the unflappable Cristiano Ronaldo – delaying the kick, eyeballing the Portuguese winger as best he could – but to no avail. Ronaldo smashed the spot-kick home but, after several players had encroached into the area, he was ordered to take it again. Cue more Germanic gamesmanship for the retake, cue an even more emphatic conversion from Ronaldo at the second time of asking. Game on.

The play swayed from one end of the pitch to the other, with both sides giving their all on an increasingly sodden pitch in pursuit of victory. After Rooney had again been denied by Lehmann, Patrice Evra won a free-kick just outside the Arsenal area. All eyes turned to Cristiano Ronaldo, including those of Lehmann, who stood helplessly as Owen Hargreaves curled the set-piece just over the defensive wall and into the bottom corner. Pandemonium, jubilation and, finally, a release of nervous tension rang around Old Trafford.

The nerves were soon back, though. Arsenal pressed manfully in the closing stages for an equaliser, but came no closer than through two headers from substitute Nicklas Bendtner, who was twice foiled by van der Sar as United hung on for an invaluable victory.

UNITED: Van der Sar; Brown, Piqué, Ferdinand, Evra; Park (Tevez 55), Carrick, Hargreaves (Giggs 89), Scholes (Anderson 55), Ronaldo; Rooney. Subs not used: Kuszczak, O'Shea

Goals: Ronaldo (54, pen), Hargreaves (72)

ARSENAL: Lehmann; Toure (Hoyte 85), Gallas, Song, Clichy; Eboue (Walcott 61), Gilberto, Fabregas, Hleb; Van Persie (Bendtner 76), Adebayor.

Subs: Fabianski, Djourou

Goal: Adebayor (48)

The three-horse race was now well and truly down to two contenders: United and Chelsea. Keen to recognise Arsenal's role in a pulsating season, Sir Alex Ferguson was magnanimous in victory. 'Arsenal were the better team in the first half,' he admitted. 'I thought we were nervous, our passing was poor and the confidence and the way we expressed ourselves was poor. I couldn't wait for half-time.

'I had Anderson and Tevez to come on and when Arsenal scored it forced my hand. I thought we were fantastic after that. Wayne could have had a hat-trick, we played some good football and Arsenal had some good moments themselves. It was just an incredible game.

I watched the Liverpool-Arsenal match and thought it was fantastic, but the quality of that game today was absolutely outstanding. You'll not get a better game this year.'

After converting the match-winning free-kick, Owen Hargreaves revealed he didn't even bother consulting usual taker Cristiano Ronaldo before curling his effort home.

'We had an earlier free-kick and I said "I'll take that", but Ronny said "It's too far for you",' revealed the England international. 'The second one was a bit closer and it was a good distance for me, so I didn't ask him! I score goals on counter-attacks, from long distance or free-kicks and, if I can get a chance to contribute, I'm very happy with that.'

While Hargreaves was the man whose goal sealed the three points, United's patched-up backline had to take plaudits for restricting the on-song Gunners to just a single goal and for laying the foundations for an enormous victory.

'It was a massive game for us,' admitted captain Rio Ferdinand. 'We don't go a goal down at home very often, but we showed true grit, determination and a great team ethic to claw our way back into the game, as we did at Middlesbrough last week.

'The three points, no matter who you play against, are important. But there are more games to be played – the title's not handed out now. We need to win our remaining games and, if we do that, we'll be champions.'

Chelsea were undoubtedly United's only serious title rivals now and, ahead of his side's match with Wigan at Stamford Bridge the following evening, Blues' manager Avram Grant seemed far from deterred by United's vital win over the Gunners.

If the Blues took maximum points off Wigan and then Everton three days later, then they would go level on points with United, ahead of the Reds' ever-tricky trip to Blackburn Rovers.

'I believe that nobody is a computer,' said the Chelsea manager. 'Pressure can affect anybody. It can take you forward in a positive way, but also you can see that even big players under pressure cannot play like they used to. It can be any team, any player.'

Prophetic words indeed, but the Israeli could not have foreseen how soon his prediction would come back to haunt him. The pressure of chasing United for so long without reward had clearly affected the below-par Blues, who were held to a 1-1 draw by Steve Bruce's side, courtesy of an injury-time strike from Emile Heskey.

The result left Chelsea five points behind United, with both sides having just four games left to play. Next stop for the Blues was Goodison Park, where they had to win to retain even the faintest hope of regaining the Reds' crown. A solitary goal from Michael Essien kept them in the hunt, but a victory at Ewood Park would take United to within touching distance of a 17th league title.

Spirits were further heightened within the United camp the day before the Blackburn game by the news that three key players had agreed new contracts. After a long and public wrangle, Wes Brown was among the trio (which also included Rio Ferdinand and Michael Carrick) to agree extensions, much to the delight of Sir Alex Ferguson.

'There's no other club for Wes Brown,' he said. 'He's a Manchester United player. We were always quietly confident he would sign. And it's good that the squad is staying together. It continues our policy of lengthening contracts at the right time and keeps the continuity of the first-team squad going.'

Little surprise, then, that the United manager and his players were in relaxed mood ahead of the trip to face former Reds' striker Mark Hughes and his ever-combative Rovers side.

'You get accustomed to the drama of the end of the season,' said Sir Alex. 'There have been a lot of dramas over the years and you gain experience from that. We've certainly got that experience because we've been there many times. I've knocked on that door hundreds of times and so have some of my players.

'On certain occasions we've enjoyed great ends to the season and at other times we've tasted defeat in the most dramatic way, such as when we lost the league to Blackburn in 1995 by a point. We had to win at West Ham on the last day, but could only draw – I remember it well, we could have scored six! So many things can happen, the important thing is how you handle those things. I'm confident we can do that in the best possible way.'

As ever, though, United would set about doing it the hard way.

Saturday, 19 April 2008, Ewood Park

Attendance: 30,316

FA Barclays Premier League
Blackburn Rovers 1 **United** 1

Brad Friedel seems to have made it his life's mission to thwart United whenever possible.

The veteran American goalkeeper produced yet another unbelievable performance against the Reds, pulling off a string of saves that beggared belief, until Carlos Tevez struck two minutes from time to salvage a potentially priceless point for the visitors.

Although the Reds never really hit top gear, but for the form of Friedel this was a match that could have been embarrassingly one-sided. Roque Santa Cruz put the hosts ahead with their first meaningful attempt of the match, side-footing home after a defensive mix-up in the 21st minute, then he and his team-mates sat back and relied on Friedel's stunning one-man show to keep them afloat.

Friedel's opposite number was Tomasz Kuszczak, who started because of Edwin van der Sar's absence through a groin tweak. Nemanja Vidic returned to strengthen the defence, however, relegating Gerard Piqué to the substitutes' bench.

The Reds' Polish goalkeeper had to be alert after six minutes as he saved from Jason Roberts with his feet. United should have taken the lead shortly afterwards when Wayne Rooney squared for Tevez, but the Argentine barely made contact with the ball, much to Rovers' relief.

United could only rue that miss when Blackburn moved into the lead. A long throw from the left wing seemed harmless enough when Vidic met the ball first, only for the ball to cannon off Rio Ferdinand's heel and into the path of Santa Cruz, who clinically slotted the ball home.

Barring a long-range effort from David Bentley, which Kuszczak had to palm over, Rovers' attacking contribution to the match had peaked. United, meanwhile, had a decent penalty shout turned down when referee Rob Styles failed to punish Steven Reid's sliding challenge on Rooney.

Ronaldo then headed a Ryan Giggs corner goalwards, only for Friedel to make his first meaningful save of the afternoon, late in the first half. The American stopper would certainly earn his money in the second half.

With some 8,000 baying United fans in the Darwen End, the second-half's unwavering soundtrack was one of roaring encouragement for the Reds. They were left heads in hands on 65 minutes when Ronaldo's angled shot crashed against the post, before Friedel came into his own.

After Ronaldo had been felled by Johann Vogel, a loose ball ran to Tevez, who spun and fired goalwards from close range. Friedel thrust out an arm to take the pace off the ball, which he just about managed with his fingertips, before plunging onto the ball on his own goal-line.

That close call sparked a period of United pressure akin to the Alamo. Brett Emerton appeared to handle Michael Carrick's goalbound header before Friedel again pulled off a fine one-handed save to deny Rooney in a one-on-one. The 36-year-old then made another stunning save, clawing John O'Shea's close-range shot around the post, despite travelling the opposite way.

From the resultant corner, even Friedel could do nothing as United grabbed the goal their efforts had so richly deserved. Nani fizzed in the set-piece, Scholes flicked the ball on and Tevez was there, unmarked, to contort in the air and direct a header into the roof of the net.

The Darwen End erupted, acutely aware of just how significant a goal it could prove to be in the title race.

BLACKBURN ROVERS: Friedel; Emerton, Samba, Nelsen, Warnock; Reid,

Bentley, Vogel (Mokoena 86), Pedersen; Roberts, Santa Cruz.
Subs not used: Brown, Ooijer, McCarthy, Dunn.

Goal: Santa Cruz (21)

UNITED: Kuszczak; Brown (O'Shea 81), Vidic, Ferdinand, Evra; Ronaldo, Scholes, Carrick, Giggs (Nani 46); Rooney (Park 90), Tevez.
Subs not used: Foster, Piqué

Goal: Tevez (88)

Although United had missed the chance to retain a five-point lead over Chelsea, defender Nemanja Vidic was more than satisfied to have avoided defeat at Ewood Park.

'It's a big point,' the Serbian centre back said afterwards. 'At the end of the day we were losing 1-0 with ten minutes to go and we equalised. So we're happy. We had three or four chances in the second half and maybe we could have done better on a few occasions, but you have to give credit to Brad Friedel.

'We lost an early goal, but we still believed we could score and get a result. It's always tough at Blackburn; it mightn't have been the best performance, but we got a good result. We still have three games to play in the league and the aim is to win all those matches if we want to be champions.'

United's vocal travelling support sang long and loud throughout the match, and their efforts drew praise from midfielder Michael Carrick, who said: 'The fans were unbelievable again and they probably sucked the ball in for us in the end! They're always great at Old Trafford, but when we come away from home the fans are something else.'

Lifelong United fan Wes Brown prepared for the Reds' next outing – a daunting trip to Barcelona – by signing his new contract. 'Manchester United is a fantastic club and I am delighted to have signed a new deal,' he said. 'To be part of a team I have supported all my life is a great honour. I can see this team winning many trophies in the coming seasons and it will be great to share in that success.'

Brown was among the travelling party who returned to Barcelona almost nine years after the Reds' last trip to Catalonia, 1999's infamous Champions League final victory over Bayern Munich. While it was impossible to ignore parallels with the past, Sir Alex Ferguson was keen for his young side to focus on their own futures.

'I don't know what the older players, the ones who were here that night, have said to the younger players,' he said from the team hotel. 'That victory is not lost on anyone – it's shown that many times on television or on videos.

'But even more important is what this team can achieve themselves, making their own history. They are good enough to do that. This team is for today. They don't need to be reminded of the past or be worried about it.'

United's burgeoning squad were allowed a sneak peek at the future – and at the team who would potentially lie in wait for them in Moscow – by watching Liverpool take on Chelsea at Anfield in the first leg of the other semi-final. An injury-time own goal from John Arne Riise cancelled out Dirk Kuyt's opener for the hosts, handing Avram Grant's side a slight advantage for the second leg.

It was the third time in four years that the two sides had met at the Champions League semi-final stage and, predictably, it yielded a cautious, mediocre 90 minutes. The eyes of the world expected a far more open, enjoyable clash when United and Barcelona met 24 hours later.

Wednesday, 23 April 2008, Nou Camp

Attendance: 95,949

UEFA Champions League Semi-final, first leg
FC Barcelona 0 **United** 0

Those who sat down to gorge on a feast of attacking football will not have been satisfied. With two of the richest attacking arsenals on the continent going head to head, it was hardly conceivable that 90 minutes could yield only two chances of note.

The first fell to Cristiano Ronaldo after just two minutes. Gabriel

Milito inexplicably handled the Portuguese winger's header inside his own area to concede a penalty, which Ronaldo subsequently blazed wide.

Samuel Eto'o wasted Barca's best opportunity, smashing wide from 15 yards in the second half as a superb defensive display from Sir Alex Ferguson's side neutralised the Catalans' potent attack. Barca, for their part, were also in solid form at the back.

With the stakes so high, the two teams opted to remain at arm's length. Barcelona probed cagily with more attacking intent, while United stuck steadfastly to a gameplan of containment and countering.

On one of United's rare forays into enemy territory, just before the half-hour mark, referee Massimo Busacca could very easily have given Ronaldo a second chance from the penalty spot.

Seizing on a slack pass from Andres Iniesta, the winger burst through on goal, only to have his route unceremoniously blocked by Rafael Marquez, who showed little interest in playing the ball. Busacca quickly waved away the claim, however, much to Ronaldo's chagrin.

The Mexican defender was later booked for a barge on Ronaldo, a caution that ruled him out of the second leg in Manchester. Half-time came and went, the only interruption in a steady flow of Barcelona possession and probing.

A brief flurry of attacking intent from the hosts, with the impressive Lionel Messi pulling the strings, saw Michael Carrick make a timely interception to deny the Argentine, before Eto'o fired wastefully wide after being fed by Xavi's neat backheel.

Carrick then smashed a shot into the side netting after engineering space for himself inside the Barca area, but that was United's final meaningful attack of the evening. The notion of nicking an away goal was now an afterthought, and maintaining a clean sheet absolutely vital.

With the Reds so resolute at the back, Barca resorted to pot-shots from distance in an attempt to beat Edwin van der Sar. The Dutchman beat away an effort from substitute Thierry Henry, before holding the Frenchman's free-kick and another long-ranger from Andres Iniesta as the game drifted towards the unlikeliest of stalemates.

FC BARCELONA: Valdes; Zambrotta, Marquez, Milito, Abidal; Deco (Henry 77), Toure, Xavi; Messi (Krkic 62), Eto'o, Iniesta.
Subs not used: Pinto, Gudjohnsen, Sylvinho, Giovani, Thuram

UNITED: Van der Sar; Hargreaves, Brown, Ferdinand, Evra; Rooney (Nani 76), Carrick, Scholes; Park, Ronaldo, Tevez (Giggs 85).
Subs not used: Kuszczak, Anderson, Piqué, O'Shea, Silvestre

After a surprisingly tentative match at the Nou Camp, all the immediate post-match talk was of the man who came closest to finding the back of the net – Cristiano Ronaldo.

'You can't blame him,' said Owen Hargreaves, of the winger's missed penalty. 'You're not going to score them all. He's scored more than he's missed and I think maybe he changed his mind at the last moment. It probably would have changed the flow of the game had we scored, but it's fine.

'I think we'd have taken 0-0 before the game. Defensively I thought we were strong and didn't allow Barcelona any clear chances. They had a lot of possession and kept the ball well, but they didn't really penetrate us and that was the strategy going into the game.'

Having seen their original gameplan of containing Barcelona work a treat, United were confident of overturning the Catalans at Old Trafford six days later with a truer display of their attacking capabilities.

'We looked very solid as a team and put in a very good performance defensively,' said Michael Carrick. 'In a perfect world we would have liked to score, but it's not to be. It's not the end of the world, a draw's not a bad result for us.

'We know now that if we can win next week at home, we go through. It's a different game at a different place, so we'll be looking to attack more – that's for sure. But we're not going to do that in a stupid way. They've got some world-class players. They're not a side you can take lightly, and we're all aware of that. We know the threats that they possess and it's probably going to be another tight affair. Hopefully we'll come out on top.'

The trip to the Nou Camp was the first of three massive games in six days for United. With a Saturday noon kick-off against title rivals Chelsea to come at Stamford Bridge, the Reds opted to stay and train in Barcelona before flying straight to London for the chance to effectively end the Blues' hopes of regaining the Premier League trophy.

'There is a great incentive for us,' said Sir Alex Ferguson. 'What we have had to do is get the players recovered from Barcelona. We've had the disadvantage of a day's less rest than Chelsea and then there is the travelling. We'll do our best. We'll get the players rested and, hopefully, we will be all right for Saturday.

'I said in December that I was looking over my shoulder at Chelsea because I thought they would be a big threat to us, and I've been proved right. They're a strong and an experienced, powerful side, and never at any stage in the season did we dismiss them. We showed good concentration levels against Barcelona and we'll need to produce the same again on Saturday. I've got a good bunch of lads and I'm confident they'll be ready.'

Saturday, 26 April 2008, Stamford Bridge

Attendance: 41,828

FA Barclays Premier League
Chelsea 2 **United** 1

The Premier League title race was blown wide open after a late Michael Ballack penalty gave Chelsea victory over an under-strength United side at Stamford Bridge.

Sir Alex Ferguson and his players were left fuming at the decision to punish Michael Carrick for handball five minutes from time, after Wayne Rooney had cancelled out the German's first-half opener.

A frustrating afternoon for United was worsened when Rooney limped off, having aggravated the hip injury he sustained at Black-

burn Rovers, while Nemanja Vidic's run of ill-fortune continued
when he was stretchered off after taking an accidental knee to the
face from Didier Drogba.

For much of the second half it seemed as though United were on
course for either one or three points, enough to keep Chelsea at arm's
length or essentially end the title race right there in west London.
The hosts were fuelled by the need to win and dominated the first
half as United struggled to find any cohesion in the baking sun.

With the second leg of the Champions League semi-final against
Barcelona just three days away, it was no surprise to see changes to
the Reds' starting line-up. Darren Fletcher made a surprise return
from a month-long injury absence and Mikael Silvestre replaced
Patrice Evra at left-back. Nani, Anderson and Ryan Giggs all started,
with Cristiano Ronaldo and Carlos Tevez named on the bench.

Chelsea flew out of the traps, and the ever-impressive Michael
Essien twice shot narrowly off target as Avram Grant's side called
the tune. Joe Cole came closest to putting the hosts ahead, but his
improvised snapshot cannoned off the top of Edwin van der Sar's
post and away to safety.

Just when it seemed as though United had weathered the storm
until half-time, Drogba did well to work space on the right edge of
the penalty area, clipped in a lovely cross and Ballack steamed in to
power a header past van der Sar.

The onus was now on United to attack, and the balance of play
shifted to the Reds immediately after the restart. There was far more
vim and vigour about the visitors' attacking play, but there was a
huge slice of fortune involved when they drew level ten minutes
after the break.

Ricardo Carvalho blindly played a casual back-pass towards his
own goal, straight to Rooney. Despite clearly being in discomfort, the
striker sprinted goalwards, cut across John Terry and fired a clinical
low shot inside Petr Cech's right-hand post. So sore was Rooney's
hip, he was unable to celebrate fully and hastily waved his joyous
team-mates away. Inevitably, he was substituted shortly afterwards.
His replacement – a fresh Cristiano Ronaldo – trotted into the fray.

The Portuguese winger stung Cech's palms with a shot from distance, as did Ryan Giggs, as United looked to end the title race and Chelsea's proud unbeaten home record, which had lasted over four years.

That record remained intact, however, when Essien's cross struck Carrick's arm and, after consulting his assistant referee, Alan Wiley pointed to the spot. With typical German precision, Ballack hammered home the kick to send Chelsea fans into rapture.

Not that there weren't any late scares for the Blues. In a frantic finale, United twice had efforts cleared off the line. First Ashley Cole hacked away Ronaldo's low effort with Cech well beaten, then Andriy Shevchenko blocked a Darren Fletcher header right on his own goal-line, as Chelsea held on to take the title race to the wire.

CHELSEA: Cech; Ferreira (Anelka 67), Terry, Carvalho, A. Cole; Essien, Ballack, Mikel, J. Cole (Makelele 87); Kalou (Shevchenko 81), Drogba. Subs not used: Cudicini, Belletti

Goals: Ballack (45, 86, pen)

UNITED: Van der Sar; Brown, Vidic (Hargreaves 14), Ferdinand, Silvestre; Fletcher, Carrick, Anderson (O'Shea 65), Nani, Giggs; Rooney (Ronaldo 64). Subs not used: Kuszczak, Tevez

Goal: Rooney (56)

'Seething' would be a fair description of Sir Alex Ferguson's post-match mood, having seen his side suffer from the latest in a long line of marginal refereeing decisions.

'It's a major decision that's cost us the game,' he churned in reference to the spot-kick given against Michael Carrick. 'To give a penalty for that in a game of such importance, on the linesman's say-so, is absolutely diabolical. Granted the ball hit Carrick's hand, but he couldn't get out of the road. He didn't lift his hands above his shoulders or above his head, and the ball was going straight to Rio

Ferdinand anyway. The referee should have seen that.

'Earlier, when Ronaldo came on, he was grappled almost to the floor by Ballack at a corner and it was a clear penalty kick. And when Carrick went down in the same way, the referee was right there, but again he didn't give it. The game hinged on major decisions and, unfortunately, they didn't go our way.

'We were knocked out of the FA Cup after not getting a penalty kick. We should have had a penalty from Mike Riley at Middlesbrough when their player dived and saved the ball. And the linesman we had today, Glenn Turner, flagged Ronaldo when he was through and five yards onside.

'Then last week at Blackburn, Rob Styles, who's turned down five penalty kicks for us this season, didn't give one out of three. If we don't get the decisions we deserve, we're going to have to perform really well.'

While Sir Alex was clearly irked to see his side beaten by a referee's intervention, experienced campaigner Ryan Giggs mused that Lady Luck had indeed been on Chelsea's side.

'When you concede a late goal it's always hard to take, especially having got ourselves back in the game,' said the winger. 'The luck just didn't go for us. Sometimes you get the breaks and Chelsea had them today. They cleared two shots off the line, they were given a penalty and Ronaldo got a dubious offside call when through on goal.

'We've got to pick ourselves up now. There's no bigger game than Barcelona. We want to win the league and we want to reach the Champions League final, and it's still in our hands. We showed our battling qualities in the second half today, and we'll need them in the next two games.'

The rage and frustration in the United camp was highly publicised in the following days, with Rio Ferdinand quick to apologise for accidentally catching a Chelsea steward when he kicked a wall, and a number of squad members scuffling with Stamford Bridge groundstaff during the warm-down.

A timely tonic was received when Cristiano Ronaldo retained his

Professional Footballers' Association Player of the Season award, beating off competition from Fernando Torres, Steven Gerrard, David James, Cesc Fabregas and Emmanuel Adebayor.

The Portuguese winger saw his previous year's Young Player of the Season award taken off him by Arsenal midfielder Fabregas, but he remained elated at being recognised once again by his peers.

'I feel very happy,' he said in an acceptance speech. 'When you work all season to do something for the team, and then at the end the PFA give you this award, it is a great moment. It is an honour, a pleasure and a great motivation to carry on, to work more and get better. This is a good moment for me, but it is not just my award, my team-mates have helped me a lot this season. They give me good passes to score goals – and I score.'

The impending arrival of Barcelona – fresh from a La Liga defeat at Deportivo La Coruna – in Manchester gave Ronaldo and company little time to dwell on their defeat at Chelsea. Nemanja Vidic and Wayne Rooney were serious doubts after their Stamford Bridge battle wounds, so Sir Alex Ferguson called upon Old Trafford to provide the vocal backing to roar United to Moscow.

'I thought the Barcelona supporters were tremendous [last week],' he said in his programme notes. 'Despite the frustrations of not being able to see their team score, they rallied round their players. And with 95,000 in the Nou Camp, they made a fearsome noise.

'We must match their support; hopefully even better it. So show your colours, wave your scarves, hoist your flags and make your presence felt. With your help we can do it. The players won't let you down. This tie is absolutely wide open.'

As part of a club campaign entitled 'Show Your Colours', Sir Alex and his players encouraged all United followers to get behind the side against the Catalan giants. The idea's crowning glory was a pair of mosaics held up at the Stretford End and Scoreboard End, the former showing the European Cup flanked by the poignant numbers 68 and 99, while the latter simply read 'Believe'.

Amid a deafening atmosphere, the like of which Old Trafford has rarely known, players, staff and fans were united in belief – only 90 minutes stood between the Reds and Moscow.

Tuesday, 29 April 2008, Old Trafford

Attendance: 75,061

UEFA Champions League Semi-final, second leg
United 1 **FC Barcelona** 0 (United win 1-0 on aggregate)

Nine years after missing out on a deserved place in the 1999 Champions League final against Bayern Munich, Paul Scholes sealed his own redemption with a stunning goal to book United's place in the 2008 showpiece.

The midfield schemer struck an unstoppable 14th-minute shot that arced high into the top corner of Victor Valdes' goal, prompting wild jubilation around Old Trafford.

United, to a man, were heroic. So, too, were the fans, as Barcelona – and in particular pocket trickster Lionel Messi – probed tirelessly in pursuit of a route back into the tie, only to meet a Red wall of noise and defiance from all those gathered inside the famous old stadium.

This was never vintage United. Shorn of key duo Wayne Rooney and Nemanja Vidic, the attacking instinct had to be curbed, particularly as the concession of an away goal would leave the Reds needing to score at least twice.

Nerves jangled for the entire 90 minutes, and with good cause. Less than a minute had elapsed when Scholes felled Messi right on the chalk of the United penalty area, but referee Herbert Fandel ruled – correctly – that the foul had taken place just outside the 18-yard line.

That early scare apart, United's defensive gameplan was identical to that adopted in the Nou Camp – one of total, unerring concentration and complete decisiveness. Rio Ferdinand shone, barely allowing Samuel Eto'o a sniff of goal, in tandem with the flawless Wes Brown. Owen Hargreaves bombed about like a natural right-back, in similar style to Patrice Evra. Neither full-back gave consideration to being one booking away from missing the final, throwing themselves into challenges and generally marauding around as if their lives depended on it.

Missing a Champions League final, as Paul Scholes can attest, is a nightmarish experience. The biggest stage of all, and no part to play. It was ultimately fitting that the veteran midfielder should give himself a second chance with a strike fit to grace any theatre in world football.

Seizing on an aimless clearance from Gianluca Zambrotta, Scholes took a touch some 25 yards from goal, before slicing an unstoppable half-volley high into the top right corner of Valdes' net. Bar the small section of Barcelona fans, Old Trafford writhed and leapt in euphoric unison.

Now everybody believed. Now, with something to hold onto, United could encourage Barca attacks and hit on the counter. It was a plan that very nearly reaped dividends as first Ji-sung Park sidefooted narrowly wide, then Nani headed the Korean's cross inches past the post just before half-time.

Save for a couple of near-misses from Deco snap-shots, United had kept the Catalans at arm's length brilliantly. Not only were the defence outstanding, the entire midfield and attack put in a memorable shift of defending from the front line. None embodied the Reds' gritty determination more than Carlos Tevez, who must surely have been engulfed in steam when he took off his boots afterwards.

United's resolute nature made life frustrating for the visitors, but Barcelona's ball retention and patience made for a nervy, excruciating second half for all. Chances were few and far between for either side, but there were plenty of hearts in mouths when substitute Thierry Henry planted a header straight at Edwin van der Sar ten minutes from time.

That, wonderfully, was Barca's last attack of note. When the final whistle sounded, after six life-sapping minutes of injury time, the shrill chorus that had soundtracked the previous 90 minutes erupted into a prolonged roar. Follow, follow, follow, because United are going to Moscow.

UNITED: Van der Sar; Hargreaves, Ferdinand, Brown, Evra (Silvestre 90); Nani (Giggs 76), Carrick, Scholes (Fletcher 76), Park; Ronaldo, Tevez. Subs not used: Kuszczak, Anderson, O'Shea, Welbeck

Goal: Scholes (14)

FC BARCELONA: Valdes; Zambrotta, Puyol, Milito, Abidal; Messi, Xavi, Toure (Gudjohnsen 88), Deco, Iniesta (Henry 60); Eto'o (Bojan 71). Subs not used: Pinto, Edmilson, Silvinho, Thuram

'I just hope my pacemaker's working – if not, I'm in trouble,' quipped a beaming Sir Alex Ferguson after booking a second appearance in a Champions League final. 'It was excruciating, that's what it was. The pain and the agony – I always feel that to get success, the players have to endure that. All the hard work, all the pain and torment you go through in football is rewarded by a result like tonight's.'

The irony of Paul Scholes' status as matchwinner was not lost on his team-mates, who were delighted that the midfielder had managed to exorcise some personal demons.

'You could see his reaction, it was a big relief for him,' said Mikael Silvestre. 'He wasn't involved in '99, but now he is taking the team with him to Moscow. It's good for him, he fully deserves it. He is a great professional. He is a local lad so it means a lot to him.'

'It was a great goal, unbelievable,' added Wes Brown. 'I'm just glad it was Scholesy, he deserves it. He's got us into the final.'

But who would be lining up against the Reds? For Sir Alex, the next stop was Stamford Bridge and the United manager watched on as Chelsea edged a thrilling second leg against Liverpool, running out 3-2 winners (4-3 on aggregate) after extra-time. The destination of the Premier League and Champions League trophies would be decided by two teams.

Now came the real nitty gritty for United. What a month May promised to be.

Chapter Eleven

MAY – DOUBLE CHASERS

There games to go, two trophies on offer. The stakes were never higher, but United's epic victory over Barcelona had dramatically raised spirits after the disappointment of losing at Stamford Bridge.

Such grand situations demand the best of the finest players, and Cristiano Ronaldo had his sights set on a silver-lined May. With a memorable Double on the horizon, the winger was in greedy mood.

'We're in the Champions League to win it, as much as the league,' he said. 'We took our opportunity [against Barcelona] and now we're in the final of the Champions League. Nothing could be better.

'Manchester always plays to win, the players want to win something this season and we have a great opportunity to do that in the Premier League and Champions League. Now we need to relax a little bit, do some good work and try to achieve our goals.'

Ronaldo's mood was further improved when he retained the Football Writers' Association (FWA) Footballer of the Year award, an achievement that made him only the second player to win both the FWA and PFA awards in successive seasons, after former Arsenal striker Thierry Henry (in 2002/03 and 2003/04).

An overwhelming favourite to scoop the award after his stunning season, the Portuguese winger saw off the challenges of Liverpool striker Fernando Torres and Portsmouth goalkeeper David James, who finished second and third respectively.

FWA chairman Paul Hetherington commented: 'Ronaldo's award is no surprise after his brilliant form this season and incredible goalscoring record and he is, of course, essentially a winger.

Cristiano was an overwhelming winner and, given his age, he has the potential and ability to dominate this award for years in an unprecedented way.'

Inside Carrington, however, nobody would be looking past the forthcoming visit of West Ham. Not the Premier League finale at Wigan, nor Chelsea in Moscow; short-term focus was the name of the game.

'We can't look ahead to Moscow just yet,' warned Ryan Giggs. 'We have big games to play before that. We first have to make sure we go out against West Ham and get the right result.

'Hopefully the crowd will be just as passionate as they were against Barcelona. It does make a difference, especially to the opposing team. It was such a ferocious atmosphere on Tuesday; it was brilliant.

'West Ham are an unpredictable side. They have a lot of quality, but they've also had a lot of injuries, which hasn't helped them. We need to be wary of them, especially at this stage of the season. It will be tough and tense, but we're up for it and we can't wait to get out there.'

Despite the pressure of the situation, Owen Hargreaves was brimming with confidence that the Reds would return to winning ways in the Premier League.

'The most important thing is we have the ability and the belief in each other to do it,' declared the midfielder. 'We are all very confident that, even with the setback against Chelsea last week, we can win our final two games and clinch the title.

'There's a great combination of qualities in the squad. The experience we have from Gary Neville, Ryan Giggs, Paul Scholes, Edwin van der Sar and Mikael Silvestre is vital, and then you've got the young guns like Wayne Rooney, Cristiano Ronaldo, Carlos Tevez, Nani, Anderson – some of whom are chasing their first title.

'We've also got the most experienced manager in the business, a manager that has been in this situation on many occasions before. That gives everyone confidence.'

Confidence was further boosted by the news that Patrice Evra would be fit to face the Hammers, having been stretchered off in injury time against Barcelona, although Sir Alex faced a conundrum about the potential returns of Wayne Rooney and Nemanja Vidic.

'Wayne may be on the bench,' the manager told the pre-match press conference. 'But we've got a major final to think about and we're not going to rush him.'

Sir Alex also confirmed that concussion victim Vidic would most likely miss the game on doctor's advice, but would be in contention to start against Wigan in the final league game of the season.

Victory over the Latics would see the Reds retain the title, but only if they could beat West Ham first.

Saturday, 3 May 2008, Old Trafford

Attendance: 76,013

FA Barclays Premier League
United 4 **West Ham United** 1

The job was half done. A scintillating first-half display had United home and hosed by the interval, although it took Michael Carrick's 59th-minute goal to settle the Reds' nerves.

United had raced into a three-goal lead inside half an hour, only for a stunning Dean Ashton overhead kick to reduce the arrears and a needless sending-off for Nani to hand the visitors a numerical advantage.

Ultimately, though, the Hammers offered little by way of a serious threat, and the Reds were able to coast to a vital win, despite starting with the same XI that had battled to victory over Barcelona.

An early goal was the order of the day, to prevent anxiety creeping in, and it was duly delivered by Ronaldo inside four minutes. The winger cut in from the right flank, advanced towards goal and hammered a shot that took a deflection off the back-pedalling George McCartney and flew inside Rob Green's near post.

The strike ended a run of four games without a goal – Ronaldo's longest goal drought of the season – and took his tally to 39 for the campaign. Number 40 followed shortly afterwards, after Wes Brown had somewhat fortunately survived a strong appeal for handball inside his own area.

On 24 minutes, Owen Hargreaves – again excellent as a makeshift right-back – manoeuvred space on the right wing and curled a left-footed cross towards the back post. Rookie Hammers defender James Tomkins misjudged the ball's flight and missed it, and a startled Ronaldo was on hand to divert the ball in from six yards with a potentially painful combination of upper thigh and groin.

If there was a hint of scrappiness, or good fortune, about the Reds' second goal, there was none whatsoever about the third, which followed two minutes later. Former Hammer Carlos Tevez picked up the ball on the left flank, motored inside and thumped an unstoppable 30-yard effort over the despairing dive of Green.

Arguably the finest goal of the Argentine's United career to date, and there was little surprise that it drew warm acclaim from the away supporters as well as the jubilant home contingent.

That mutual back-slapping was reprised just two minutes later when West Ham hauled themselves back into the game with an equally brilliant goal, one that was even afforded appreciation from some fans in the Streford End. Wes Brown failed to clear Bobby Zamora's chipped pass, and sent it looping up into the air. Dean Ashton back-pedalled, never taking his eye off the ball, leapt high and sent a spectacular overhead kick past a motionless Edwin van der Sar.

The game had been a thrilling spectacle for its opening third and, such was the Reds' attacking dominance, it seemed inevitable that United would build on their lead before the interval. Shortly before the break, however, those ambitions were scrapped when Nani was sent off. Having tangled with Lucas Neill off the ball, the young winger reacted to the Australian's baiting with an ill-advised headbutt. Both players fell to the ground but, after seeking the advice of his assistant, referee Mike Riley brandished the red card to Nani.

So poor were West Ham in attack, however, that United fans needn't have worried. Save a wayward shot from Scott Parker, the

Hammers offered nothing going forward. Just before the hour, Carrick took advantage of acres of space in the centre of the park, advanced and shot low towards goal. Green probably had it covered, but a telling deflection off Neill left the England goalkeeper totally wrong-footed, and United could start looking ahead to Wigan at the JJB Stadium.

Substitute Darren Fletcher side-footed against the upright late on, but the closing stages were played out at half-pace as United sought to retain energy. After all, they were just one victory away from the title.

UNITED: Van der Sar; Hargreaves, Ferdinand, Brown, Evra; Nani, Carrick, Scholes (O'Shea 73), Park (Giggs 61); Ronaldo (Fletcher 64), Tevez.
Subs not used: Kuszczak, Anderson

Goals: Ronaldo (4, 24), Tevez (26), Carrick (59)

WEST HAM UNITED: Green; Pantsil, Neill, Tomkins, McCartney; Noble, Mullins (Sears 75), Parker, Boa Morte (Solano 52); Ashton (Cole 57), Zamora.
Subs not used: Walker, Collinson

Goal: Ashton (28)

Nothing was in the bag just yet, but Sir Alex Ferguson still led his players on a lap of honour around Old Trafford, in order to thank the fans for a season of superb support.

'The fans were fantastic again today,' said the United manager. 'It's strange to do a lap of honour when you've not won anything, but the fans deserve it. We wanted to honour them because they've been superb this season. Against Barcelona they were out of this world. Hopefully we can all celebrate in a big way next Sunday at Wigan.'

Sir Alex's buoyant mood came in spite of Nani's unsavoury actions, and the boss made it clear that he was far from impressed by the youngster's antics.

'The game was marred by immaturity from Nani, real immaturity,' he conceded. 'He retaliated when he didn't need to and the referee didn't have any option but to send him off after he'd spoken to the linesman. Nevertheless, I'm sure he'll learn from it.'

It didn't take long for the winger to recognise his mistake, as he announced: 'I know my action was a thoughtless one. I also have to say I was provoked and attacked, but I regret what I did and publicly want to ask for forgiveness.'

Nani would be on the sidelines when the Reds took on Wigan eight days later in a make-or-break title decider. With West Ham out of the way, the state of play was even simpler – two victories for two pots. Wes Brown, for one, was in confident mood.

'Two more wins and we've got two trophies. That's what we're aiming for,' said the defender. 'We've played well all season. To throw it away now would be very disappointing. We know the title is ours if we win at Wigan and we're all looking forward to Moscow. It won't be easy, but we want both trophies and we'll do everything we can to get them.'

Chelsea's 2-0 victory at Newcastle meant that the title race would indeed go down to the wire – just as Sir Alex Ferguson had predicted some five months earlier. Goal difference separated the Reds from the Blues, but stalwart winger Ryan Giggs was happy for United to be masters of their own destiny.

'It's in our hands, which is all you can ask for,' he insisted. 'It's going to be a tough game. Wigan have got some decent players, they showed that when they went to Chelsea and got a draw. But no matter what happens at Stamford Bridge [where Chelsea would entertain Bolton], it's still in our hands and we've got to be professional and do our job.'

Immediately after beating Newcastle, Chelsea's players made pointed calls for Wigan to provide United with a stern challenge. The presence of ex-Reds' defender Steve Bruce at the Latics helm fuelled the Blues' outbursts, but the former club captain was having none of it.

'Everybody who knows me knows me better than that,' Bruce declared. 'Am I going to say to the team: "Just roll over and let United win"? That's not going to happen. Make no mistake; we'll be trying our utmost.'

With the Latics already guaranteed to avoid relegation after a surprise victory at Aston Villa, however, Owen Hargreaves was convinced that United's greater need to succeed would prove telling at the JJB Stadium.

'We are full of confidence,' said the midfielder. 'Wigan have done themselves a favour by beating Villa, so this game doesn't mean a lot for them. But to us it means everything. We've got 90 minutes to play and it's a great position to be in. We've had no midweek game so we've put in some good training and, hopefully, we will be ready.

'At the start of the season if somebody had offered us one game to win the league, we would have jumped at that. We've worked so hard all season, not just the players, but the staff who put all their time and energy in at this club. That's what makes this a special place. So for them to see us win the league would be a fantastic moment. We'll go out on the pitch on Sunday and give everything we have for 90 minutes.'

The players were making all the right noises ahead of the must-win trip across the north-west, and Sir Alex Ferguson was happy just to sit back and let them get on with winning the game.

'It doesn't matter what the Wigan players are saying or what the Chelsea players are saying. If we win our game, that's it,' the manager told reporters at the pre-match briefing.

'You hope you get the breaks, you hope this, you hope that and you hope the next thing. You could wish for too many things. The important thing is to have trust in your players. I trust my players and I will let them get on with it. Their form this year has been terrific, they've played some fantastic football. They've excelled, they've done everything I could possibly ask from a squad.

'It will be nailbiting for the fans, but we're in the right position. If we win our game we win the league, so it's a great incentive for us. We go into the game with a great chance. We will also have a fantastic support on Sunday and that's a big plus for us.'

An estimated 8,000 United fans made the short trip to Wigan.

Having roared the Reds to Moscow and to within 90 minutes of the title, they were hoping for plenty more to sing about at the JJB Stadium.

Sunday, 11 May 2008, JJB Stadium

Attendance: 25,133

FA Barclays Premier League
Wigan Athletic 0 **United** 2

As ever, United's way was the hard way. But, after an afternoon of nerves and tension, the dust settled to reveal that Manchester United were league champions for the 17th time.

Goals in either half from Cristiano Ronaldo and Ryan Giggs sealed a 2-0 victory and the Premier League title for the tenth time since the competition's inception. There was a fitting air about the identity of the goalscorers – undoubted player of the season Ronaldo and Giggs, making his 758th appearance for the club and equalling Sir Bobby Charlton's all-time appearance record.

The Reds' victory rendered Chelsea's match with Bolton inconsequential. Ironically, after all the hype surrounding Wigan's need to exceed, it was the Trotters who shone, holding the Blues to a 1-1 draw at Stamford Bridge and ensuring United won the title by two clear points.

United went into the make-or-break clash buoyed by the return of Nemanja Vidic and Wayne Rooney from injury, as Sir Alex Ferguson fielded a strong attacking side. With so much at stake, however, the Reds were nervous in the opening exchanges, and the hosts had the first meaningful efforts as Jason Koumas twice shot wastefully off target from outside the area.

Although Rooney and Paul Scholes missed half-chances, the hosts continued to make the better openings and should have moved ahead from opportunities at two set-pieces. First Emmerson Boyce fired over the bar, then Marcus Bent headed off target from close range.

They were two huge let-offs for United and the Reds took full advantage just after the half-hour mark. Amid scrambled scenes inside the Wigan area, Boyce fouled Rooney and referee Steve Bennett pointed straight to the penalty spot. After a lengthy delay, soundtracked by shrill home support, Ronaldo stepped up, sent the goalkeeper the wrong way and side-footed a shot inside Kirkland's left-hand post.

The Wigan contingent were irate, and their mood became even more aggrieved shortly afterwards. Paul Scholes, already booked, barged Wilson Palacios to the ground, but escaped with a stern lecture from referee Bennett.

To add further drama to the occasion, the mid-afternoon sun turned to heavy rain, before thunder and lightning cracked around the JJB Stadium. As if those inside the ground weren't jumpy enough already.

Half-time came and went with United ahead and Chelsea being held to a goalless draw. So far so good and, but for a fine save from Chris Kirkland, Ronaldo's blistering free-kick would have ended the game as a contest just after the restart.

Shortly afterwards, United's players and the supporters behind Kirkland's goal were bellowing for a penalty when Titus Bramble clumsily felled Scholes inside the area. It looked like a clear spot-kick, but Bennett declined to award it. Instead he gave a corner, from which Ronaldo headed just off target.

When Kirkland produced a pair of fine saves to deny Rooney and then Carlos Tevez, United nerves were set jangling. Chelsea didn't help the situation by taking the lead at Stamford Bridge through Andriy Shevchenko, and neither did Emile Heskey, who headed onto the roof of Edwin van der Sar's net with just 20 minutes remaining. Had it dropped in, the title race would have been flipped on its head.

Ultimately, though, that scare proved a timely wake-up call for United. Ryan Giggs and Owen Hargreaves replaced Scholes and Ji-sung Park, and it was record-equalling winger Giggs who, in the most fitting of fashions, ensured a season's work wouldn't be going to waste.

Rooney cut in from the left wing, spotted some criminally slack marking from the Latics' defence and slid a pass to Giggs. The experienced campaigner took one touch to cushion the ball, then slotted a shot low past Kirkland and sparked scenes of unabashed delirium among the euphoric United supporters.

'We're gonna win the league,' they bellowed, as one. Although Wigan did mount a spirited late response, with Giggs clearing off the line from a wayward Wes Brown header and Maynor Figueroa striking the outside of the post, they were right.

With the Premier League title retained, attentions would soon inevitably switch to Moscow and the small matter of the Champions League final. For just one sweet evening, however, the Reds could kick back and relax. They were champions.

WIGAN ATHLETIC: Kirkland; Boyce, Bramble, Scharner, Figueroa; Brown (King 81), Koumas, Palacios, Valencia; Bent (Sibierski 70), Heskey. Subs not used: Pollitt, Taylor, Skoko

UNITED: Van der Sar; Brown, Ferdinand, Vidic, Evra; Park (Giggs 68), Scholes (Hargreaves 67), Carrick; Ronaldo, Rooney, Tevez. Subs not used: Kuszczak, Saha, Silvestre

Goals: Ronaldo (33, pen), Giggs (80)

For man-of-the-hour Ryan Giggs, celebrating his status as the Reds' joint all-time appearance-maker could wait. He was a league champion for the tenth time and that was what mattered.

'It feels great,' he said of his record-extending tenth title. 'I'm not bothered about individual records, this is what it's all about – championships. We knew it would be a tough game and it was. We did well in the first half and got that first goal. Then it was a case of holding on.

'The second was a great goal just to settle us down. We felt a little more comfortable after that. Winning the league feels brilliant and, hopefully, we can win another trophy in ten days' time.'

For Sir Alex Ferguson, an afternoon of nervousness was made worthwhile by the chance to lift the Premier League trophy yet again and, although he suffered at times, the manager was absolutely elated at the final whistle.

'It was a tough one alright and being away from home today made it more difficult,' he admitted. 'In fairness, we played well for most of the game. There were some nervous moments and when the rain came we were wondering how things would go, because anything can happen on a wet surface.

'Just after half-time we started to get a grip of it. We missed a few chances and the goalkeeper made some great saves. I was saying to myself, "Please give us that second goal." Of course, my oldest player, ten medals today, gets it – Ryan Giggs. Fantastic. I'm very proud; proud to have survived for so long. It's a great club and it's much easier for me than it is for anyone else. How would I do without this?'

After watching his young side move to within one title of equalling Liverpool's long-standing record tally of 18 titles, Sir Alex was quietly confident about overhauling the Reds' Merseyside rivals.

'I think it will come,' he predicted. 'This side's young. It's developing all the time and there are plenty of years left in them. They'll do it in their own time.'

Having returned from injury to set up two goals, Wayne Rooney paid tribute to his manager at full-time. After over two decades at the Old Trafford helm, Sir Alex's status as one of the game's greatest ever managers was never in question for Rooney.

'He's brilliant. It's a privilege to play for him every week,' insisted the striker. 'He's been in the game for so long, but his determination to win is stronger than ever. All credit to him for staying with the club for all this time.

'We were under a little bit of pressure towards the end of the season, but we hung in there. We knew that coming into the last two games, if we got six points we'd be champions. We could see the finish line. It was in our hands and we weren't going to let it slip.'

Having watched his side retain their crown, Sir Alex couldn't help but let his mind wander ahead to the Champions League final in Moscow.

'The great thing is we're bouncing into it,' he smiled. 'We can look forward to it. If we'd lost the title today, it would have been difficult. When we lost it at West Ham in 1995, we lost the FA Cup final the following week. We were dead then. We're not dead now, we're alive. If we win the European Cup, this has to be my best team.'

There was one more stop to be made before attentions could fully switch to Moscow – Old Trafford, for the players' annual end-of-season awards dinner. There was time only for them to shower, grab the trophy and board the coach back from Wigan. Upon arriving in Manchester, they were afforded a rapturous reception from the crowd amassed outside the North Stand.

Once inside the players were let off the leash and the partying could begin. Two of the younger players – Danny Welbeck and Richard Eckersley – may not have been old enough to keep up with their senior counterparts, but they still had plenty of cause to celebrate after scooping the Jimmy Murphy Academy Player of the Year and Denzil Haroun Reserve Player of the Year trophies respectively. And 24 hours later the pair helped United overcome Bolton Wanderers in the Manchester Senior Cup final.

The first team awards were, unsurprisingly, dominated by Cristiano Ronaldo. The Portuguese international, fresh from scoring his 41st goal of an unbelievable season, won the Fans' Player of the Year, Players' Player of the Year and Goal of the Season awards – the latter for his unstoppable free-kick against Portsmouth in January.

'It's a fantastic feeling. I didn't expect to win all three,' he admitted during his acceptance speech. 'I'm very happy and I have to say thank you to the fans, my team-mates and everyone. It's a great night for me.

'The fans have been fantastic. Not just to me, but every player, singing all the time. This gives us extra motivation to play better. The supporters help us all the time and I thank them for that.'

The individual accolades continued for Ronaldo the following day when he picked up the Barclays Player of the Season and Barclays Golden Boot awards. The Portuguese wing wizard also collected a merit prize for passing 30 league goals.

Inevitably, the player who had become arguably the planet's finest was already looking ahead to performing on the biggest stage. In just nine days' time, Chelsea would be waiting at the Luzhniki Stadium, and so would the chance to complete a remarkable Double.

'We all want to win the Champions League, but you never know what will happen in a final – you have a 50/50 chance,' admitted Ronaldo. 'I'm very happy and proud to be playing in a Champions League final for the first time. We have a great opportunity to do the Double and all the lads believe. So why not?'

Forty-eight hours after sealing Premier League glory, celebrations turned to preparations for the Reds as the countdown to the Champions League final began in earnest.

Sir Alex admitted he already had his starting XI in mind, but with only 18 places available for the game, including seven spots on the bench, the boss knew he had some tough decisions to make.

'There are going to be some very good players I have to leave out from the 24 that can play. It's not going to be easy and it'll be heartache for some of them,' insisted Sir Alex, who was voted Manager of the Year by the League Managers' Association the day after his tenth title triumph.

'The consolation for anyone not playing in the final is to be on the bench, because they do at least feel part of it. I just hope that, at some point in the Champions League, they extend the substitutes to 11 players as they do in World Cup games. That would be justified in a final. The dilemma I have should be taken from me.

'I've had to do it in the past, but it doesn't get any easier with time, if anything it becomes more difficult. It was made easier for me in 1999 in the sense that Paul Scholes and Roy Keane were suspended and Henning Berg was injured. In Rotterdam [in the 1991 European Cup-Winners' Cup final] I had to leave Neil Webb out of the squad and my own son Darren as well, and that wasn't easy. I won't look forward to it, but I know I have to make the decision and it's an important one – games can sometimes be won by your subs and we're in a good position in that sense.'

Arguably United's greatest super-sub of them all, Ole Gunnar

Solskjaer, whose place in Old Trafford folklore was guaranteed by 1999's injury-time toe poke in Barcelona, called on his former team-mates to believe in their potential ahead of the Moscow showpiece:

'This side can win it and hopefully start something bigger,' insisted the Norwegian striker turned Carrington coach. 'You want the players to get the feeling that this is where they want to be every year. Hopefully it will inspire them and motivate them to believe what they really can achieve. I think this team could go on to win more Champions Leagues than us in 1999 because of the talent and the age of the players.'

With United having booked their place in the final in this year of all years, talk inevitably turned to how victory would act as the most fitting tribute to the 23 people who perished in the Munich air disaster some 50 years earlier. But Munich survivor and 1968 European Cup winner Sir Bobby Charlton was defiant in his belief that the players should focus on winning the trophy for themselves, rather than for those who lost their lives.

'It wouldn't be fair to put total responsibility on them to win the Champions League to help commemorate the 50th anniversary of the tragedy. I would never put pressure on these players. They have their own careers and Munich is a long time ago,' insisted Sir Bobby, who would attend the final with fellow survivors from the crash.

'These players know they will make their own history if they win the European Cup. That's what it should be about for them. But there's no doubt that if they can beat Chelsea in the final, there will be a lot of satisfaction among anyone who was connected with Munich.

'It would be perfect, as it was Sir Matt Busby who pioneered the idea of English clubs competing in Europe and the Babes, who would have done so well in it but for the tragedy. That history is not lost on these players. They appreciate and are aware of what it's all about. This team deserves to add the European Cup to the title.'

One man with more determination than most to reign supreme in the Russian capital was Patrice Evra. The Frenchman was a losing finalist in 2004 with Monaco, who were beaten 3-0 by Jose Mourinho's Porto side. Evra was intent on avenging that defeat and used a unique analogy to illustrate the confidence he felt about United's chances.

'I went to the Champions League final in a Fiat with Monaco, now I'm going to Moscow in a Ferrari with Manchester United,' he insisted. 'But even if you're in a Ferrari, you still have to make sure you drive it well. So we will have to play our best against Chelsea if we want to win.

'For me this game is now the most important of my life. I don't want to lose for a second time. When I first came to Manchester I said I didn't just want to get to a Champions League final again, I wanted to go there and win it. The competition holds bad memories for me after losing with Monaco – I'm determined to put that right.'

Another player set for a second chance of a different kind was Paul Scholes. The midfielder was famously suspended for the 1999 final against Bayern Munich, along with skipper Roy Keane, but Sir Alex, who never normally succumbs to sentimentality, said after the Reds' semi-final victory over Barcelona that he would make an exception to ensure Scholes was handed a starting berth in the Luzhniki Stadium. And team-mate Ryan Giggs felt there was no player more deserving.

'I'm not telling the manager who to pick,' he insisted, 'but Scholesy deserves to play because he's a great player. His form has been brilliant and his goal against Barcelona got us to the final. To play with a player like him is a privilege. He does things others can't do. The disappointment of 1999 was massive for him and Roy, having played such an important part in getting us to the final. I'm glad he's got another chance now.'

Fresh from picking up another title medal and signing a new five-year contract, you'd have thought things couldn't have got any better for Rio Ferdinand. At the club's media open day for the final, the defender admitted the last couple of weeks had indeed been memorable, but remained adamant his season would end on a sour note unless United defeated Chelsea in Moscow.

'I'll tell you next week after the game how good a time this has been for me,' he smiled. 'If we win the Champions League then I'll say it's been fantastic for me personally. If not, then the season will have ended on a disappointing note.

'To be able to stay here for the next five years is something I'm very happy about,' he added. 'You see the surroundings. I'm in every day training at Carrington, playing in front of 76,000 fans every other week ... what more could you ask for?'

Team-mate Michael Carrick was in complete agreement as he became the latest player to commit his future to the Reds by signing a new four-year contract in the lead-up to the final.

'This is a fantastic club and it's a pleasure to be part of this great squad,' declared the midfielder. 'I believe this team will be together for many years to come and to win back-to-back titles in my first two seasons is a dream come true.'

Another player keen to secure his long-term future at Old Trafford by making his move to United a permanent one was Carlos Tevez. The Argentine striker had initially joined on loan, but admitted he would sign a contract immediately if it was put in front of him.

'I would certainly love to extend my stay, I am very happy here,' he said. 'I would go and sign right now if the opportunity was there. From day one, everyone has treated me well and the fans even shout "Argentina", which has made me feel right at home. Now to have the opportunity to win two big trophies is fantastic. The atmosphere around the squad is amazing.'

Whether or not the Argentine would be part of the manager's starting XI in the final remained to be seen, as the Reds' 24-man squad arrived at their Russian HQ on Monday evening.

The players stuck to British Summer Time to ensure the three-hour time difference in Moscow did not affect their preparations. The final itself was due to kick-off at 10.45pm local time, but the Reds viewed it as a typical 7.45pm start.

There were plenty of fans and well wishers stationed around the hotel lobby the following day, including ex-Red Andrei Kanchelskis, who had stopped by to catch up with some of his former team-mates and, of course, Sir Alex to wish them good luck.

The Reds headed off to the Luzhniki Stadium around tea-time for a pre-final training session on one of the most talked about pitches in Europe. Concerns had been raised about the recently installed grass pitch in place of the Luzhniki's usual artificial surface, but Sir Alex was not worried when asked about it during the pre-match press conference.

'I've got no concerns,' he said. 'UEFA have done their best. I'm delighted they relaid it. You have to remind yourself that Old Trafford in December and January isn't the best. I think it will be fine.'

There may have been no concerns over the pitch, but eyebrows were raised when Nemanja Vidic failed to appear at the Reds' training session, while striker Louis Saha was also a notable absentee. On Vidic, Sir Alex said simply: 'Nemanja is on a different training programme to the rest of the squad, but he will definitely play.'

Chelsea had their own injury worries later that evening when they sampled the Luzhniki pitch for first time. Defender Ashley Cole started the session, but was forced to pull out midway through after he was on the receiving end of a two-footed challenge from team-mate Claude Makelele. The left-back was in clear discomfort as his right ankle was examined by the Blues' medical staff, and even though he rejoined his team-mates in a practice match, he was unable to complete the session and left early for more treatment.

If fit, Cole seemed likely to be up against his old adversary Cristiano Ronaldo. All eyes would be on the winger to deliver on the big stage, an ability that had been called into question on occasion during the campaign. Sir Alex believed the Portuguese star could play a key role in firing the Reds to European glory, so too Wayne Rooney, but insisted United, unbeaten in the competition all season long, would not be relying solely on the contributions of their deadly duo.

'Rooney and Ronaldo are still young and I suppose a lot of their big future is ahead of them,' explained the manager. 'In terms of their ability, their nerve and their courage to play there are few better and Wednesday night is a great challenge for them. But it's a challenge for every one of our players and we can't look to depend on two young lads as our saviours. I will be relying on all 11 players to see us through and that gives us a massive chance.'

As he pondered the possibility of a second Champions League triumph, Sir Alex admitted that the fear of never experiencing European success again had driven him on to build his third great United side. And he remained convinced his players could deliver when it mattered on Wednesday night.

'You fear many things, but sometimes that drives you on. I felt it was an important time for us when we started to make another change and began to rebuild again,' he explained, in reference to United's early elimination from the competition in three successive seasons between 2003/04 and 2005/06.

'It's not easy to manage change and when you see a team starting to break up due to age, injuries or merely because others are not maintaining the level they should be at. But bringing in these young players over the last two or three years gives you optimism you can do it again. If I didn't think like that with players like Rooney, Ronaldo, Giggs and Scholes then I really am a pessimist.'

While team selection would be crucial, fans and pundits alike were equally as interested in how Sir Alex would line his team up tactically. Would he look to combat Chelsea's three-man midfield or would he set up to make the most of his side's natural attacking prowess?

'Tactics will come into a good part of the game,' he suspected. 'Chelsea are a physically stronger team than most in the Premier League, but we don't need to match that. We have to pay attention to it, of course, but it's important we play our own game. My players have the nerve and courage to win. I trust them to deliver.'

That trust would be fully rewarded, but not before a dramatic series of events on a rain-sodden night in Moscow.

Wednesday, 21 May 2008, Luzhniki Stadium

Attendance: 69,552

UEFA Champions League final
United 1 **Chelsea** 1 (United win 6–5 on penalties)

Some things are just meant to be. Fifty years on from Munich and forty years after Sir Matt Busby had led United to their first European triumph, fate contrived to crown the Reds Champions of Europe for a third time on a dramatic, unforgettable evening in Moscow.

After 120 minutes of football had failed to separate the Premier League's top two sides, it came down to the lottery of a penalty shoot-out. Cristiano Ronaldo's miss handed Chelsea the advantage, but John Terry's ill-timed slip with the cup within touching distance sent proceedings into sudden death. Fittingly, record breaker Ryan Giggs converted United's final penalty, before Edwin van der Sar sealed victory, brilliantly saving from Nicolas Anelka to send United's travelling army delirious with delight.

Earlier, during normal time, Cristiano Ronaldo had put the Reds in front with a 26th-minute header, before Frank Lampard equalised in first-half injury time.

Sir Alex Ferguson surprised many pundits, and no doubt his opposite number Avram Grant, by opting to stick Owen Hargreaves on the right, while Michael Carrick and Paul Scholes anchored the midfield and Cristiano Ronaldo took up the left-flank position. Wayne Rooney and Carlos Tevez were the front pairing of the 4-4-2 formation. It was the first time the 11 had ever started together.

As for the bench, Gary Neville and Louis Saha were understandable absentees after spending much of the campaign troubled by injury. The biggest shock was the omission of Ji-sung Park, who had been one of United's most impressive performers in the semi-final win over Barcelona.

The Luzhniki Stadium was a sea of colour and noise before kick-off with the travelling Reds in typically good voice. United were the livelier outfit early on, but found themselves temporarily down to ten men on 20 minutes while Paul Scholes received treatment for a bloodied nose after a clash with Claude Makelele. Thankfully Scholes was back in time to play his part in the opening goal.

Neat interplay between the midfielder and Wes Brown after a throw-in on the right flank gave Brown time to pick out a cross for Ronaldo. Rising high above marker Michael Essien, the Portuguese winger expertly directed his header past the motionless Petr Cech for his 42nd goal of a staggering season.

Chelsea, who had offered little in attack, almost drew level on 34 minutes. Didier Drogba headed Lampard's deep cross back across goal, Rio Ferdinand dithered with Michael Ballack breathing down his neck, and the German's presence – and slight shove – forced the United skipper into heading towards his own goal. Despite the point-blank range of the header, Edwin van der Sar was alert enough to beat it away to safety.

United broke forward from the resulting corner, with Wayne Rooney finding Ronaldo with an exquisite 40-yard cross-field pass. The winger controlled it brilliantly and delivered a perfect cross onto Carlos Tevez's head. Cech blocked the diving effort from the Argentine and was also on hand to parry Michael Carrick's follow-up shot from the edge of the box. It was an awesome double save.

The Reds were clearly growing in confidence and Ronaldo in particular was giving Chelsea's stand-in right-back Essien a torrid time. Two minutes before the break Hargreaves won possession, broke forward and fed Rooney on the right. He fizzed in an early daisy-cutter that evaded Makelele at the near post. Tevez was waiting just behind him, but was unable to poke the ball goalwards.

At the other end, Ferdinand was booked for a foul on Lampard right on the edge of the box, but Ballack curled the subsequent free-kick over van der Sar's crossbar, much to the delight of the elated United fans behind the goal.

That jubilation turned to deflation on the stroke of half-time, however, when Chelsea drew level. When the marauding Essien's shot cannoned off both Vidic and Ferdinand, it dropped to Lampard in the area. Van der Sar raced to meet him but slipped at the vital moment, allowing the Chelsea midfielder to side-foot the ball home.

Buoyed by their ill-deserved equaliser, Chelsea began to take a grip of proceedings after the break. Essien broke forward down the right and, after holding off the attentions of Ronaldo, cut inside and hit a powerful left-foot drive. Van der Sar slipped again, but thankfully for the Reds the shot flew over the bar.

United's backline was on red alert thereafter – Vidic brilliantly headed clear as Drogba lay in wait to convert Ashley Cole's cross, before Ferdinand twice did the same as the Blues' attacking barrage continued. Michael Carrick then hooked Florent Malouda's inviting free-kick away from danger. The Reds breathed another sigh of relief 12 minutes from time when Drogba curled a right-foot shot against van der Sar's left-hand post with the Dutchman well beaten.

The openings were all falling to Chelsea, who had dominated the second period. Ryan Giggs entered the fray just before the start of extra-time, thus breaking Sir Bobby Charlton's all-time appearance record in his 759th match for the Reds. But the occasion was almost spoiled when Lampard spun to clip a shot against the crossbar four minutes into the first period of extra-time.

Seven minutes later Giggs almost capped his record-breaking night in the most fitting of fashions with a winning goal. Patrice Evra brilliantly burst into the area before pulling the ball back, and Giggs' toe-poked effort was goalbound until John Terry somehow headed the shot over the bar.

The second half was marred by ugly scenes which saw Chelsea reduced to ten men. The Blues reacted angrily to perceived poor sportsmanship after Tevez had kicked the ball out for a throw-in rather than return it to the Blues, following a break while players were treated for cramp. It was a case of selective memory from the Chelsea players, who chose to ignore that Salomon Kalou had done exactly the same thing in the first period of extra-time. During the scuffle, Drogba needlessly aimed a slap at Vidic and was sent off for his troubles, while Tevez and Ballack were both shown yellows for their part in the fracas.

A further booking, for a foul by Essien, was to be the last noteworthy event before the game headed for penalties. There United would have their glory, but not before Ronaldo had his spot-kick saved by Cech, to put Chelsea temporarily in the driving seat. When Terry squandered his opportunity to win it for the Blues, Anderson scored to put United ahead – then Kalou and Giggs both netted, before Anelka stepped up for the final decisive penalty, saved superbly by van der Sar. History had been made, as United ruled Europe once again.

UNITED: Van der Sar; Brown (Anderson 120), Ferdinand, Vidic, Evra; Carrick, Hargreaves, Scholes (Giggs 87) Ronaldo; Rooney (Nani 101), Tevez.
Subs not used: Kuszczak, O'Shea, Fletcher, Silvestre

Goal: Ronaldo (26)

Penalty shoot-out
Scored: Tevez, Carrick, Hargreaves, Nani, Anderson, Giggs
Missed: Ronaldo

CHELSEA: Cech; Essien, Terry, Carvalho, A. Cole; Makelele (Belletti 120), Ballack, Lampard, Malouda (Kalou 92), J. Cole (Anelka 99); Drogba.
Subs not used: Cudicini, Shevchenko, Mikel, Alex

Goal: Lampard (45)

Penalty shoot-out
Scored: Ballack, Belletti, Lampard, A Cole, Kalou
Missed: Terry, Anelka

Seconds after confirming United's new status as European champions, Edwin van der Sar was engulfed by his delirious team-mates. Sir Alex Ferguson danced a jig of delight before embracing his players and staff, having finally finished on the winning side in a big game penalty shoot-out – he had previously lost three with Aberdeen and three with United.

For the Reds manager victory was the realisation of an ambition he had harboured since first tasting Champions League glory nine years ago. And it felt just as good second time round.

'This is an amazing achievement, it's fantastic. As a club, we started the sojourn into Europe in 1955. And we deserve to get this trophy now,' he beamed. 'I think we deserved to win the game. In the first half we were fantastic and we should have been 3-0 up, but they scored right on half-time, they got a lucky break there, and I thought Chelsea were the better side in the second half. We got better in extra-time and I'm just delighted for all the people here and my players. I'm very proud of my team and I think this has got the makings of our best ever side.'

Hero of the hour van der Sar was full of emotion after receiving his second winners' medal, a full 13 years after scooping his first.

'Nights like this are what you dream of. It's been a long time since I won it and it feels fantastic, especially in the way we won it,' grinned the goalkeeper, who had also experienced the pain of losing a shoot-out in the 1996 final when Juventus beat Ajax.

'It was the last penalty – saving it – I don't have any words for it. What can I say? It's great. You see it coming, you save it and then you get up and you know the game's over. You have two, three or four seconds on your own, arms in the air and everything goes through your mind. You see your team-mates coming towards you and it's just happiness; one of the greatest feelings you can ever have.'

The veteran stopper also paid tribute to record-breaker Ryan Giggs, who hoisted the trophy aloft with captain-for-the-night Rio Ferdinand.

'It's incredible to think Ryan has been part of this club for over 17 years,' insisted van der Sar. 'He has enormous determination, great fitness and top quality and he works hard every day in training. He's a top professional.'

Having become United's all-time record appearance-maker, converted the decisive penalty in the shoot-out and claimed his second Champions League triumph ten days after securing a tenth domestic title, the man himself was overcome by tears of joy at the finale.

'I can take it in a lot more at this stage of my career,' he admitted.

'In 1999 I was 25 and it was a blur, but I will try to enjoy this a little bit more because there won't be too many more of these for me.

'I hope we can do it again next season. That's the challenge now for this club and these players, to go on. We don't want to be waiting for nine years until the next time again. We want to be competing for the Champions League every year. We can kick on, where we didn't last time. The difference between now and 1999 is that this is a young team. I'm sure the manager is going to add to the squad, it has the potential, the experience and the players to go on to even more great things.'

For Rio Ferdinand, skippering the Reds to victory in Moscow was the perfect end to a superb season's work. The England international described the feeling of winning as the best he'd ever experienced, but insisted it was the kudos that came with it that represented the most satisfying part of the achievement.

'I said before the game that you're only really considered a great player at this club when you win the Champions League,' explained Ferdinand, who was due to take the next spot-kick had Anelka not missed. 'There have been a lot of top players at United, but to win this competition and be revered by the fans and everyone associated with the club by becoming a European champion sets you apart from everyone else. It's the best feeling I've ever had. Not many players get to experience it. We want to be back here next year and experience this feeling again because it's fantastic.'

The jubilant squad headed back to their hotel at around 4.30am local time for the party of all parties with their families and friends. During the celebrations, Sir Alex made a speech to thank everybody for their efforts over the course of a glorious campaign, before he and Sir Bobby Charlton presented Ryan Giggs with a specially inscribed watch from his team-mates to mark his club appearances record.

A few hours later the players and coaching staff were more than a little bleary-eyed as they headed to Moscow's Domodedovo airport. Chief executive David Gill said everyone had made the most of the chance to let their hair down and admitted he only got to bed around

7am. Wes Brown confessed he got just one hour's sleep, while Nemanja Vidic revealed he had not even had as much as that!

Although an official victory parade would have to wait until later in the summer, there were still plenty of United fans on hand to welcome the squad back to Manchester when they touched down around 9.30pm on Thursday evening, albeit four hours later than planned because of earlier delays.

Having had chance to reflect on an unforgettable occasion in Moscow, including the fact that the Reds were within one kick of losing the cup, Sir Alex ventured that divine intervention had once again played a part, just as it did in 1999.

'It was such an emotional occasion on Wednesday. I said the day before the game we would not let the memory of the Busby Babes down. And fate played its hand in John Terry slipping,' he concluded. 'We had a cause and people with causes become difficult people to play against. I think fate was playing its hand in the final. I feel very, very proud.'

The manager's desire and hunger for more silverware had clearly not diminished; in fact, the fire in his belly appeared to be burning brighter than ever.

'The euphoria evaporates very quickly for me,' he confirmed. 'The next day I'm already thinking about next season. When you win something like this you have to look at the players the following year and make sure the hunger is still there. Defending the trophy is not easy. But the players will improve and I hope we can do it. They are certainly good enough.'